WITHDRAWN

Hostels U.S.A.

Praise for previous editions of Hostels U.S.A.:

WITHDRAWN

"Eminently practical and fun to browse through, this guide belongs in every backpack."

—*San Jose Mercury News*

"A hip, humorous, irreverent guidebook that 'nails it' when it comes to evaluating the whole hostel experience."

—*Independent Publisher*

"A spirited and opinionated guide . . . the author rates the accommodations based on a combination of hospitality, cleanliness, safety, 'party potential,' and those intangible elements that can make the difference between heaven and hell."

—*Chicago Tribune*

"This is the only guide of its type that rates the hostels it describes."

—*Library Journal*

"If you love to travel but don't have a fortune to spend on accommodations during your journeys, *Hostels U.S.A.* is the book for you."

—*Navy Times*

D1320072

Help Us Keep This Guide Up To Date

Every effort has been made by the author and editors to make this guide as accurate and useful as possible. However, many things can change after a guide is published—hostels open and close, phone numbers change, buildings come under new management, etc.

We would like to hear from you concerning your experiences with this book, and how you feel it could be improved and kept up to date. If you have learned about a new hostel and think it should be reviewed in this book, please let us know. While we may not be able to respond to all comments and suggestions, we'll take them to heart and we'll also make certain to share them with the author. Please send your comments and suggestions to the following address:

The Globe Pequot Press
Reader Response/Editorial Department
P.O. Box 480
Guilford, CT 06437

Or you may e-mail us at:
editorial@GlobePequot.com
Thanks for your input, and happy travels!

HOSTELS SERIES

Hostels *U.S.A.*

The Only Comprehensive, Unofficial, Opinionated Guide

SEVENTH EDITION

Paul Karr

gpp®

travel

Guilford, Connecticut

The prices, rates, and general information listed in this guidebook were confirmed at press time, but under no circumstances are they guaranteed. We recommend that you contact establishments to obtain current information before making firm travel plans.

Text design: Sheryl Kober
Maps: XNR Productions Inc. © Morris Book Publishing, LLC

Co-concept, original research, and writing: Evan Halper
Contributing freelancers include but are not necessarily limited to: Barney Beal, Ron Butchko, Win Cahill, Andrew Donaldson, Dan Eisenberg, Gabe Freid, Paul Gerards, Monica Hancock, James Hogan, Mandy Horan, Kathleen Karr, David Kociemba, Michael LeRoux, Ross Metzman, Jaqueline Quintana, Jessica Rendell, Kadie Renner, Shawn Richardson, David Robinson, Denise Rubinfeld, Patricia Shea, Mark Terry, Nick Thompson, Suzan Verberne, Carey N. Williams, Katharine Wroth, Jim Yingst.

ISSN 1540-4390
ISBN 978-0-7627-4779-5

Printed in the United States of America

10 9 8 7 6 5 4 3 2 1

Contents

Acknowledgments

Thanks to that rust-red Chevy Cavalier and assorted other trains, planes, and automobiles for all those miles and to Ryan Adams, Oasis, and a host of others for musical sustenance. Very special thanks to the hardworking, prize-winning, muck-raking journalist Evan Halper, who helped us create this series and contributed a ton of hard work and clear-eyed writing at the outset.

Thanks to the many friends and family who gave bed, board, and/or friendship during these travels. Thanks also to certain hostel managers for inspiring discussions and for demonstrating by example how to run the best kind of hostel. Thank you to the hardworking freelancers for invaluable research and writing assistance; the good folks at Magellan's for kindly helping sponsor our initial forays; and Martin Levin and Bob Halper for early counsel. Thanks also to Globe Pequot's editorial staffers, including especially the late Laura Strom, who bought our idea and championed this series; to Hostelling International for its encouragement and assistance; anyone else who provided information, companionship, or shelter; and (what the hell) planet Earth, just for always being there in a pinch.

Thanks, finally, to a world of friends met or made on the road. So many of them shared their corner of the world, or otherwise made the work enjoyable and useful.

Thank you all.

How to Use This Book

What you're holding in your hands is what became the first attempt of its kind: a complete listing and rating of hostels in the United States. Dozens of hostellers from countries all over the globe were interviewed in the course of putting this guide together, and their comments and thoughts run throughout its pages. Who knows? You yourself might be quoted somewhere inside.

We wrote this guide for two pretty simple reasons. First, we wanted to bring hostelling to a wider audience. Hostels continue to grow in popularity, particularly with older travelers, but most North American travelers still don't think of them as options when planning a local trip. We wanted to change that because—at its best—the hostelling experience brings people of greatly differing origins, faiths, and points of view together in a convivial setting. You learn about these people, and also about the place in which the hostel is situated, in a very personal way that no textbook could ever provide.

Second, we wanted very much to give people our honest opinions of the hostels described here. You wouldn't send your best friend to a fleabag, and we don't want readers traveling great distances only to be confronted with filthy kitchens, nasty managers, or dangerous neighborhoods. At least, we thought, we could warn them about unsafe or unpleasant situations ahead of time.

On the other hand, of course, we would also tip our friends off to the truly wonderful hostels—the ones with treehouses, cafes, and free breakfasts, the ones with real family spirit. So that's what we've done. Time after time on the road, we have heard fellow travelers complaining that the guidebooks they bought simply listed places to stay but didn't rate them. Well, now we've done it—and we haven't pulled a single punch or held back a bit of praise.

How This Book Was Written

The editor and a cadre of assistants have been fanning out across the country with notebooks and laptops in hand since 1996. Sometimes we identified ourselves in advance; sometimes we just popped in for surprise visits. We counted rooms, turned taps, tested beds. And then we talked with managers and staff.

Before we left, we also took the time to interview plenty of hostellers in private and get their honest opinions about the places they were staying or had already stayed.

The results are contained within this book: actual hosteller quotes, opinions, ratings, and more.

What Is a Hostel?

If you've picked up this book, you probably know what a hostel is. On the other hand, a surprising number of people interviewed for this book weren't sure at all what it means.

So let's check your knowledge with a little pop quiz. Sharpen your pencils, put on your thinking caps, and dive in.

1. **A hostel is:**
   A. a hospital.
   B. a hospice.
   C. a hotel.
   D. a drunk tank.
   E. none of the above.
   (correct answer worth 20 points)

2. **A hostel is:**
   A. a place where international travelers bunk up.
   B. a cheap sleep.
   C. a place primarily dedicated to bunks.
   D. all of the above.
   (correct answer worth 20 points)

3. **You just turned thirty. Word on the street has it that you'll get turned away for being that age. Do you tell the person at the hostel desk the grim news?**
   A. No, because a hostel is restricted to students under thirty.
   B. No, because a hostel is restricted to elderly folks over sixty-five.
   C. No, because they don't care about your midlife crisis.
   (correct answer worth 10 points)

4. **You spy a shelf labeled FREE FOOD! in the hostel kitchen. What do you do?**
   A. Begin stuffing pomegranates in your pockets.

B. Ask the manager how food ended up in jail.

C. Run for your life.

(correct answer worth 5 points)

5. **Essay question. Why do you want to stay in a hostel?**
    (extra credit; worth up to 45 points)

Done? Great! And the envelope, please . . .

1. **E. None of the above.** The word hostel is German, and it means "country inn for youngsters" or something like that. In French, it's called an auberge de jeunesse, and in Italy, it's called an ostello.

2. **D. All of the above.** You got that one, right?

3. **C.** No age limits or restrictions here!

4. **A.** Free means free.

5. Give yourself 15 points for every use of the word "friends," "international," or "cool," okay? But don't give yourself more than 45. Yes, we mean it. Don't make us turn this car around right now. We will. We mean it.

What? All you wrote was "It's cheap"? Okay, okay, give yourself 20 points.

So how did you do?

100 points:	Born to be wild
80–100:	Get your motor runnin'
40–80:	Head out on the highway
20–40:	Lookin' for adventure
0–20:	Hope you don't come my way

Don't be embarrassed if you flunked this little quiz, though. Hostel operators get confused and blur the lines, too. You'll sometimes find a campground, retreat center, or college setting aside a couple bunks—and calling itself a hostel anyway. In those cases we've used our best judgment about whether a place is or isn't a hostel.

Also, we excluded some joints—no matter how well-meaning—if they (a) exclude men or women, (b) serve primarily as a university residence hall (with a very few special exceptions), or (c) serve you a heavy side of religious doctrine with the eggs in the morning.

In a few cases our visits didn't satisfy us either way; those places were either left out, set aside for a future edition, or briefly described here but not rated.

The bottom line? If it's in this book, it probably is a hostel. If it isn't, it's not, and don't let anyone tell you otherwise. There. 'Nuff said.

Understanding the Ratings

All the listings information in this book was current as of press time. Here's the beginning of a sample entry in the book, from a hostel in Seaside, Oregon. It's a fairly typical entry:

Seaside International Hostel ✳✳✳✵

930 North Holladay Drive, Seaside, OR 97138
(503) 738-7911; (888) 994-0001

  Fax: (503) 717-0163
  Web site: www.seasidehostel.net
  E-mail: seaside@teleport.com
  Rates: $20–$23 per person; $41–$53 for private room
  Credit cards: DISC, JCB, MC, VISA
  Beds: 56
  Private rooms: 7
  Affiliation: None
  Office hours: 8:00 a.m. to 9:00 p.m.
  Extras: Espresso bar, cafe, earplugs, VCR, hikes, canoes, kayaks, tours, kitchen, laundry, ironing board, Internet access, lockers

First things first. See those little pictures at the bottom of the listing? Those are icons, and they signify something important we wanted you to know about the hostel. We've printed a key to these icons on the facing page.

The overall hostel rating consists of stars or a turkey sitting at the top of each entry. It's pretty simple: Five stars means top notch. A turkey means bad.

We've used these symbols to compare the hostels to one another; only a select number of hostels earned the top rating of five stars, and a few were considered unpleasant enough to merit a turkey. You can use this rating as a general assessment of a hostel.

Sometimes we didn't give any stars at all to a hostel that was a mixed-bag experience. Or, for one reason or another—bad weather, bad luck, bad timing, remoteness, an inability to get ahold of the staff, or our own confusion about the place—maybe we just didn't feel we collected enough information to properly rate that hostel for you.

Key to icons

 Attractive natural setting

 Ecologically aware hostel

 Superior kitchen facilities or cafe

 Offbeat or eccentric place

 Superior bathroom facilities

 Romantic private rooms

 Comfortable beds

 A particularly good value

 Wheelchair-accessible

 Good for business travelers

 Especially well-suited for families

 Good for active travelers

 Visual arts at hostel or nearby

 Music at hostel or nearby

 Great hostel for skiers

 Bar or pub at hostel or nearby

 Editors' choice: Among our very favorite hostels

That said, here's a key to what these ratings mean:

✳✳✳✳✳	Best of the best; fun, clean, and pleasant
✳✳✳✳	Excellent
✳✳✳	Generally decent; average to above-average
✳✳	Barely adequate
✳	Not recommended
🐤	Bad news
NR	Not rated, mixed bag, jury's out

The rest of the information is pretty much self-explanatory:

Address is usually the hostel's street address, occasionally its mailing address.

Phone is the primary phone number.

E-mail is the staff's e-mail address, for those who want to get free information or book a room by computer.

Web site (this hostel didn't have one) indicates a hostel's Web address.

Rates are the cost per person to stay at the hostel. Expect to pay somewhere around $15 to $17 per person as a rule, more in cities or popular tourist areas. For private or family rooms, we've listed the total price for two people to stay in the room; usually it's higher than the cost of two singles, sometimes considerably so. Single or triple room rates will vary; ask ahead if you're unsure what you'll pay.

Note that these rates sometimes vary by season, or by membership in a hostelling group such as Hostelling International (HI); we have tried to include a range of prices where applicable. Most HI member hostels, for instance, charge $2 to $4 extra per day if you don't belong to one of Hostelling International's worldwide affiliates.

Also, some hostels charge about $1 to supply sheets and towels if you haven't brought your own. (Sleeping bags, no matter how clean you think they are, are often frowned upon.) Finally, state, provincial, or local taxes may also add slightly to the rates quoted here.

Credit cards can be a good way to pay for a bed—especially in a foreign country (you get the fairest exchange rates on your home currency); here, we have listed all the cards accepted by the hostel. More and more hostels are taking them, and even if we haven't listed any credit cards, things may have changed. When in doubt, call ahead and ask.

Here are the credit card abbreviations we use in *Hostels U.S.A.*:

AMEX: American Express
DISC: Discover Card
JCB: Japan Credit Bureau
MC: Master Card
VISA: Visa

Season indicates what part of the year a hostel is open—if it's closed part of the year. (Since this hostel has no "Season" line, that means it's open year-round.) We've made our best effort at listing the seasons of each hostel, but schedules sometimes change according to weather or a manager's vacation plans. Call if you're unsure whether a hostel will be open when you want to stay there.

Beds: This is the hostel's self-reported number of total capacity. Generally speaking, they count bunks as one (available) bed and double beds in private rooms as two beds.

Private rooms or **family rooms** are for a couple, a family with children, or (sometimes) a single traveler. Sometimes it's nice to have your own room on the road: It's more private, more secure, and your snoring won't bother anyone. Unlike Euro-hostels, most American hostels offer at least one private room. But often it's hard to get; call in advance if you know you want one.

Private bathrooms belong to a certain private room; nobody else (in theory) can use 'em. This luxury is pretty unusual in any sort of hostel, but you've got a better shot here than most anyplace else in the world; a few places do actually offer them.

Affiliation indicates whether a hostel is affiliated with Hostelling International or any of several smaller hostel groups. For more information about what these organizations do, see "A Word or Two About Affiliations" in the next chapter.

Office hours indicates when staff are at the front desk and answer the phones, or at least would consider answering the phones. Keep in mind that nothing is fixed in stone, however; some hostel staff will happily field calls in the middle of the night if you're reasonable, while others can't stand it. Try to call within the listed hours if possible.

A good rule of thumb to follow: The smaller a place, the harder it is for the owner/manager to drag him/herself out of bed at four in the morning just because you lost your way. Big-city hostels, however, frequently operate just like hotels—somebody's always on duty, or at least on call.

Extras list some of the other amenities that come with a stay at the hostel. Some—but not all—will be free; there's an amazing variety of services and almost as big a variety in managers' willingness to do nice things for free. Laundries, for instance, are almost never free, and there's usually a charge for meals, lockers, bicycle or other equipment rentals, and other odds and ends. On the other hand, some hostels maintain free information desks. Some give you free meals, too.

With each entry we've also given you a little more information about the hostel, to make your stay a little more informed—and fun. Here's the last part of the hostel entry that began above:

Best bet for a bite:
The Stand on Avenue U (great Mexican)
Insiders' tip:
Hiking Tillamook Head
What hostellers say:
"Great coastline."
Gestalt:
Whole latte fun
Hospitality: *A*
Cleanliness: *A*
Party index: 🎉🎉

What does all that stuff mean?

Best bet for a bite tells you where to find food in the area; usually we'll direct you to the cheapest and closest supermarket. But sometimes, in the interest of variety—and good eatin'—we'll point you toward a health food store, a place rich with local color, or even a fancy place.

Insiders' tip is a juicy secret about the area, something we didn't know until we got to the hostel ourselves.

What hostellers say relates what hostellers told us about a hostel—or what we imagine they would say.

Gestalt is the general feeling of a place, our (sometimes humorous) way of describing what it's about.

Safety describes urban hostels only; this hostel is not in a big city, so there's no safety rating. If it had been, though, we would have graded it based on both the quality of the neighborhood and the security precautions taken by the hostel staff, using this scale.

A:	No worries
B:	Pretty safe
C:	Somewhat dodgy
D:	Use great caution
F:	Dial 911

Hospitality rates the hostel staff's friendliness toward hostellers (and travel writers).

A:	Friends for life
B:	Smile city
C:	Take a chill pill
D:	Hostile hostel
F:	Very hostile

Cleanliness rates, what else, the general cleanliness of a place. Bear in mind that this can change—rapidly—depending on the time of year, turnover in staff, and so forth. So use it only as a general guide.

A:	Immaculate
B:	Spic-'n'-span
C:	Gettin' grungy
D:	Animal House
F:	Don't let the bedbugs bite

The **party index** is our way of tipping you off about the general scene at the hostel:

Rage all night
Party hearty
Lively
Mellow
Downright quiet

Finally, **How to get there** includes directions to the hostel—by car, bus, train, airplane, or even ferry. Often these directions are complicated, however; in those cases, managers have asked (or we recommend) that you call the hostel itself for more precise directions.

A Short History of Hostelling

*H*ostelling as we know it started around 1907, when Richard Schirmann, an assistant schoolteacher in Altena, Germany, decided to make one of the empty classrooms a space for visiting students to sleep. That was not a completely unique idea; Austrian inns and taverns had been offering reduced rates and bunk space to students since 1885. But Schirmann would develop much grander plans. He was about to start a movement.

His idea was to get students out of the industrial cities and into the countryside. Schirmann was a strong believer that walking and bicycling tours in the fresh air were essential to adolescent development and learning. But such excursions were impossible without a place to spend the night. His logic was simple: Since rural schoolhouses were deserted during weekends and holidays, why not make use of those spaces?

The caretakers of the school he chose agreed to serve as houseparents, and some fast ground rules were established. Students were responsible for piling up the tables and benches in the classroom and laying out thin straw sacks on the floor. At some ungodly early morning hour, the students were to restack the straw mats and reorganize the classroom as they found it. Boys and girls slept in separate rooms but were treated as equals. Detractors cried scandal, wondering aloud what was going on in these schoolrooms after dark.

The experiment worked, sort of. Altena became a haven for student excursions into the countryside, but finding shelter in other communities proved to be difficult. Sometimes the situation would become dire. Late one night in the summer of 1909, Schirmann decided it was time to expand his movement beyond Altena. His goal was to establish a network of hostels within walking distance of one another. Beginning in a schoolhouse with straw mats, Schirmann eventually acquired the use of a castle. It still stands—the Ur-hostel, if you will—in Altena, and it's still used as a hostel, believe it or not.

After World War I the movement really began to spread. By 1928 there were more than 2,000 hostels worldwide. Today tens of thousands of hostellers stay at Hostelling International–affiliated hostels each year, hailing from everywhere from Alaska to Zaire. Thousands more stay at independent hostels.

The goal of a single association of hostels located within a day's walk of one another will probably never be realized. Still, you're likely to find a promising brew of cultural exchange and friendship over pots of ramen noodles and instant coffee almost anywhere you go.

In that sense, perhaps, Richard Schirmann's dream has been realized after all.

A Word or Two about Affiliations

A majority of hostels in this book are affiliated with Hostelling International (HI); the rest we've labeled accordingly.

HOSTELLING INTERNATIONAL has long been the backbone of U.S. hostelling. The organization is part of the International Youth Hostel Federation, which has about 4,000 member hostels in about eighty countries worldwide. Member hostels are held to a number of regulations, such as maximum number of beds per shower, even a minimum amount of space that must exist between top bunks and the ceiling.

Overall, the HI hostels tended to earn higher marks from our reviewers than independent hostels. They regularly own the nicest buildings and keep the floors cleanest. The organization's mission statement trumpets its contribution to "the education of young people," so be warned that some of its most popular hostels attract youth groups like molasses does flies. Families and senior travelers are also attracted to the Hostelling International network.

Liquor is supposed to be off-limits at most of these places, and guests tend to be an orderly bunch. Many of the giant urban hostels are purpose-built facilities owned by the organization itself, often resembling well-equipped college dormitories. Some of these HI-owned hostels have developed impressive educational programs that incorporate volunteers from the local community and so forth.

The bulk of HI hostels, however, are independently owned. These joints are as varied in personality as their owners. A common thread that runs through them is a respect for the educational dimension of hostelling. Owners reiterate that hostels offer more than just a cheap sleep; they often join HI out of respect for the organization and its goals.

There is one last breed of HI hostels, the so-called home hostel—usually a spare bedroom or two in somebody's home. It goes without saying that your freedom (and partying) can be strictly limited at such places, but we've found that some of them are great if you can abide by the rules and enjoy getting to know your hosts. You'll definitely get more attention at these places.

INDEPENDENTS are what we call all the other hostels. Some owners opt not to join an organization. Membership costs are high, and they feel the return on such an investment isn't enough. Such a decision does not reflect on the quality of the hostel. It would be foolish to write a hostel off simply because it is not affiliated.

On the other hand, there's no guarantee of quality, and the standards, upkeep, noise level, and beer flow tend to vary wildly from place to place.

Hostel Memberships and International Booking

First things first: We advise you to get a Hostelling International membership before you ever even set out on your trip.

There are a few ways to become a member in the United States. The easiest way is to join online (go to www.hiusa.org for details). You can also call Hostelling International's U.S. customer service department at (301) 495-1240 (press 3 at the prompt). Or you can visit one of the official hostels listed in this book; nearly all of them sell memberships.

An annual membership still costs $28 per person for adults (ages eighteen to fifty-four), $18 for seniors age fifty-five and older. Kids can join for free. You can also purchase a lifetime membership for $250.

If you want to try some hostels before committing to the responsibility of owning a card, you can also obtain a guest membership; just pay a small supplement of about $3 US at an "official" hostel, which stamps your "guest card" each night you pay it. After six stamps, presto! You're a member. As a bonus, many hostels have established discounts for hostellers at businesses in the towns where hostels are located. You might get 10 percent off a meal at a restaurant, discounted train tickets or museum entrance fees, or other perks.

Hostelling International–American Youth Hostels

8401 Colesville Road, Suite 600
Silver Spring, MD 20910
(301) 495-1240
Fax: (301) 495-6697
Web site: www.hiusa.org

Hostelling International–Canada

205 Catherine Street, Suite 400
Ottawa, ON K2P 1C3, Canada
(613) 237-7884
Fax: (613) 237-7868
E-mail: info@hihostels.ca
Web site: www.hihostels.ca

Youth Hostels Association of England and Wales

Trevelyan House
Dimple Road, Matlock, Derbyshire DE4 3YH
+44 (0) 1629–592600

Fax: +44 (0) 1629–529702
E-mail: customerservices@yha.org.uk
Web site: www.yha.org.uk

Scottish Youth Hostels Association

7 Glebe Crescent
Stirling FK8 2JA, Scotland
+44 (0) 1786 891400
Fax: +44 (0) 1786 891333
E-mail: info@syha.org.uk
Web site: www.syha.org.uk

An Óige (Irish Youth Hostel Association)

61 Mountjoy Street
Dublin 7, Republic of Ireland
+353 (0) 1 830 4555
Fax: +353 (0) 1 830 5808
E-mail: mailbox@anoige.ie
Web site: www.irelandyha.org

Hostelling International–Northern Ireland

22-32 Donegall Road
Belfast BT12 5JN, Northern Ireland
+44 (0) 28 90324733
Fax: +44 (0) 28 90315889
E-mail: info@hini.org.uk
Web site: www.hini.org.uk

If you're the type who needs the security of knowing where you're staying each night of your trip, you might also want to participate in the International Booking Network (IBN), whereby certain participating hostels—usually located in big cities or major tourist areas—call ahead to another IBN hostel (located in the same sorts of areas) and secure your bunk, even in high season if it's humanly possible. Most ask for an advance notice of three to seven days; if there's any room, you'll get priority—you only need prepay for your bed with a Visa, MasterCard, or Discover Card (plus a $5 US booking fee) and you're in. The system is fairly straightforward. However, be prepared to eat the cost of the whole bed if you need to cancel on short notice.

How to Hostel

*H*ostelling in the United States is, generally speaking, easy as pie. Plan ahead a bit and use a little common sense, and you'll find check-in goes pretty smoothly.

Reserving a Bed

Getting a good bunk will often be your first and biggest challenge, especially if it's high season. (Summer is usually high season, but in some areas of the United States—the Rockies, for instance, and parts of Vermont—winter is the toughest time to get a bed.) Hostellers often have an amazingly laissez-faire attitude about reservations; many simply waltz in at midnight expecting a bed will be available.

Sometimes it is. Sometimes it isn't.

Most every Hostelling International abode takes advance reservations of some form or another, so if you know where you're going to be, use this service. Be aware that many hostels require a credit card number to hold a bed, and some require you to send a deposit check. Many hostels also maintain their own toll-free reservation numbers; we've included these numbers wherever they're available.

Some HI hostels are also affiliated with the worldwide International Booking Network. You can make advance reservations for a very small fee online at www.hiusa.org.

Independent hostels are sometimes more lax about taking solid reservations, though they're also a lot more willing to find extra couch space or a spare mattress in case you're squeezed out. Calling a few days ahead to feel the situation out is always a good idea.

If you can't or won't reserve, the best thing to do is get there super-early. Office opens at 8:00 a.m.? Get there at 7:00. No room, but checkout ends at 11:00 a.m.? Be back at 11:05 in case of cancellations or unexpected checkouts. The doors are closed again till 4:30 in the afternoon? No problem. Come back around 4:00 p.m. with a paperback and camp out on the porch. That's your only shot if you couldn't or wouldn't reserve ahead, and hostellers are pretty respectful of the pecking order: It really is first come, first served. So come first.

Paying the Piper

Once you're in, be prepared to pay for your night's stay immediately—before you're even assigned a bunk. Take note ahead of time which hostels take credit cards, checks, and so forth. Think you're being cheated with the bill? Remember that most hostels charge $1 or so per night for linens if you haven't brought your own. (You always have the option of bringing your own, however, and we recommend it. See below.)

Other charges could include a surcharge for a private room and charges for phone calls from your room, if a phone is included (very unusual).

You might also need to leave a small deposit for your room key—usually about $5, sometimes more—which you'll get back when you check out, unless you lost the key in the meantime. Sometimes you will be required to show some form of photo identification to check in. Very occasionally, you'll even be forced to leave a passport or driver's license with the front desk. This is annoying and possibly illegal, but a few hostels still get away with it. Scream bloody murder, threaten to sue—but you might still get shut out unless you play along.

Remember to pay ahead if you want a weekly stay. Often you can get deep discounts, though the downside is that you'll almost never get a refund if you decide you can't stand it and leave before the week is up.

If you're paying by the day, rebook promptly each morning; hostel managers are very busy during the morning hours, keeping track of check-ins, checkouts, cleaning duties, and cash. You'll make a friend if you're early about notifying them of your plans for the next day. On the other hand, managers hate bugging guests all morning or all day about whether they'll be staying on. Don't put the staff through this.

Some hostel managers have the curiously softhearted habit of letting the rent slide a few days. We can't figure why; when managers do this, a day often becomes a week or a month. Even if this courtesy is extended to you, don't use it except in an emergency. You never know who they'll hire to get that money out of you later.

Okay, so you've secured a bed and paid up. Now you have to get to it. This may be no easy task at some hostels, where staff and customers look and act like one and the same. A kindly manager will probably notice you bumbling around and take pity. As you're being shown to your room, you're also likely to get a short tour of the facilities and a briefing on the ground rules.

Knowing the Ground Rules

There's one universal ground rule at every hostel: You are responsible for serving and cleaning up after yourself. And there's a corollary rule: Be courteous. So while you're welcome to use all the kitchen facilities, share the space with your fellow guests—don't spread your five-course meal out over all the counter space and rangetop burners if other hungry folks are waiting. And never, ever leave a sink full of dirty pots and pans behind. That's bad form.

Hostel guests are almost always asked to mark their name and check-in date on all the food they put in the refrigerator. Only the shelf marked free food is up for grabs; everything else belongs to other hostellers, so don't touch it. (Hostellers get very touchy about people stealing their grub.) Some of the better-run hostels have a spice rack and other kitchen essentials on hand. If you're not sure whether something is communal, ask. But don't assume anything is up for grabs unless it is clearly marked as such.

Alcohol is still a major issue at some hostels. Hostelling International rules officially forbid it on the premises of HI hostels. We were not surprised to see this rule bent or broken in some places, but inquire with a smile on your face before you bring that brew inside. Independent hostels are a lot more forgiving; some even have bars.

Then there's the lockout, a source of bitter contention among hostel factions. A few rural and small-city Hostelling International hostels throw everybody out in the morning and don't let them back in until the early evening. Lockouts tend to run from around 10:00 a.m. to 4:00 p.m., during which time your bags might be inside your room—but you won't be.

The practice has its pros and cons; managers usually justify a lockout by noting that it forces travelers to interact with the locals. The real reason is usually that the hostel can't or won't pay staff to hang around and babysit you all day. On the other hand, some hostels become semi-residential situations stuffed with couch potatoes. A lockout sure solves that problem.

In the reviews, we've identified those hostels that enforce lockouts. Usually you wouldn't want to be hanging out in the hostel in the middle of the day anyway, but after several sleepless nights of travel—or when you're under the weather—daytime downtime sure is appreciated. So beware.

Some hostels also enforce a maximum limit on your stay—anywhere from three days, if the hostel is really popular, to about two weeks. You will know if such a policy is in effect the moment you walk into a place. If there are lots of cigarette butts, slackers, or dirty clothes hanging around, it's the curse of the dreaded long-termers: folks who came for a day and stay for a lifetime just to avoid finding work. So a maximum-stay rule can be a very good thing. On the other hand, you might find yourself wanting to spend more than three days in some great place—and be shown the door instead.

Savvy budget travelers have learned how to get around this unfortunate situation, of course: They simply suck it up and spend a night at the "Y" or a convenient motel—then check back into the cheaper hostel first thing in the morning. But we didn't tell you to do that. Uh-uh.

Etiquette and Smarts

Again, to put it simply, use common sense. Hostellers are a refreshingly flexible bunch. All these people are able to make this system work by looking after one another; remember, in a hostel you're a community member first and a consumer second. With that in mind, here are some guidelines for how to act:

- The first thing you should do after check-in is get your bed made. When you're assigned a bed, stick to it. Don't spread your stuff out on nearby bunks, even if they are empty. Someone's going to be coming in late-night for one of them, you can bet the backpack on it.
- Be sure to lock your valuables in a locker or the trunk of your car. Good hostels offer lockers as a service; it might cost a little, but it's worth it.
- Set toiletries and anything else you need in a place where they are easily accessible. This avoids your having to paw through your bag later at night, potentially disturbing other guests from their slumber. The same goes for early-morning departures: If you're taking off at the crack of dawn, take precautions not to wake the whole place.
- If you're leaving early in the morning, try to make all arrangements with the manager before going to bed the night before. Retrieve your key deposit before the desk closes if possible, and settle up any other debts. Managers are usually accommodating and pleasant folks, but guests are expected to respect their privacy and peace of mind by not pushing things too far. Dragging a manager out of bed at four in the morning to check out—or for some other trivial matter—is really pushing it.
- Be sure to mind the bathroom. A quick wiping of the shower floor with a paper towel after you use it is a common courtesy.
- Finally, be sure to mind the quiet hours. Some hostels have curfews, but very few force lights-out. If you are up after hours, be respectful. Don't crank the television or radio too loud. (Save that for the beach and for annoying people staying in much nicer digs.)

Packing

Those dainty hand towels and dapper shaving kits and free soaps you get at a hotel won't be anywhere in sight at the hostel. In fact, even some of the base essentials may not be available; you're on your own, so bring everything you need to be comfortable.

There are only a few things you can expect the hostel to supply:

- a bed frame with a mattress and pillow;
- shower and toilet facilities;
- a working kitchen with communal pots, pans, and dishes;
- a common room with some spartan furniture; and
- maybe a few heavy blankets.

Some of the more chic hostels we've identified in this guide may be full-service. Heck, we've stayed in hostels that provide the food for you to cook—not to mention generous spice racks. But they are the exception to the rule.

Bring this stuff to keep your journey through hostel territory comfortable:
- A passport is strongly advised, even if you are traveling domestically. Many urban hostels keep a very tight filter on who may check in. (The exception is Hostelling International affiliates, which are required by policy to admit all paying guests.) A passport gives you a sense of legitimacy as a traveler. Be aware that a few American hostels simply will not allow American visitors to stay due to concerns about transiency—and we have done our best to identify those in the write-ups. HI hostels are not supposed to take in hostellers who live in the area, for obvious reasons, but sometimes this rule is bent in dire emergencies.
- Hostelling International membership cards are a good thing to have on hand. They can be purchased at most HI-member hostels ($28 annually per adult 18 to 54, $18 for seniors 55 and older). This card identifies you as a certified super-hosteller and gets you the very cheapest rate for your bed in all HI (and also some unaffiliated) hostels. At $2 to $4 per night, these savings can add up fast.
- Sometimes that membership card gets you deals at local restaurants, bike shops, and tours, too. Again, it will be easier to deal with the front desk at some of the more cautious hostels (even nonmember ones) if you can flash one of these cards.
- Red alert! Do not plan on using a sleeping bag in most hostels. A good number of places simply won't allow it—problems with ticks and other creatures dragged in from the great outdoors have propelled this prohibition into place. The alternative is a "sleep sack," basically two sheets sewn together with a makeshift pillowcase. You can find them at most budget travel stores, or make your own. Personally we hate these confining wraps, and we rarely get through the night in one without having it twist around our bodies so tightly that we wake up wanting to charge it with attempted manslaughter. Our preferred method is to bring our own sets of sheets,

though that might be too much extra stuff if you're backpacking it. Some hostels give you free linen; most that don't will rent sheets for about $1 to $2 per night. You don't get charged for use of the standard army surplus blankets or the musty charm that comes with them.

- Some people bring their own pillows; those supplied tend to be on the frumpy side. This is a good idea if you're traveling by car and can afford the space.
- We definitely suggest earplugs for light sleepers, especially for urban hostels—but also in case you get caught in a room with a heavy snorer.
- A small flashlight is a must—not only for late-night reading but also to find your bed without waking up the entire dorm.
- A little bit of spice is always nice, especially when you have had one too many plates of bland pasta. You'll find the cost of basil, oregano, and the like in convenience stores too high to stomach once you're on the road. Buy it cheap before you leave and carry it in jars or small plastic bags.
- Check which hostels have laundry facilities. It's much easier to do the wash while making dinner than to waste a day sitting around with the cast of The Shining at a local Laundromat.
- Wearing flip-flops or other plastic sandals in the shower might help spare you a case of athlete's foot.
- Be sure your towel is a quick-drying type. Otherwise you'll wind up with mildew in your pack—and in your food.

Transportation

*T*ake a careful look at your transportation options when planning a hostel journey. You should be able to fly from city to city and take a bus or train to urban hostels without a problem, but you could have trouble getting to rural hostels without a car.

By Airplane

The U.S. airline business is crazy: Deals and rip-off fares come and go with frightening regularity. Supply, demand, season, the stock market, and random acts of cruelty or kindness all appear to contribute to the quixotic nature of fares.

As a result, there is no one piece of simple advice we can give you, other than this: Find a travel agent who cares about budget travelers, then trust that agent with all the planning. You can cruise the Internet if you like, and you might find an occasional great deal your agent doesn't know about. Just make sure the sellers are reputable before giving out your credit-card number.

When planning, try to make longer flights between hubs if you can, then backtrack if necessary. You want to fly into Los Angeles, New York, and Miami instead of San Diego, Buffalo, or Tampa, if you can help it. Places like Atlanta, Orlando, Dallas, Houston, Pittsburgh, Memphis, Newark, and Boston have all become hubs for cheaper domestic and international flights.

If you really must fly from point to point within the United States and will be coming from outside North America (sorry, Americanos), the VUSA pass—it means "visiting the USA and Canada"—can be a big help. The pass cheapens certain flights considerably, though you must buy it in your home country before leaving.

Cheap-ticket brokers (also called consolidators or bucket shops) are a great bet for saving money, but you have to be fast on your feet to keep up; the deals appear and disappear literally daily. London and New York are major centers for bucket shops.

By Bus

Bus is, generally speaking, the cheapest way to travel. Service is okay, though a bus might only come once every few days to some very remote areas. Check ahead of time to be sure. We have included bus directions wherever possible to help you figure out what to do. Still confused? Call the hostel directly to clear things up.

Also remember that it can take somewhat longer to get where you're going, especially if the bus stops a lot on the way. Be ready, too, for possible stopovers in bus stations in the middle of nowhere, and the comfort level often won't be high. Who needs it? Probably you if you're broke, because tickets can be super-cheap. Some lines also offer even more affordable unlimited travel passes.

Greyhound (800-231-2222; www.greyhound.com) offers by far the most extensive system of bus transport in the United States. Greyhound sometimes offers spectacular price cuts for cross-country travel, as well as passes allowing you to ramble all over this great land for less than a train ticket would cost.

Where Greyhound doesn't go, smaller local lines fill in the rest of the gaps fairly capably. They're the ones that will get you to most of those small-town hostels, so grab as many schedules at the airport or bus station as you can.

By Car

If you're from the United States, skip these first few paragraphs.

Speeds and distance in the United States are measured in miles. One mile is about 1.6 kilometers; 100 miles is roughly 160 km. Here are some common speed limits you might see on road signs, with their metric equivalents:

Miles	KILOMETERS
35 mph	56 km per hour
50 mph	80 km per hour
55 mph	88 km per hour
65 mph	104 km per hour
70 mph	112 km per hour

When deciphering a map, U.S. distances will always be given in miles. To convert miles to kilometers, multiply by 1.6.

Stop signs are red, octagonal, and obvious. Streetlights are also simple: Red means stop, yellow means slow down, green means go. A green or blinking green arrow means go ahead and turn; a yellow arrow means slow down before you turn. In the United States and much of Canada, you're allowed to make a right turn when the light is red—after making a complete stop. Don't do it unless there's no traffic, and never do it if a sign says no turn on red.

Gas is measured in gallons, and there are roughly four liters to the U.S. gallon. Gas prices are listed per gallon, so divide by four to estimate the price per liter you'd pay back home. A ten-gallon fill-up generally costs around $35 these days, less in the South and more in the Northeast. Prices depend partly on geography, partly on the OPEC-set and economic demand–driven price of crude oil, and partly on each state's gas taxes. Natural disasters (think hurricanes,) tensions in the Mideast, and increased demand from industrializing economies also affect prices. Gas is almost always cheaper off the interstate—especially where there's a lot of competition—than it is on the interstate.

U.S. cities are as traffic-clogged as those in other countries, and possibly more dangerous: Accidents are frequent, and angry drivers sometimes even shoot at one another. Our advice? Never drive in a big city between the "rush hours" of 7:00 to 9:00 a.m. or 4:00 to 7:00 p.m. if you can help it. Use back roads (U.S. highways can be a nice alternative) instead of huge interstates, freeways, and beltways—unless you need to make time over great distances.

Keep an eye on your speed, though. Speeding probably won't get you more than a fine, which could be heavy, but driving while intoxicated could land you in jail—immediately.

Knowing a bit about how cars work—like when to check the oil and how to change a tire—is useful. Many travelers join AAA (www.aaa.com), the largest auto club in the world; one of the benefits you get for the $50 to $70 annual fee is an "800" number to call for emergency towing.

Car rental companies are a dime a dozen, but their rates can fluctuate dramatically. In a city, the name brands often offer the best deals, but shop around. In smaller-town hostels, check at the desk; a local firm will occasionally have a "hosteller special" available. The biggest hassle about renting a car is that it can run up to $500 to return it any place other than where you picked it up—a major headache. Also, you usually need a major credit card and must be over age twenty-one to rent with most.

Remember to check with your home insurance company about whether you're already covered for driving rental cars—often you are, even though the company will use pressure to get you to buy needless extra insurance for $8 to $12 per day. On the other hand, don't skip it if you're not already covered.

The lowest cost choices seem to be National (unlimited mileage with rentals), Alamo (special 10 percent discounts for Hostelling International members), Budget, and Rent-a-Wreck. They're in all the big cities, as are other big American rental companies like Enterprise, Avis, and Hertz (more expensive, but also gives small discounts to HI members). Smaller, local rental companies sometimes undercut the big guys, but they might charge more for mileage or refuse to do a one-way rental.

Auto Driveaway (www.autodriveaway.com) gets solid reviews from folks who have time to stick around and wait for a car that needs driving. The company—really a series of small offices in major cities across the United States and Canada—pairs you up with someone who needs a car moved from one place to someplace else. All you have to do is put down a few hundred dollars for a deposit, pay for the gas, and leave the tank full when you deliver. Remember, however, that there is a time frame in which you need to deliver the car and that you're not allowed to stray too far off a designated route. You get the deposit back when you turn over the car, although you might have to cash the refund check in that particular city.

Other local companies with similar names often provide a similar service to smaller, more out-of-the-way destinations, but they may be less flexible about deposits or drop points. Check the local Yellow Pages or Internet under Auto Transportation or Auto Driveaway.

Purchasing a used car is a popular (if a bit risky) choice for many foreign travelers. Try to know a thing or two about cars if you're going to go this route, rather than spend hundreds of dollars for a set of wheels—only to put twice that much into repairs on your cross-country journey. Remember that registration and proof of insurance, at the very least, will be required before you hit the road and that they can take a little time to obtain.

By Train

Amtrak (800-USA-RAIL; www.amtrak.com) is the United States' railroad network. Service in the busy coastal corridors gets much higher marks than it does on cross-country routes, and the train can be a surprisingly expensive option if you need a sleeping car. Still, seats are comfortable and the ride is usually smooth, so planning your trek around the Amtrak schedule may not be a bad idea.

Cross-country travelers should look into the USA Rail Pass, a terrific combination deal giving a rider unlimited coach travel on trains in the United States. Three types of passes are available: for fifteen days/eight segments; thirty days/twelve segments; and forty-five days/eighteen segments. Travel must begin within 180 days of the date you buy the pass, but they're no longer valid in Canada—sorry, Charlie. The passes cost $389 to $749 per adult, half-price for children ages two to fifteen. More fine print: You have to pick the passes up at the first station on your itinerary, wherever that's going to be; bring a passport or U.S. identification card to the station. Also, these passes do not absolve you of needing tickets and reservations for each Amtrak leg you take: You still gotta go online or to a ticket window and reserve seats, even though the pass pays for them.

Other Resources

*T*here's surprisingly little out there about hostelling and hostels—that's why you're reading this, right?—but we did find a few sources. Most simply list phone numbers and addresses.

Remember that hostels are constantly opening, closing, renovating, being sold, and changing their policies. So not everything written in a guidebook will still be true by the time you read it. Be smart and call ahead to confirm prices, availability, and directions, rather than rolling into town depending on a bed—and getting a nasty surprise like a vacant lot instead. We know; it has happened to us. With that in mind, here's what else is around:

Hostels Canada (Globe Pequot, 2000) is perhaps the finest guide to Canadian hostelling ever written—complete coverage of more than 125 hostels north of the border. And we know because we wrote it. Seriously, though, there's more hostelling info than you can shake a stick at between those two covers, especially if you'll be heading north at some point. A great value for the price.

Hostels in the U.S.A. is the official U.S. guidebook for Hostelling International. It provides the same basic information as this book, without the opinions, but little else besides maps to most of the member hostels. The directions are sometimes a bit difficult to follow. The North American handbook comes out early each year and is available free at HI-affiliated hostels.

Or contact Hostelling International directly. The American headquarters are located at 8401 Colesville Road, Suite 600, Silver Spring, MD 20910, and you can call 'em at (301) 495-1240.

Hostelling International's Web site, www.hiusa.org, keeps you fairly up to speed on U.S. doings. It features snappy graphics, membership info, write-ups on some of the member hostels, the basics of the organization, a nice section on volunteering and getting involved, and links to other hostels around the world. We especially like the festivals page, describing festivals around the country—plus links to nearby HI hostels.

The HOSTELS

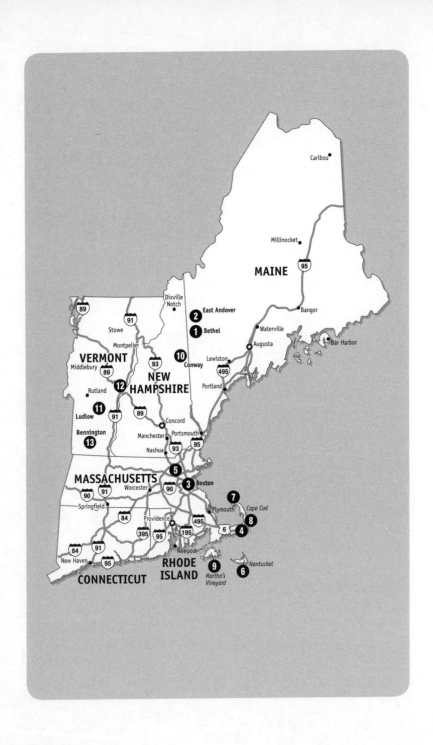

New England

Page numbers follow hostel names

MAINE

The SnowBoarding House Hostel

646 West Bethel Road, Bethel, ME 04217

(207) 824-4224; (800) 533-3607

Fax: (207) 824-8511
Rates: $19 per Hostelling International member
Credit cards: DISC, MC, VISA
Beds: 18
Private rooms: None
Affiliation: Hostelling International
Office hours: 8:00 to 10:00 a.m.; 5:00 to 10:00 p.m.
Extras: Kitchen, laundry, Internet access

*T*his place popped up on our radar a few years back; it's the second to open in the rugged mountains of western Maine. Originally a spring-to-fall, eighteen-bed joint with laundry, kitchen with nice checked floor, and access to the Internet, it has since gone four-seasons on us. Cool, since you can only snowboard in Maine's (lonnnnnng) winter. Cleanliness remains spotty, though this is on the edge of the Maine woods, so you're already coming with a bit of a rough expectation, right? But we also came expecting a laid-back groove and dudes who like to rip it up on the slopes. Well, that's what we expected; instead, the place was super-sedate (and not always in a good way), with little to no party atmo, and the vibe just wasn't what it could be. Sigh. Ponying up more dough with four friends and splitting a condo at Sunday River just might be a more attractive option for full-out party/ski hostelers.

At least we can say this for it: West Bethel is rural, but it's cool rural—there are tons of rivers to raft, lakes to canoe and/or fish, mountains to climb, woods to ski or snowshoe, and fall foliage to peep at in the area. Apple orchards serve up plenty of ripe ones in the fall, too. And there's an ace natural foods store just north of the center of the attractive town of Bethel. White Mountains National Forest is very close at hand (well, by car, anyway) if you're up for some seriously high peaks, and a supremely beautiful stretch of the Appalachian Trail breaches the Maine–New Hampshire border just 10 miles away.

How to Get There:

By bus: Nearest bus stop is in Gorham, New Hampshire, 12 miles away.
By car: Take Maine Highway 26 to U.S. Highway 2 to Bethel, then continue 4 miles west on US 2.

The Cabin in Maine ✹✹✹✷

497 East Andover Road, East Andover, ME 04226
(207) 392-1333

   E-mail: thecabin@megalink.net
   Web site: www.thecabininmaine.com
   Rates: $14 per person; $25 for private room
   Credit cards: None
   Beds: 10
   Private rooms: 1
   Affiliation: None
   Office hours: 6:00 to 9:00 a.m.; 4:00 to 9:00 p.m.
   Extras: Laundry, kitchen, bikes, canoes, hiking equipment, parking, shuttle service, barbecue, library, piano, guitar, meals ($), TV, tepee, snowshoes, skis, garden

*W*estern Maine is often ignored by travel writers, yet it's rife with stunning scenery and choice vistas from the mountain peaks that dominate the landscape and provide visitors with year-round activities ranging from skiing to hiking. Most lodging in the area, which extends roughly from Bethel to Rangeley, is priced out of range for most budget travelers except during the muddy spring or the short summer. (Fall brings loads of Appalachian Trail through-hikers and fans of fall foliage; winter is the star attraction here, as resorts vie for the skier's attention.) Fortunately, the managers at this hostel run a good—if small—hostel. You'll find a friendly retired couple, nicknamed "Honey & Bear," who started the place during the mid-1990s and truly seem to enjoy interacting with their guests. Hostellers continue to rave about their friendliness and warmth.

Your sleeping quarters are either a mixed-gender dorm room with eight beds or the one private room with a queen-size bed. One bathroom serves all who are staying the night.

The couple goes out of their way to accommodate late arrivals and will try not to turn any sleepy body away.

The location is extremely rural and peaceful; fields and woods surround the place, so don't be surprised if you happen to spy a moose or deer casually grazing by the roadside. (Be alert for these animals when driving, as collisions with them are alarmingly common in these parts.) The town of Andover is pretty typical of western Maine—a mixture of back-to-the-land types, loggers, and others. Culture is pretty thin on the ground, but who cares? There's plenty to do out of doors.

For starters, we'd hightail it to the little natural foods store just outside Bethel and grab some gorp and other trail food and head for the hills. Bring a bucket or container of some sort in late July or early August in case you come across patches of wild blueberries. You'll probably meet through-hikers along the way, ripe with the scent of too many days without a shower, but if you can handle that, this makes a good diversion. Just remember the two house rules: No dogs, no drugs. Once you've got those two down, the rest is mashed potatoes and gravy.

How to Get There:

By bus: Call hostel for pickup from bus stations in Pinkham Notch, Gorham (New Hampshire), or Portland (Maine).

By car: Take Route 2, turning north on Route 5; continue 8 miles, make a right on covered bridge road and keep left up the hill when you join East Andover Road.

MASSACHUSETTS

BOSTON HOSTELS: A SUMMARY					
	RATING	PROS	CONS	COST	PAGE
Fenway Hostel	✸✸✸✸	plush	pricey	$35	p. 35
Boston International Hostel	✸✸✸✸	central	big	$28–$45	p. 33
Boston Backpackers		central	noisy	$25-$35	p. 31

Boston Backpackers

232 Friend Street, Boston, MA 02114

(617) 723-0800

Rates: $25–$35 per person

Credit cards: None

Beds: 48

Private rooms: 1

Affiliation: None

Office hours: 9:00 a.m. to 9:00 p.m.

Extras: Lockers, raffles, pool, movies, laundry, TV, bar, restaurant, kitchen, free Internet access

If sipping a Guinness and watching the Sox on the tube in an Irish pub just downstairs from your hostel bed is your idea of heaven on earth, you might think about booking this place, which is steps from Boston's historic North End. Think again. Because if nirvana also includes a good night's sleep and a spacious kitchen in which to make your breakfast, this definitely isn't the place for you. The doors to the rooms squeak, and when you're sharing the bedroom with nine people, that's a big deal. With music thumping through the floor (from the bar, which means until last call), the place has all the ambience of a highway hotel above a truckers' bar. And it's far, far from sparkly clean; beware, if you enjoy clean digs.

There are a lot of freebies here, though. Almost anything you'd have to pay for elsewhere comes free at the B-B: linens, storage, Internet access, and so forth. The only advantage, as we've noted, is the location: It's near the North End, so there's great Italian food and street life to check out 24/7. There's shopping at the covered market in Faneuil Hall (second-largest tourist attraction in the United States, don't ya know), hoops at the TD Banknorth Garden (home of the world-champion Celtics, as well as the currently nonchampion Bruins), and the Freedom Trail is also a must-see (or, rather, must-walk). Afterward there's a satellite dish at the hostel that allows the intrepid explorer to watch soccer and rugby games from all over the globe.

How to Get There:

By airplane: From airport, take the Orange or Green T (subway/underground) Line to North Station. Exiting North Station, walk with TD Banknorth Garden (Fleet Center) on your left and continue walking down Causeway Street until Friend Street. Turn left onto Friend Street to hostel.

By bus: Greyhound and Trailways bus companies stop at South Station. From South Station, take the Red T Line to Downtown Crossing station and change to Orange Line going three stops to North Station. Follow walking directions above.

By car: From Interstate 93, take exit 25; turn left on Causeway Street, then left on Friend Street. Proceed to hostel.

By train: Amtrak stops at South Station. From South Station, take the Red T Line to Downtown Crossing station and change to Orange Line, going three stops to North Station. Follow walking directions above.

Boston International Hostel

12 Hemenway Street, Boston, MA 02115

(617) 536-9455

Fax: (617) 424-6558

E-mail: bostonhostel@bostonhostel.org

Web site: www.bostonhostel.org

Rates: $28–$45 per Hostelling International member; $80–$133 for private room

Credit cards: JCB, MC, VISA

Beds: 205

Private rooms: 11

Affiliation: Hostelling International

Office hours: Twenty-four hours

Extras: Television, VCR, air-conditioning, laundry, lockers, kitchen, Internet access, light breakfast

*L*et's say that after a long day of seeing Boston's best tourist traps, you wanted to grab a burger at the oldest tavern in the nation. At the ordinary hostel, the weary backpacker would queue up to ask the harried desk staff for directions and, eventually, maybe get some.

Not at Hostelling International's Boston hostel, though, where the adventuresome can access a touch-screen computer system to get directions to many of Beantown's best nightspots. The info system here provides an address, phone number, photograph, and extremely accurate directions (down to the quarter-mile and by block, plus directions by bus and subway). You can even print out the price of that burger.

It's a useful service, too, because the hostel's party potential is out of this world. Some of the best clubs in the city are just a few blocks away on Lansdowne Street. The place is situated smack in the middle of college housing

Best bet for a bite:
Cafes on Newbury

Insiders' tip:
Dunkin' Donuts (founded in Boston) coffee excels

What hostellers say:
"Good place."

Gestalt:
Home run

Safety: *B*

Hospitality: *B*

Cleanliness: *B*

Party index: 🎉🎉🎉

for several universities and colleges, including Northeastern, the Boston Conservatory, and the Berklee School of Music.

Being surrounded by college students in the middle of Boston does have its darker side, however. The neighborhood is noisy and, like many urban centers, can be dangerous to the unwary international traveler at night. Be careful, or just stay in groups when you're straying from busy, well-lit areas.

For those who want something more mellow than a night of mosh-pitting to industrial music, there are several other great cultural experiences within an easy walk. You can catch the Green Line and watch a Red Sox game at historic Fenway Park, check out museums, or take in an outdoor concert at the renowned Hatch Shell in a park set beside the lovely Charles River.

This hostel has undergone some extensive remodeling to add space to the kitchen, redo the lighting and plastering, replace the carpeting, and rework the floors. The front desk has been streamlined, and a mural was added in the stairwell. It's basically a place of big dorms and surprising amenities: free continental breakfast, lockers, comfortable rooms with beds that got kudos for heavier bedding than the usual single scratchy blanket in many hostels, and a handy kitchen. This place, frankly, surprised us with its continuing upkeep and customer service. It's better than we expected, time hasn't taken a toll, and we'd still recommend it to almost anyone.

How to Get There:

By airplane: From Logan Airport, take free Massport shuttle to subway station, then take MBTA subway Blue Line inbound four stops to Government Center station; change to Green Line and travel outbound to Hynes stop. Walk left on Massachusetts Avenue to Boylston, then turn right. Go 1 block, turn left; hostel is on left.

By bus: Greyhound and Trailways stop in Boston. From South Station, take subway to Green Line; get off at Hynes stop. Walk left on Massachusetts Avenue to Boylston, then turn right. Go 1 block, turn left; hostel is on left.

By car: Take I-93 to Storrow Drive; follow Storrow to Fenway/Boylston exit (about ten minutes). Go to second light. Take right on Massachusetts Avenue, next right onto Haviland Street, then next right onto Hemenway Street.

By train: Amtrak stops in Boston. From South Station, take subway to Green Line; get off at Hynes stop. Walk left on Massachusetts Avenue to Boylston, then turn right. Go 1 block, turn left; hostel is on left.

Fenway Hostel

575 Commonwealth Avenue, Boston, MA 02115

(617) 267-8599

Fax: (617) 424-6558

E-mail: fenway@bostonhostel.org

Web site: www.hifenway.org

Rates: $35 per Hostelling International member; $89–$92 for private room

Credit cards: MC, VISA

Season: June 2 to August 20

Beds: 300

Private rooms: 100

Affiliation: Hostelling International

Office hours: Twenty-four hours

Extras: Lockers, laundry, Internet access

ocated right on the campus of famously party-hardy Boston University, this summertime-only joint is more like a hotel than a hostel; all rooms have no more than three beds each (these are dorm rooms, after all), and all have air-conditioning. Public facilities include a handy hosteller laundry, Internet access, and storage lockers for your stuff. It's a very high-quality place, probably best for couples and families and probably a bit dull for single travelers looking to party; you'll find no beer blasts here in summer, only during the school year (when the hostel's closed).

Kenmore Square is a great, studenty area in which to riffle through bins and bins of used records and comic books, grab a beer, or just hang. The Charles River Esplanade is nearby. The best thing to do, though, is catch a game at nearby Fenway Park—it's so close you can walk there. Join thousands of other Sox fans in this shrine of an old ballpark and

Best bet for a bite:
Around the Square
Insiders' tip:
Game On! bar is even cheaper than bleacher seats
What hostellers say:
"Yankees suuuuuuuuck!!!!!"
Gestalt:
Sox in the city
Safety: *A*
Hospitality: *A*
Cleanliness: *A*
Party index:

cheer your guts out for the latest incarnation of the Team That Finally Did It! All in all, the best hostel digs in town; grab 'em if you can.

How to Get There:

By airplane: From Logan Airport, take free Massport shuttle to subway station, then take MBTA subway Blue Line inbound four stops to Government Center station; change to Green Line and continue on westbound B, C, or D train five stops to Kenmore station. Walk 1 block west to hostel.

By bus: Greyhound stops in Boston beside South Station. From South Station, take MBTA subway Red Line inbound two stops to Park Street T station and change to Green Line; continue on outbound B, C, or D train five stops to Kenmore station and walk 1 block west to hostel.

By car: Take Interstate 90 (Massachusetts Turnpike) east to Copley Square inbound exit, turn left at Dartmouth Street and continue to Beacon Street; turn left onto Beacon Street, and merge right onto Commonwealth Avenue.

By train: Amtrak stops in Boston at South Station. From South Station, take MBTA subway Red Line inbound two stops to Park Street T station and change to Green Line; continue on outbound B, C, or D train five stops to Kenmore station and walk 1 block west to hostel.

Mid-Cape Hostel ✹✹✹✹

75 Goody Hallet Drive, Eastham, MA 02642

(508) 255-2785

Fax: (508) 240-5598

E-mail: midcape@usahostels.org

Web site: www.capecodhostels.org

Rates: $32 per Hostelling International member; $140 for single room

Credit cards: MC, VISA

Season: Late May to late September

Beds: 46

Private rooms: None

Affiliation: Hostelling International

Office hours: 8 a.m to 11:00 p.m.

Extras: Outdoor showers, barbecue, basketball, volleyball, table tennis,

---

*T*his miniature bungalow community-style hostel offers an entirely different experience from its sister hostels on Cape Cod. Visitors sleep in tiny cabins equipped with only a few head-to-toe bunk beds and a hanging lightbulb. Think of them as deluxe lean-tos.

You'll have to brave the elements to access the restrooms at night, which are housed in the centrally located main lodge—an old-fashioned bathhouse construction with exposed rafters—along with most everything else. The walls here and in the cabins are thin and the table tennis table is in regular use, so quiet is hard to come by. On the flip side, though, the crowd is as friendly as any without being rowdy (lots of families come here). The barbecue pit and screened porch are great for cookouts, and outdoor showers ease the morning crush by offering a welcome opportunity to bathe in the morning sunshine.

Eastham's off-the-beaten-path, wooded location (for the Cape, at least) makes for great wildlife watching. Management dressed the hostel surroundings with birdfeeders and is placing emphasis on environmental education through a weekly lecture series. The trade-off in terms of location, though, is that there is no direct beach access; you'll have to trek out a couple of miles to reach the surf. Another recreational option is to hop onto the Rail Trail, a converted 30-mile bike path that passes nearby.

Come early or come late, but don't come at the height of the summer season if you can help it: Camp groups hit this one hard.

Best bet for a bite:
Hole in One donut shop
Insiders' tip:
Bird sanctuary 8 miles east
Gestalt:
Summer camp
Hospitality: *A*
Cleanliness: *B*
Party index:

How to Get There:

By airplane: From Logan Airport in Boston, take Plymouth & Brockton bus line to Orleans. Hostel is 2 miles from bus stop. Rent a bike 1 block east on Main Street at the bike store if you can. Go east on Main to Rock Harbor Road (bike path runs parallel) and follow to Bridge Road on left. Go ¼ mile to Goody Hallet Drive on right. Hostel driveway is 100 yards on left.
By bus: From Boston, take Plymouth & Brockton bus line from South Station to Orleans. Hostel is 2 miles from bus stop. Rent bike on Main Street if you can. (See above directions.) Hostel driveway is 100 yards on left. (You can also take this bus from Truro, Provincetown, Plymouth, and Hyannis.)
By car: Take U.S. Highway 6 to rotary at Orleans Center; use Rock Harbor exit. Drive ¼ mile to right on Bridge Road and ¼ mile to right on Goody Hallet Drive. Hostel is 100 yards on left.

Friendly Crossways Hostel ✳✳✳✳

247 Littleton Country Road (P.O. Box 2266),
Harvard (Littleton), MA 01451
(978) 456-9386

Fax: (978) 456-9386
E-mail: info@friendlycrossways.com
Web site: www.friendlycrossways.com
Rates: $18–$27 per Hostelling International member; $48–$54 per couple (kids extra)
for private room
Credit cards: None
Season: January 2 to December 21
Beds: 14
Private rooms: 13
Affiliation: Hostelling International
Office hours: 8:00 to 10:00 a.m.; 5:00 to 10:00 p.m.
Extras: Storage, information desk, parking, piano, fireplace, library, bikes, pickups,
kitchen, meals ($)

---

*W*hen this hostel passed from the former manager on to her daughter and son-in-law, some held their breath. Could it maintain the same high standard?

Well, so far, so good. They've kept the place eco-friendly and added their own innovations, like afternoon tea and free bikes rescued from the town dump. See? This hostel recycles and composts in a big way.

The kitchen is well-equipped with cookbooks and spices; you'll also find a cozy dining room with communal tables, a fireplace, and a piano. The sleeping space befits the early Hostelling International style, with two large bunkrooms. Down the hall are a few privates and doubles. We were thrilled to see that the quilts were chock full o' brilliant carnival shades. Legend has it that they were sewn together by an actual circus fat lady, who did the deed between acts—while chain-smoking.

The only negative to this place at all is the lockout policy, which is understandable, but if you're traveling without a car you may find it a serious obstruction: the place is closed up from 10:00 a.m. until 5:00 p.m., and that's seven long hours to fill. If you can get a lift to the town train station, though, you're in luck: It will take you straight into the heart of

Boston, where there's more than enough to do for a day.

If you're sticking to the surroundings during the day, Littleton is classic New England all the way. The bright colors of leaves in fall are almost too beautiful to be believed, and sledding and cross-country skiing delight winter visitors. Hit nearby Bay Hill Pond for swimming and nature walks in warmer months. Bring the tweed to wear at night, as it can get chilly—this town is Norman Rockwell territory, even if the new bosses favor Hawaiian shirts. All in all, this is a great place for old-timers or hostel fanatics, but maybe not so hot for party-hearty types (there's an 11:00 p.m. curfew).

Best bet for a bite:
Kimball's Ice Cream
Insiders' tip:
Fruitlands Museum
What hostellers say:
"Pass the apple cider."
Gestalt:
Saturday Evening Post
Hospitality: *A*
Cleanliness: *A*
Party index:

How to Get There:
By bus: Call hostel for transit route.
By car: Take Route 2 to exit 39. Go left on Taylor Street, then left onto Porter Road, then left at the stop sign. Go 1½ miles; hostel is on right.
From Interstate 495, take exit 29B to Route 2 West. Take exit 39, go left on Taylor Street, left on Porter Road, left at stop sign. Go 1½ miles; hostel is on right.
By train: Amtrak stops in Boston. From North Station, take Fitchburg/Acton line to Littleton/495 stop. At Littleton, call hostel for pickup or directions.

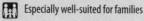

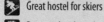

Robert B. Johnson Memorial Hostel

Surfside, 31 Western Avenue, Nantucket, MA 02554

(508) 228-0433

Fax: (508) 228-2273

E-mail: nantucket@usahostels.org

Web site: www.capecodhostels.org

Rates: $27 per Hostelling International member

Credit cards: JCB, MC, VISA

Season: Late May to late September

Beds: 49

Private rooms: None

Affiliation: Hostelling International

Office hours: 7:00 a.m. to 10:00 p.m.

Extras: Barbecue, volleyball, picnic area, travel library, piano, kitchen, laundry

*Y*ou could say this hostel has a "million-dollar location," but even *that* would be an understatement. The Surfside neighborhood that's home to this handsome former lifesaving station (built in 1873) is priced so high that most vacationers wouldn't even consider it. Yet Hostelling International situated itself on Nantucket years before the island was hip, and now the island's quaint cobblestone streets and beautiful beaches are the stuff of which New England summer hostelling dreams are made.

Walk across the street from the hostel to one of the island's best surfing beaches, or hop onto your bike and cruise around the numerous paved paths that extend for miles. The hostel is just 3½ miles from the charming downtown district where the ferry drops you. While buses make regular runs around the island, cycling and in-line skating are really the best ways to go if you can hack it. There are almost no hills, and an extensive system of pathways offers great views of the inspiring scenery. Be sure to get out into the

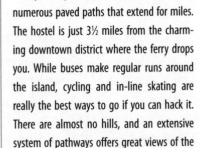

Best bet for a bite:
A&P at ferry landing

Insiders' tip:
Discount on local bike rentals

What hostellers say:
"Behave. Or I'll tell your mother."

Gestalt:
Buoys and Gulls

Hospitality: *A*

Cleanliness: *B*

Party index:

island's nature preserves: They'll pull you away from the crowds and offer a whole new island experience.

In town, the Whaling Museum always seems to get rave reviews, as do numerous bake shops. Voyeurs will be interested to know that lavish yachts can always be found floating around the downtown piers. On a nice evening you can't go wrong by getting a lobster and a few ears of corn at a seafood joint to bring back for a sunset picnic on the beach by the hostel, either. Beware, though, that whatever your plans, it's going to cost you. Everything from bike rentals to hamburgers is so inflated here that it will shock the unwary American traveler. (British or Japanese travelers, though, might see it as business as usual.)

One worrisome trend: The secret is out about this hostel, and not because of the book you're holding in your hands. It's so overwhelmingly popular, due to its bargain pricing, that Hostelling International once even asked the place to cut back on overnight bookings a bit; even the enthusiastic managers were dismayed by that, but what could they do? Teen groups hit this place hard, basically filling the forty-nine beds (packed into just four big rooms) from July 4 through Labor Day with advance bookings. So the hostel's occasionally being overrun by screaming adolescents is a risk you're going to have to take, because these are the *only* budget digs on the isle. The facilities are great, mind you; it's just that there isn't enough space to go around. But we digress. The location here is so sweet that we'd even be psyched to sleep in the backseat of a Chevy Nova (some readers doubtless have done so somewhere along the journey of life). To get a bed and kitchen use for this price is almost too good to be true. So if you can get one, do it.

How to Get There:

By bus: Ask at information booth at ferry landing about buses to Surfside.

By car or bike: Hostel is 3½ miles from Nantucket ferry wharf. Go inland on Main Street and left on Orange Street, then right on East York Street (at bake shop). Bear left onto Atlantic Avenue, which becomes Surfside Road. Stay on Surfside Road for 2 miles. At the beach go right onto Western Avenue. Hostel is on right. Taxi cost: $10; local bus: $2.

Outermost Hostel

28 Winslow Street, Provincetown, MA 02657

(508) 487-4378

  Web site: www.outermosthostel.com

  Rates: $25 per person

Credit cards: None
Season: May to October
Beds: 30
Private rooms: None
Affiliation: None
Office hours: 8:00 to 9:30 a.m., and 5:30 to 9:30 p.m.
Extras: Picnic tables, bike rentals

*T*his hostel epitomizes much of what staying in hostels is all about: "No hassles." There's no curfew and no lockout, so hostellers can come and go as they please. There's also no view, no kitchen, and very few facilities to speak of. People don't come here to be swept off their feet; they come to take advantage of close proximity to Provincetown's downtown.

What's here are five small cabins, each packed like a sardine can with four bunk beds, on a piece of property that is overshadowed by a water tower. Sad to say, little of "P-Town's" charm is reflected in this facility. The place draws some seriously mixed opinions: a few of our hostelers loved its funky charm to death, while others couldn't wait to get out. All in all, it's certainly acceptable, but not the great green experience you might expect on a Cape otherwise packed with superior-quality hostels.

The staff is as laid-back as they come, though, and you certainly won't get that "walking on eggshells" feeling that comes with some rule-heavy hostels. If hitting a local bar scene is your reason for being in town, this is the one Cape Cod hostel that gives you the freedom to do it. (Of course, in this case, the "bar scene" is a heavily *gay* bar scene—something to keep in mind before you wander through the nearest pink door.) The hostel's very convenient for folks without cars, because both the local beaches and the town's many art galleries are within easy walking distance. (You can get here by bus, so you don't actually need a car.) In addition, it seems that the hostel hosts its own party most nights, so walking to a bar

Best bet for a bite:
Pizza downtown
Insiders' tip:
Whale watching from MacMillan Wharf
What hostellers say:
"What day is it??"
Gestalt:
Cottage squeeze
Hospitality: *B*
Cleanliness: *C*
Party index:

might not even be a concern. Keep in mind, seekers of ultimate peace and quiet, that this may not be your kind of place.

How to Get There:
By bus: Call hostel for transit route.
By car: From U.S. Highway 6 east, take third Provincetown exit and turn left onto Jerome Smith Road. Make an immediate right onto Winslow Road; hostel is 2/10 mile on right.

Truro Hostel

North Pamet Road (P.O. Box 402), Truro, MA 02666
(508) 349-3889

> **E-mail:** truro@usahostels.org
> **Web site:** www.hi-travel.org
> **Rates:** $29 per Hostelling International member; $120 for single room
> **Credit cards:** JCB, MC, VISA
> **Season:** Late June to early September
> **Beds:** 42
> **Private rooms:** None
> **Affiliation:** Hostelling International
> **Office hours:** 8:00 a.m. to 10:00 p.m.
> **Extras:** Library, volleyball, piano

---

*T*ruro is the ultimate in exclusive Cape Cod communities. With its hostel set on a bluff overlooking the ocean, many real estate agents would love to get their hands on this place. The only thing standing between our snoops and the ocean was the mansion next door . . . the one that was hosting former Vice President (and almost-President) Al Gore during one of our snoops' visits.

At last thrifty travelers can take a holiday on the Cape and bask in beach sunshine without being packed like sardines at a tiny public facility. A refreshing walk down through the dunes sets you right on a lovely ocean beach away from the local traffic. In fact, you'll have to go way out of your way to find the crowds here: Truro is a tiny little rich town with an environmental conscience, and the hostel isn't even *in* the downtown.

The place is inside a turn-of-the-twentieth-century Coast Guard station that was given to Hostelling International long ago; it really does look almost like a palace. The majestic white mansion has sprawling common areas complete with huge picture windows that open onto priceless views. Everything is just as it should be, down to the quaint front porch, where guests often gather at night to drift on the swing and sing campfire songs. Yes, Virginia, really. Only the men's basement sleeping dorm could stand some improvement; bad beds and overcrowding are the norm in high season. Women are blessed with sturdy wood bunks and super views from the top floor.

Management has all the spunk you'd expect at such a stellar facility—and then some. Local music nights, evening walks along the seashore with local conservation groups, and ecology lessons are among the endeavors in which visitors can expect to take part. This place is big on encouraging hostellers to get out into the area's dunes, marshes, and cranberry bogs. Bird-watchers will want to visit the National Audubon Center 8 miles away. Cape Cod, you'll find, is much more interesting than just beaches, bistros, and bars.

Intellectual stimulation can be found 10 miles up the "arm" (Cape Cod geography lingo) in Provincetown. There are galleries galore in this big-money tourist town, plus bars, arcades, and all the other stuff you may, or may not, want to be part of your vacation. A giant monument to commemorate the landing of Pilgrims in 1620 offers a challenging climb, and whale-watching excursions leave from downtown "P-town."

Be back by 10:00 p.m., however, because the curfew here is ironclad. There are also no exceptions to the all-day lockout, so don't forget your towel! One last gripe: Teen groups overrun the place in high season. Late June and late August are when you are likely to have the most pleasant stay. Otherwise bring a set of earplugs.

How to Get There:

By bus: Take Plymouth & Brockton bus line from Boston or Hyannis to Truro. Transfer to Plymouth & Brockton line; bus drops passengers at post office. Call hostel for walking directions (about 2 miles).

By car: Take North Pamet Road exit off U.S. Highway 6. Follow signs 1½ miles to end of North Pamet Road. Hostel is on right.

Martha's Vineyard Hostel ✳✳✳✳✳

25 Edgartown–West Tisbury Road (P.O. Box 3158),
West Tisbury, MA 02575
(508) 693-2665

Fax: (508) 693-2699

E-mail: vineyard@usahostels.org

Rates: $27 per Hostelling International member; $75–$200 for private room

Credit cards: MC, VISA

Season: Mid-May to mid-October

Beds: 69

Private rooms: 1

Affiliation: Hostelling International

Office hours: 7:00 a.m. to 10:00 p.m.

Extras: Barbecue, outdoor showers, lockers, ferry and cab discounts, kitchen, Internet access, library

*N*ot only is this fabulous hostel located on exclusive Martha's Vineyard, it's also tucked away in the peaceful, sheepherding town of West Tisbury. This select area is where writers and artists have formed retreat communities alongside locals with a rich ancestry on the island. The general store remains the center of town life, and the venerable Agricultural Hall is still home to a weekly farmers' market. The hostel is right near a 4,000-acre state forest, where cyclists can access wonderfully scenic (and flat) paths that lead to other island attractions. The forest is also a prime location for quiet walks and bird-watching; just be sure to bring binoculars (and bug spray, too).

The cedar saltbox-style structure was constructed in 1955 as the first purpose-built hostel in the United States. There is nothing plastic about this place; instead, a cozy rustic feel pervades each of the rooms, and all the precious space is put to good use. Unexpectedly, several corners of the hostel are filled with interesting books, and the comfortable furniture is arranged to encourage conversation. The kitchen is worthy of awards, as well: Its circular design—complete with a lit stained-glass globe in the center—transforms the usual aggravation of crowded hostel cooking into a fun, communal experience. Long wooden dining tables create a festive, almost publike atmosphere, and the kitchen's even a great place to read in the morning as sunlight streams across the lush front yard into it.

In the dorms are firm, shiny wood bunks, although the rooms are packed to the max with them, limiting personal space. Every dorm is named after part of the Cape (for example, "Chappaquidick"), and the hallway bulletin board overflows with wise quotes. This is a so-called Sustainable Living Center, so ecology is a top priority, and information about how you can do your part abounds. There are also regular lectures and other educational programs.

The outdoor showers and toilet are a big hit, too. Hostellers seem to enjoy the luxury of bathing outdoors on misty island mornings. These outdoor facilities, as well as a row of lockers, are accessible to guests all day. Right next to them is a makeshift chicken coop, which is popular with kids.

Best bet for a bite:
Grocer near the ferry wharf
Insiders' tip:
Cycle, cycle, cycle
What hostellers say:
"What a kitchen!!"
Gestalt:
Salty dogs
Hospitality: *A*
Cleanliness: *A*
Party index: 🎉🎉

"We're as much an institution as anything else on this island," said one manager. This hostel predates the yachts of Edgartown and the arcades of Oak Bluffs; it's even pointed out by tour guides. The pride the community takes in the hostel is evident through generous discounts at numerous local businesses. That's right: You can save yourself a bundle by making use of the coupons distributed at the front desk and by taking advantage of the cheap in-house breakfast.

Don't miss this place, but do try to come during an off-peak time. Dozens of screaming camp groups parade through summer peak periods, which can be the only downer at this terrific hostel. And remember: It's isolated. You *will* want to rent a bike.

How to Get There:
By taxi: Available from Vineyard Haven ferry landing to hostel.
By ferry: Cheapest route is from Woods Hole to Vineyard Haven. Ferries from Hyannis on Cape Cod and Nantucket are also available. Parking is available on the mainland. Bring a bike or rent one at the ferry terminal. From Vineyard Haven go left on Water Street for ¹/₁₀ mile to a right on State Road. Go 3 miles until a left on Old County Road. Go 3½ miles on Old County until you reach Edgartown/West Tisbury Road. Turn left and go ¾ mile to hostel.

NEW HAMPSHIRE

Albert B. Lester Memorial Hostel

36 Washington Street, Conway, NH 03818

(603) 447-1001

Fax: (603) 447-3346

E-mail: conwayhostel@yahoo.com

Rates: $23 per Hostelling International member; $48 for single room; $38–$48 for private room

Credit cards: JCB, MC, VISA

Beds: 28

Private rooms: 4

Affiliation: Hostelling International

Office hours: 7:30 to 10:00 a.m.; 5:00 to 10:00 p.m.

Extras: Laundry, free breakfast, bike room, barbecue grill, movies, Internet access, kitchen

*T*he July 1995 opening of this hostel was a monumental event for low-budget travelers, who can now take advantage of 750,000 acres of forests, rivers, and mountains in the White Mountains National Forest without dishing out the big bucks for a "quaint" bed-and-breakfast. The only drawback is that it has changed hands a few times, and it may have been sold again (or even sold and totally closed down as a hostel) by the time you read this.

If it's a green-friendly hostel you crave, then this is the place. Everything about this hostel—from the sustainably harvested wood walls and nontoxic paint to the compost bin in the kitchen—is focused on reducing, reusing, or recycling.

Sustainability aside, this converted farmhouse is a great place to stay and offers some special touches. The common room has several couches, there's a gigantic kitchen, and rooms are clean. Most visitors opt to stay in the dorms, divided by sex, but private rooms are available.

Location is also great. There are two business districts in the area: Conway and North Conway. The latter—complete with tacky outlet stores and fast-food chains—bears more resemblance to a strip mall than a secluded paradise. The hostel, though, is in Conway, a charming village of the *It's a Wonderful Life* ilk. The husband-and-wife proprietors will help you find the best deals on everything from mountain biking clinics to ice cream cones to kayak rentals.

During the weekend we stayed, the guest list included a half-dozen "gearheads" in town for a conference on rock climbing. With lots of several-hundred-foot rock faces, the area is famous among climbers. If you are into that kind of thing, be sure to catch one of the hostel's Friday night slide shows. Presentations vary but often focus on the most extreme sorts of life-threatening outdoor enjoyment.

Biggest setback? The only other hostel accessible from here by public transportation is in Boston, so unless you've got wheels and gas, it's pretty hard to work it into a New England trip. Also note an $8 per night bedding charge and a half-price deal for kids under age thirteen.

How to Get There:

By bus: From Boston, Concord Coach Lines (800-639-3317) makes one or two trips per day. From stop, walk north to Main Street, turn right, then left onto Washington Street.

By car: Drive U.S. Route 302 until it intersects with New Hampshire Highway 16; follow Highway 16 (Main Street) into the town of Conway (not North Conway); turn north onto Washington Street at light, continue ¼ mile. Hostel is on left.

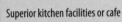
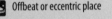
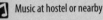
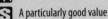
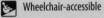
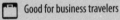

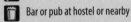
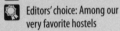
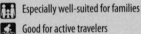

VERMONT

Trojan Horse Lodge

44 Andover Street, Ludlow, VT 05149

(802) 228-5244

E-mail: thlodge@aol.com

Web site: www.members.aol.com/thlodge

Rates: $23–$28 per person

Credit cards: MC, VISA

Season: June to August and November to March

Beds: 18

Private rooms: None

Affiliation: None

Office hours: 8:00 to 10:00 a.m.; 4:00 to 9:00 p.m.

Extras: Television, VCR, games, canoe rental (sometimes), kitchen, lockers

Set in a former carriage barn—a building constructed of tongue-and-groove wood—the Trojan Horse is one nice place to stay the night if you're bumping around Vermont's Black River Valley. Rich Gray, a jack-of-all-trades, runs the hostel when he isn't working as a master electrician or carving tree stumps into some whimsical shape. Wife Paula helps out, too.

This is Vermont, so you sleep in what used to be the hayloft of the barn. It is now a series of clean bunkrooms (six beds to a room) with big windows. Both the sleeping quarters and the big, friendly common room stay pleasantly cool during the hottest summer days.

There's a television and VCR, but we'd rather walk around the place admiring fruit trees and the herb garden, swing in the

Best bet for a bite:
Art of the Chicken
Insiders' tip:
Book ahead for winter weekends
What hostellers say:
"Great for relaxing."
Gestalt:
Mountain magic
Hospitality: *B*
Cleanliness: *A*
Party index:

swings, rent a canoe, head into town to see about renting a bike, or check out the nearby rivers and streams, which are fine for fishing or even dipping toes. Hiking abounds, as well, especially in fall, when the maples come alive. Skiing is obviously a big draw in wintertime (when the rates go up $5 a day) because there's a nice ski hill just a short jaunt away.

There's not much to complain about, except perhaps that the hostel is left unlocked all day. Vermont is about as safe a place as you'll find on the continent, though, so never mind about that. This is a good place in any season.

How to Get There:
By car: Take Vermont Highway 100 or 103 to Ludlow; go south on 100 for ½ mile. Hostel is on left.

Hotel Coolidge Hostel ❂❂❂
39 South Main Street (P.O. Box 515), White River Junction, VT 05001
(802) 295-3118; (800) 622-1124
> **Fax:** (802) 291-5100
> **E-mail:** reservations@hotelcoolidge.com
> **Web site:** www.hotelcoolidge.com
> **Rates:** $25–$35 per Hostelling International member
> **Credit cards:** AMEX, DISC, MC, VISA
> **Beds:** 26
> **Private rooms:** 16
> **Affiliation:** Hostelling International
> **Office hours:** Twenty-four hours
> **Extras:** Meals, laundry, fireplace, kitchen

*T*ucked inside the aging Hotel Coolidge sits a little (though hardly cheap) hostel. The innkeeper is extremely enthusiastic about the hostel section of his building. For years a place of rest for weary Central Vermont Railway workers, this hotel is now a place for train-traveling backpackers to hop off the Amtrak run from New York—the station's right across the street. That makes this a great town for railroad buffs; if you're not one, though, you might find the place lacking. Anyway, check in, unpack, and head out trolling through the eateries, gift shops, sports bars, and brewery, all within walking distance.

This hotel has history coming out the wazoo. The entire building was transported here in 1849 by a riverboat captain, and actress Lillian Gish stayed in the hotel while making the classic 1920 silent film *Way Down East*. There are just two beds to a hostel room here, and check out what else you get in each one: a sink and mirror, chairs, linens, towels, blankets, steam heat, and ceiling fans. They're fairly comfortable compared with most hostel

Best bet for a bite:
Polka Dot diner
Insiders' tip:
Tubing the Connecticut
What hostellers say:
"Old World."
Gestalt:
Kinda Coolidge
Hospitality: *B*
Cleanliness: *A*
Party index:

digs, once you get used to the odd decor—white walls trimmed with, um, off-white curtains. Obviously, it's easy to get a private room. Heck, every room is a private room.

Bathrooms are simple, clean, and (thanks to inside latches) private; they also have hampers and mirrors. The common room consists of the usual kitchen, TV, and couch setup. Drawbacks? Some feel the hostel—along with the hotel—is getting tired, musty, and outdated. We can't deny that. This is not a place for those looking for modernity or creature comforts.

The hostel wing spills right into the Briggs Opera House, where year-round entertainment plays to hotel and hostel guests alike. All areas of this hotel, in fact—well, except people's bedrooms, but you get the point—are accessible to hostellers, a switch from most hostel-hotel combos we've stayed in.

For eats, the somewhat pricey cafe on the premises serves a selection of coffee, teas, and pastries, though it's worth the extra cash if you want to kick back with one of the many books that line the walls and shelves of the place while sipping tea. Lots of other diners, cafes, and restaurants line the streets of working-class White River, too, so you could also pick from a grinder (a hoagie or sub to you non–New Englanders), organic sprouts and local cheeses from the food co-op, or some fresh pastas to make in the kitchen from an Italian joint. White River isn't really a travel destination in and of itself unless you're into trains or mills, but if you're passing through the area, the surrounding hills and waters mean there's lots to do year-round. The manager, an outdoors enthusiast, can direct you to all the best canoeing, skiing, and tubing opportunities. Dartmouth College's green lawns and awesome bookstores aren't far away at all. Don't visit the area without conquering a portion of the Appalachian Trail, either, especially if you're coming mid-September through October: The famous trail passes nearby.

Just as fun, the nearby Catamount Brewing Company gives tours three times a day. With a biiiiiig free tasting at the end. (Yes!) You'll learn lots of—okay, maybe too much—interesting stuff about beer, but as your eyes glaze over during the Louis Pasteur digressions, keep your eyes on the prize.

Like we said, good thing the hostel is within walking distance.

How to Get There:

By bus: Greyhound stops in White River Junction. From bus terminal, call hostel for directions.
By car: Call hostel for directions.
By train: Amtrak stops in White River Junction. From station, walk across Main Street to #17.

Greenwood Lodge Hostel

Vermont Highway 9, Box 246, Woodford (Bennington), VT 05201
(802) 442-2547
   Fax: (802) 442-2547
   E-mail: campgreenwood@aol.com
   Rates: $25 per Hostelling International member; $57 for single room
   Credit cards: None
   Season: Mid-May to late October
   Beds: 9
   Private rooms: None
   Affiliation: Hostelling International
   Office hours: 9:00 a.m. to 9:00 p.m.
   Extras: Pond, piano, boats, volleyball, pickups (sometimes), kitchen, camping, Internet access

---

*E*ven though it's been significantly downsized in recent years (just nine beds at last count), Greenwood Lodge is a potential hospitality heaven tucked into the Green Mountains. Owners Ann and Ed Shea strive to make every visitor feel at home at their mountaintop hostel, and they mostly succeed. The couple, who taught school in New York before returning to Ed's native Vermont, constantly work on big and small improvements to their 120 acres and their hostel/campground. The Sheas have made getting around easy for all guests by widening hallways and adding ramps and roll-in showers.

A guest feels immediately at home inside the lodge. The main room features a piano, television, lots of windows, benches and comfy couches, and farm implements galore. Ed wanted a farmhouse look—he's got it—but there's an added lightness and style that keeps it from being too cute.

The site also hosts about forty campsites, and the Sheas encourage campers and hostellers to interact, emphasizing that "they're all travelers." Bennington is just 8 downhill miles away (watch out on the way back) and features lots of shops and restaurants. There is no transportation from town other than an expensive taxi, but creativity always works.

A location at the edge of the Green Mountain National Forest means there is access to the Long Trail. Opportunities for walking, biking, boating, and swimming also abound. For Americana and staples, there's True's General Store, where they actually still sell penny candy.

The Sheas say they "didn't know a hostel from a hole in the ground" when a friend convinced them to try starting one up in the late 1970s. From a hole in the ground to the top of a mountain: They've sure come a long way.

How to Get There:
By airplane: Nearest airport is Albany, New York (one hour away); from there, take bus or rent car.
By car: From Bennington, drive east on State Highway 9; turn in at Prospect Mountain entrance, then left at gates.
By train: Amtrak stops in Albany, New York, and Brattleboro, Vermont; take bus or rent car.

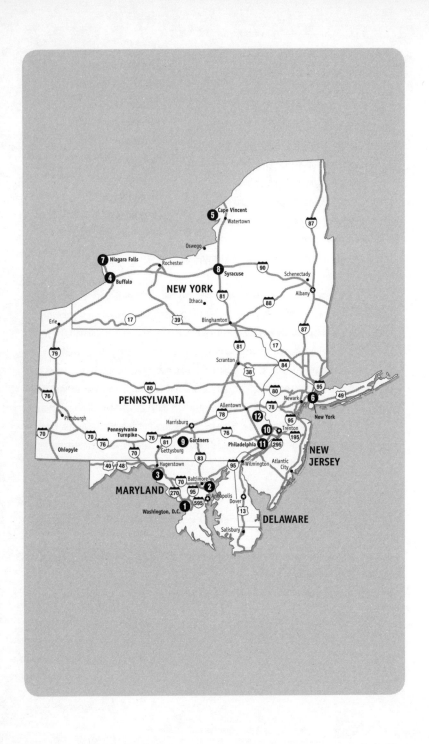

Mid-Atlantic

Page numbers follow hostel names

DISTRICT OF COLUMBIA

WASHINGTON, D.C., HOSTELS: A SUMMARY

	RATING	PROS	CONS	COST	PAGE
Hilltop Hostel	✹✹✹	great neighborhood	aging	$22	p. 56
Hostelling International– Washington, D.C.	✹✹✹	programs, facilities	poor location	$26–$30	p. 58
Washington International Student Center	✹✹	fun area and crowd	packed dorms	$24–$28	p. 60

Hilltop Hostel ✹✹✹

300 Carroll Street NW (Takoma Park), Washington, DC 20012

(202) 291-9591

Web site: www.hosteldc.com

Rates: $22 per person; $45 for private room

Credit cards: None

Beds: 40

Private rooms: 3

Affiliation: None

Office hours: 9:00 a.m. to midnight

Extras: Game room, foosball, pool table, television, VCR, laundry, kitchen, hammock, free parking, free lockers (bring padlock), summer barbecues, free local phone, Internet access

The District of Columbia is lucky to have this hostel, located outside the city in the user-friendly Takoma Park neighborhood. Described as a sort of Addams Family–like building with New Orleans–style balconies, it was a Victorian hotel long before Watergate got famous and is listed on the National Historic Register.

Dorm rooms here are small, with no more than six happy campers to a room, and there are separated-by-gender bathrooms. (The place does get stuffy in summer, though.) Other amenities include a pool table and television room for movie nights. Guests can also help themselves to free local phone calls—and no, the phone is not tapped. Heh-heh. Management keeps the atmosphere light but fun by encouraging folks to mingle in the big backyard, where they stoke up the barbecue during the summer months or when an impromptu mood hits.

There's a satellite television, with plenty of soccer and Australian-rules football among hundreds of other channels. As a couch-potato countermeasure, a ground-floor balcony was extended to make room for a dining table. There's a popular hammock in the nice yard and a kitchen—painted white, purple, and orange—for hostellers to cook in. If there's any complaint, it's that the party vibe is beginning to take a toll on the physical condition of the place—not only in terms of cleanliness, but wear, tear, staff professionalism, and a general downsliding of the situation. Stay tuned for updates on that.

The Takoma Park neighborhood is one of the safest and most livable in D.C., we're told. Lots of residents here are stay-at-home professionals who keep a close eye on what's going on, so it's not just a jazzy place to be. It's much safer than downtown, if not nearly so multi-cultural. A twenty-four-hour convenience store across the street from the hostel serves as a mini–police station, adding to the safety factor.

(Takoma Park is even a *nuclear-free* town, many of the residents being ex-hippies who went corp and fixed up all the old Victorian mansions as a kind of boho retreat from the big city. They shop in Tibetan stores, bead stores, and the like while sipping gourmet coffee.)

If you're a serious culture vulture, though, all the museums are just a ten-minute hop away on D.C.'s fabulous Metro subway. The Metro station is just 50 yards away. For a small price you can be whisked away to all the free Smithsonians and National Gallery of Art you can take in.

How to Get There:

By airplane: Large airport outside Washington. From Ronald Reagan National Airport, take Metro Yellow Line to Gallery Place Station; change to Red Line and continue to Takoma Station. Exit platform at Carroll Street. Hostel is at #300.

Best bet for a bite:
One of the pupuseria *(pupusa shops)*
Insiders' tip:
Takoma Station Tavern for jazz
What hostellers say:
"Right on!"
Gestalt:
Capital gang
Safety: *B*
Hospitality: *B*
Cleanliness: *C*
Party index:

By bus: Greyhound stops in Washington. From bus terminal, exit onto First Street and turn left; walk 3 blocks to Union Station. Take Metro Red Line to Takoma Station; exit platform onto Carroll Street. Hostel is at #300.

By car: Take the Takoma exit off the Beltway (I-495) and follow New Hampshire Avenue. Make right on East–West Highway, follow until you reach Carroll Street, make right at church. Hostel is opposite the 7-Eleven on left.

By train: Amtrak stops in Washington. From Union Station, take Metro Red Line to Takoma Station; exit platform onto Carroll Street. Hostel is at #300.

Hostelling International–Washington, D.C.

1009 Eleventh Street NW, Washington, DC 20001

(202) 737-2333

   Fax: (202) 737-1508
   E-mail: reserve@hiwashingtondc.org
   Web site: www.hiwashingtondc.org
   Rates: $26–$30 per Hostelling International member; $69 for single room
   Credit cards: MC, VISA
   Beds: 250
   Private rooms: 7
   Affiliation: Hostelling International
   Office hours: Twenty-four hours
   Extras: Television, VCR, travel store, snack bar, arcade, smoking lounge, pool table, kitchen, lockers, Internet access ($), breakfast, laundry, bike rentals

---

*O*n our way here once, we ran into a nice Kiwi chap who told us he'd passed through and simply adored this hostel, but left with a frightening impression of D.C.'s nightlife. Having visited our nation's capital on past occasions, and finding it full of said nightlife, we were baffled by his impressions of the city. Then we got here and saw what he was talking about.

The hostel is okay overall, but the neighborhood it's located in is (how can we put it nicely?) kinda-to-really bad. A new event arena sponsored by a giant telecom company attracts performers of all stripes, but watch yourself when going to the supermarket because that area did not seem very safe to us.

At least the hostel is like a self-sustained community with something always going on. There are two and a half floors of common space, from the basement arcade to the well-stocked travel store, in this 250-bed building. The entire second floor is reserved for the expansive and rightly praised kitchen—complete with glass-door refrigerators—and dining room. It's a great resource in this part of town, where most of your only other affordable options are fast-food joints or greasy spoons. The small included breakfast is also a boon, though showers got a thumbs-down for weak pressure.

Best bet for a bite:
Chinatown (but be careful)
Insiders' tip:
Lots of hostel programs
What hostellers say:
"I'm all museumed out."
Gestalt:
Capitol gang
Safety: *C*
Hospitality: *B*
Cleanliness: *B*
Party index:

The sleeping facilities are fine, as are the bathrooms. You may find yourself sharing a floor with a school group or teen tour. The place is big enough that it shouldn't be a bother, so long as you don't mind giggling adolescents running around. We'd also like to note that recent management changes have improved customer service considerably; whereas staff were once borderline rude and uninformative, they're getting more responsive and knowledgeable. A lingering cleanliness issue, as well, has been addressed at last.

At least once each day there is some kind of event. Mostly these are free tours of the White House or Capitol with a knowledgeable guide. Guests rave about how informational the jaunts are and about how they allow you to cut the long lines (group privilege) in which every other poor solo sap must wait for hours. The group pub night is also great fun.

For sightseeing on your own, the hostel location isn't bad. Most of the major sites are within walking distance, and there is a Metro stop only a few blocks away. But it's at night that you may begin to feel isolated from the rest of the city, and a little nervous. Your best bet for going out at this time is taking a cab to and from the subway (or directly to your destination).

Those with cars should be warned that parking is gonna cost you a lot. Your best bet, should you have brought wheels, is to suck it up and pull into the neighboring Days Inn garage.

How to Get There:
By airplane: From Reagan National Airport take Metro Blue Line to Metro Center. Walk 3 blocks north on Eleventh.

From Dulles or BWI take Washington Flyer bus to Capital Hilton and walk 5 blocks east on K Street. Hostel is at intersection of K and Eleventh Streets.

By bus: From bus terminal walk 2 blocks south on First Street to Union Station. Follow directions by train.

By car: Hostel is downtown at the intersection of Eleventh and K Streets.

By train: Amtrak stops in Washington. Take Metro Red Line from Union Station to Metro Center. Walk 3 blocks north on Eleventh to hostel. You can also get a bus at Union Station.

Washington International Student Center

2451 Eighteenth Street NW, Washington, DC 20009

(202) 667-7681; (800) 567-4150

> **Web site:** www.dchostel.com
>
> **E-mail:** DCStudentcenter@aol.com
>
> **Rates:** $24–$28 per person
>
> **Beds:** 46
>
> **Private rooms:** 1
>
> **Affiliation:** None
>
> **Office hours:** 8:00 a.m. to 11:00 p.m.
>
> **Extras:** Television, air-conditioning, free breakfast, free parking, pickups, kitchen, Internet access

---

What do you get when a place that's already half-bad slides farther down the slippery slope of hostel quality? A place like this. The folks who brought you the Venice Beach and Marina Hostel in Los Angeles have set up shop in the nation's capital with yet another laid-back joint, but quite frankly it's a mixed bag. On a good day, spontaneous beer parties, club outings, hallway basketball, and other such camaraderie define the spirit of the Washington International. On a bad night, though, be prepared for unfriendly loungers hogging the TV and downing massive amounts of hard liquor.

At the least you have a good excuse for getting outside. Adams Morgan, the hostel's immediate neighborhood, is the hippest and most promising place in the city for the set that wants to shed their suits (and in this town of bureaucrats and politicos, sometimes it seems as if there's a dress code) to hang loose. Think of it as Washington's Left Bank or East Village. The nightlife is incredible, the atmosphere lively, and the ethnic restaurants abundant, so put on your dancing (or walking) shoes and have a little fun in the 'hood.

Just don't count on a great time within the walls of the hostel. Management moved out here to chill after experiencing L.A. overload. They may have become a little too laid-back, however; the tiny bathroom is a bit skanky, while staff have been rude on several visits. Guests sleep too close together on old metal bunks with foam mattresses. Be warned: These are triple bunk beds, with the top reaching within a foot of the ceiling. (Try to avoid getting stuck up there in the nosebleed section; it makes for a mighty rude awakening.) The kitchen isn't very large, so we recommend sampling some of the cheap and great ethnic food in the area rather than attempting to navigate this hostel's cooking facilities.

At least there's no curfew (hooray). It's well-placed for transit, too. The subway is a ten-minute walk from the hostel, and a bus to the White House is available right around the corner. Be sure to check the convenient information boards posted on the wall, thoughtfully written in several languages, or just read or hang out in a common room replete with newspapers, magazines, and satellite TV. Also keep in mind that the free parking in front of the hostel is a godsend in this city. It may not be a great bunk, but hey—at least you can park your car here without paying an arm and a leg. Hopefully the car will be there when you wake up in the morning . . . if you could sleep, that is.

Best bet for a bite:
Millie and Al's sports bar (pizza 'n' beer)
Insiders' tip:
Ethiopian restaurants abound on the block
What hostellers say:
"I am so outta here."
Gestalt:
Political party animals
Safety: *C*
Hospitality: *D*
Cleanliness: *D*
Party index:

How to Get There:
By bus: Greyhound stops in D.C. Call hostel for free pickup.
By car: Call hostel for directions.
By train: Amtrak stops in D.C. Call hostel for free pickup.

MARYLAND

Baltimore Hostel ✳✳✳✳

17 West Mulberry Street, Baltimore, MD 21201

(410) 576-8880

Fax: (410) 230-4590

Web site: www.baltimorehostel.org

E-mail: info@baltimorehostel.org

Beds: 44

Price: $25 per Hostelling International member; $60 for private room

Affiliation: Hostelling International

Office hours: 8 a.m. to 11 p.m.

Extras: Internet access, lockers, air-conditioning, kitchen, TV room, piano

---

*T*his Hostelling International–affiliated hostel always had location *and* history on its side, but it was shuttered for too long. Now it's back after an eight-year hiatus. The hostel's located inside an 1857 mansion, across the street from the famous Baltimore Basilica and not far from the (other) Washington Monument. And it gets everything else right, too, so far. Yay!

The place is pretty much what you'd expect: four-, eight-, and twelve-bed dorm rooms and the usual rules at HI hostels. Some great extras at this place include a free U-make-yer-own pancake breakfast, Thursday night pasta dinners, Friday night movies, free Wi-Fi; a deck and patio; and a "no lockout and no curfew" policy. Staff are friendly and accommodating. There's a basement area with a TV, and a common room upstairs with a piano to tinkle. The keys of. Only drawback: They will charge you an extra ten bucks if you want to check in after 11 p.m.

Fans of the TV show *Homicide: Life on the Street* (count us in) or *The Wire* will want to check out primo locations from those shows, such as Fells Point and the Inner Harbor. Even Camden Yards, home to the (pathetic)

Best bet for a bite:
Jimmy's in Fells Point (diner food)

What hostellers say:
"Not bad!"

Insiders' tip:
Baltimore farmers' market nearby

Gestalt:
Streets of Baltimore

Safety: *C*

Hospitality: *A*

Cleanliness: *B*

Party index: 🎉🎉🎉

Baltimore Orioles and a nearby Ruthian baseball museum, is within walking distance, though we'd take a cab at night.

How to Get There:

By car: Contact hostel for directions.

By bus: From the bus station, don't walk. Take #27 bus to Saratoga Street stop. Walk east on Saratoga Street 3 blocks to Liberty Street; turn left and walk 1 block, then turn right onto Mulberry Street. Hostel is on your right.

By train: Amtrak stops at Penn Station. From station, take #3 bus along Saint Paul Street to corner of Mulberry and Cathedral Streets. Hostel is across street.

By subway: Metro stops at Lexington Market. From station, walk north on Howard Street 2 blocks to Mulberry Street. Turn right and walk 2 more blocks; hostel is on right.

Harpers Ferry Hostel

19123 Sandy Hook Road, Knoxville, MD 21758

(301) 834-7652

> **E-mail:** mail@harpersferryhostel.org
>
> **Web site:** www.harpersferryhostel.org
>
> **Rates:** $20 per Hostelling International member; $50 for private room
>
> **Credit cards:** None
>
> **Season:** April to November (open rest of the year for groups only)
>
> **Beds:** 36
>
> **Private rooms:** 2
>
> **Affiliation:** Hostelling International
>
> **Office hours:** 7:00 to 9:00 a.m.; 6:00 to 10:00 p.m.
>
> **Extras:** Laundry, fireplace, volleyball, kitchen, campground, grill

---

*T*his hostel, which is actually set across a bridge (and a state line) from the famously historic town of Harpers Ferry, West Virginia, is pretty plain, but it's set at an absolutely gorgeous convergence of two rivers.

Despite standard bunkrooms, a nice kitchen and dining room let you get to know fellow hostellers without tripping over one another's feet. A flat grassy expanse outside allows room for lounging around, playing a game of volleyball, or camping, if you've brought a tent. The place's laid-back attitude is just right for this neck of the woods, too, though you may get asked to do a communal chore or two.

What to do? The main attraction here Is the surrounding countryside, of course, and because the Appalachian Trail passes nearby, there obviously are hiking trails at hand. Harpers Ferry also has lots of historic sites, enough to take up a good day or so if you're really into old structures. The Appalachian Trail Conference is headquartered in Harpers Ferry, too, in case you're thinking about walking the trail sometime.

For a real treat, though, you might try tubing down the Potomac River during summer. Vendors renting inner tubes set up all along the river, and you'll see kids lining up for a shot. It's a heck of a lot of fun, especially on those steamy southern nights when nothing wants to wring the humidity out of you. Find out, too, about biking on the local canal; we're told that you can go all the way south to Washington, D.C., or north to Philly in a few days, camping at lovely riverside campgrounds en route.

How to Get There:
By car: Drive U.S. Highway 340 to Potomac River. On Maryland side of the river, just before the bridge, exit onto Keep Tryst Road, then make sharp right onto Sandy Hook Road; follow sharp right bend. Hostel is on left as you begin to go downhill.

NEW YORK

Buffalo Downtown Hostel

667 Main Street, Buffalo, NY 14203

(716) 852-5222

Fax: (716) 856-3764

E-mail: stay@hostelbuffalo.com

Web site: www.hostelbuffalo.com

Rates: $25 per Hostelling International member; $60 for single room

Credit cards: MC, VISA

Beds: 48

Private rooms: 4

Affiliation: Hostelling International

Office hours: 8:00 to 10:00 a.m.; 5:00 to 10:00 p.m.

Extras: Laundry, bike storage, kitchen, wheelchair-accessible, Internet access

*N*ow there's a reason to go to Buffalo *besides* world-famous chicken wings and Bills football: a swell hostel that's flanked by a burgeoning theater scene in a (gasp) thriving downtown. Upstate New York and, for that matter, nearby Ontario are blessed with this solid hostel offering, which is seemingly only getting better and friendlier with time—and believe us, *that* is rare in the hostelling world.

Like most other Hostelling International entries in big-city markets, this one is a keeper from moment one. Heavy-duty wooden bunks are praised by hostellers for being among the most comfortable hostel beds they've ever slept in. There's a semiprivate room furnished with two single beds for couples. There's not much else in the room besides bunk beds and chairs.

Two dorms sleep four, three sleep eight, and one sleeps fourteen (that one's used mostly by groups). The kitchen is outfitted for legions of hungry hostellers with everything from chopsticks and woks to a microwave. Management does its best for the environment by encouraging recycling and supplying a local nature preserve with compost during the summer.

Communing goes on in a large common room that has (thank goodness) no television, but rather (yes!) a guitar. Do your best Ryan Adams or Patti Griffin impression, then sink into comfy couches and peruse the paperbacks or roll the dice with your bunkmates. For

Best bet for a bite:
Anchor Bar for the eponymous
Buffalo wing
Insiders' tip:
Parkside Candy
What hostellers say:
"I'm shufflin' off to Buffalo."
Gestalt:
Buffalo thrill
Safety: *A*
Hospitality: *A*
Cleanliness: *A*
Party index: 🎉 🎉

international and domestic couch potatoes, a television and VCR *are* located in the basement; there's even yet another lounge on the third floor. (That's where you can catch up on your *Friends* reruns.) A rec room offers a pool table and stereo, and the kitchen is good for hobnobbing (and scarfing free eats).

Buffalo's downtown definitely has its act together in the form of transportation and entertainment. The hostel is near Chippewa Street, where there are tons of nightlife options. For budding thespians, several theaters are minutes away and can be accessed by the Metro Rail. These theaters are known to sell half-price rush seats to hostellers. The hostel also offers a tour of the local bars on Fridays. For a step back in time, check out the glorious Parkside Candy, a real old-fashioned soda fountain where a scene in the Robert Redford film *The Natural* was shot. This nostalgic spot is quite a hike from the hostel, so you might want to visit it on public transportation. One caution: If you come during winter, the city will appear dead, because everyone's inside avoiding the bitter chill.

This hostel is a terminus for several bicycle outings, one of the more interesting being the BAT (Buffalo and Toronto), a ride from Buffalo to Toronto and back that takes about two days. Best of all, use it as a base for trips to Niagara Falls.

How to Get There:

By airplane: Take the #24 bus to downtown bus station, turn right and walk 2 blocks to Main Street, then walk or take the Metro Rail to the Theater District station.
By bus: From downtown bus station, exit through the front doors, walk left 1 block to Main Street, and 1 block left to Metro Rail station. Take Metro Rail to Theater District station.
By car: From the Peace Bridge go east on Porter Avenue, which becomes North Street, to Main Street. Turn right onto Main and go south half a mile. Turn left on Virginia Street, then go right on Washington Street. Continue 2 blocks; look for the hostel sign.
By train: Exchange Street station. Take the Metro Rail 2 blocks from the train station. Get off at the Theater District station.

Tibbets Point Lighthouse Hostel ✹✹✹✹✹

33439 County Route 6, Cape Vincent, NY 13618

(315) 654-3450

E-mail: lighthousehostel@tds.net

Rates: $15 per Hostelling International member; $40 for private room

Credit cards: None

Season: May 15 to October 15

Beds: 26

Private rooms: 2

Affiliation: Hostelling International

Office hours: 7:00 to 9:00 a.m.; 5:00 to 10:00 p.m.

Extras: Barbecue, kitchen, television, birdhouse, museum, pickups

*T*he inspirational sunsets alone should make a visit to this awesome hostel worthwhile. This lighthouse, built in 1869, is situated between the Saint Lawrence River and Lake Ontario and induces a mesmerizing trance as the sun's golden evening rays set. The placid seaway is dotted with radiant little islands, many of which are historic landmarks. A couple of hostellers were so moved by the site that they even decided on the spot to have their wedding there.

Set in the old keeper's quarters of the lighthouse, the hostel is a cozy little house kept immaculate by Jean Cougler (a.k.a. "Ma Tibbets"). She takes no bull. At your arrival she goes over all the offenses that will get you kicked out. So get on her good side; then she'll be a fantastic help. "I'm just going to lay down the law. But I do have a heart of gold," she said.

There are dozens of interesting things to see nearby, and Tibbets Point is a great base. The hostel is at the tip of the Thousand Islands region (there are actually nearly 1,900 islands), which remains one of the most

Best bet for a bite:
All-U-can-eat breakfasts around town

Insiders' tip:
Great cliffs at Wellesley Island nature center

What hostellers say:
"What a view!"

Gestalt:
Cape crusader

Hospitality: *A*

Cleanliness: *A*

Party index:

breathtaking natural views in the eastern United States. "I tell 'em, plan on spending three days and I'll send you someplace new every day," Cougler told us.

For some of the most fantastic views of the islands, check out the nearby state parks. Or, for something different, you might wander over to Boldt Castle, a 120-room Rhineland castle replica with Italian gardens and a drawbridge. There's also the option of taking a scenic ferry ride to Kingston, Ontario. That city—one of Canada's oldest and its first capital—offers more than fourteen museums.

Or you might just want to hang out at the hostel. It has a daytime lockout (sigh), but outdoor lounge chairs are still an ideal spot to dream away the day. Whatever you plan on doing, reserve early. It is not uncommon for this hostel to be booked weeks in advance.

How to Get There:

By bus: Contact hostel for transit details.

By car: Take Interstate 81 to exit 46 (Watertown). Take New York Highway 12F and then State Highway 12E to Cape Vincent. Turn left on Broadway, go 2½ miles to end.

By ferry: Ferry leaves regularly from Kingston, Ontario, to Wolfe Island, New York. Walk or cycle 7 miles across Wolfe Island; catch Wolfe Island–Cape Vincent ferry. At dock, turn right on Broadway and continue 3 miles to end.

NEW YORK CITY HOSTELS: A SUMMARY

	RATING	PROS	CONS	COST	PAGE
International House	★★★★★	nice	expensive	$55	p. 78
New York International	★★★★★	facilities	location	$32	p. 82
Big Apple	★★★★★	nice rooms, location	fills up	$39–$60	p. 69
Chelsea International	★★★★	location	tight quarters	$28	p. 73
Gershwin Hotel	★★★	swanky hip	no kitchen pricey	$40–$45	p. 75
Jazz on the Park	★	musical	beery	$26–$33	p. 80

New York City

There's no place on earth like the Apple. It's the city that brought you the Yankees, Mets, Jets, and Rangers; Fifth Avenue; the Lady of the Harbor; Madison Square Garden; Ed Koch; Donald Trump; Broadway; 9/11; A-Rod; and so much more. Everyone in the world wants to be here and see here, sooner or later, and tourist traffic has never been better. That, of course, means hostels have sprung up in New York—though not as many as you'd think. There's a gigantic Hostelling International–affiliated joint, of course (in a slightly iffy location), plus a bunch of smaller, independently owned competitors.

However, you've got to be careful when booking a bunk in NYC. The city has finally begun cracking down on illegal and dangerous hostels of late (three were closed down in one fell swoop in late 2007). In fact, a lot of places that advertise themselves on the Internet as being hostels don't seem to really *be* hostels. In reality they could be flophouses, illegal apartment rentals, and so on; as such, they're most likely not up to city safety or fire codes, so you're taking a bit of a risk and you're wasting your hard-earned and -saved cash. We'd recommend contacting only the hostels in this book, if it were up to us.

Of the few legitimate hostels/hostel chains in the city, we haven't found many we want to write home about. Check the table for a quickie summary, and read the descriptions carefully. This is one place you don't want to cut corners to save a dollar and end up miles from the action in a dive.

Big Apple Hostel ✺✺✺✺
119 West Forty-fifth Street, New York, NY 10036
(212) 302-2603

Fax: (212) 302-2605
E-mail: mail@bigapplehostel.com
Web site: www.bigapplehostel.com
Rates: $39–$60 per person; $125–$175 for private room
Credit cards: MC, VISA
Beds: 120
Private rooms: Yes
Affiliation: None
Office hours: Twenty-four hours

Getting to New York: A Quick Primer

By airplane: Three large airports serve the city: LaGuardia, JFK, and Newark Liberty (in New Jersey). Make sure you know which one you're flying into and out of! (Travel agencies will occasionally route you in and out from different airports to save you dough. *Read the tickets*.) Each airport has rows of taxis (figure $45 from JFK, up to $30 from LaGuardia; Newark fares vary with the traffic), buses, and—except for LaGuardia—convenient trains. You can even take the city subway into the city from JFK (cheapest way; two bucks at press time), though it takes nearly an hour to do it.

Assuming you won't use a limo or split a cab, here's our skinny on getting into town (always talk to your hostel too about the best strategy):

- From **JFK** you can take regular **shuttle buses** (about $10 to $12 or so) that stop at the city's two main train stations (Grand Central and Penn), or **Super-Shuttle vans** that go where you tell them to (a little more expensive). Ask at the airport's "Ground Transportation" desk for both of these options. Travel time for buses depends on the traffic; figure an hour. You can also avoid traffic by taking a short ride on a cool monorail called the **AirTrain** ($5) to Jamaica station. From there you change to either the "**A" train of the city subway** ($2 at press time; forty-five minutes or more), which gets you near Penn Station and Times Square, or the **Long Island Railroad** ($2.50 to $7.00; twenty to twenty-five minutes) which goes to Penn Station. Here's a great tip: On weekends the trip on the LIRR is discounted through the MTA's CityTicket program.

- From **LaGuardia**, once again, you can take regular **shuttle buses** (about $10 to $12 or so) that stop at the city's two main train stations, or Super-Shuttle vans. Travel time is quicker than from JFK; figure thirty to forty-five minutes depending on the traffic.

- From **Newark** airport, taxis are expensive. Buses will get you to Forty-second Street, slowly. But it's easiest to take the **AirTrain** monorail ($5) to Newark Penn Station, then switch to **any New Jersey Transit train or Amtrak train** going into New York City (about $7 extra). From Penn Station, the last stop, you can take a cab, subway, or walk to where you're going.

By bus: Unless you take one of the new East Coast bus services (Megabus, BoltBus, and so on) that are springing up from Boston, Philly, and D.C., you'll probably go Greyhound—in which case you'll arrive at the big, ugly Port Authority bus station at Forty-second Street and Eighth Avenue, which is actually very central. There are subway connections, buses running along Forty-second Street, taxis—and you're 1½ blocks from Times Square by foot.

By car: The quickest way is probably I–95 to the Henry Hudson Parkway (south); get off where you need to, and bring a map. Parking garage rates are outrageous, but so are the fines attached to parking tickets if you read the signs wrong; deal with it. Consult hostel listings for parking tips. In some neighborhoods you can park for free overnight, but always check with the hostel staff, and again, read the signs on the streets carefully.

By train: Amtrak trains roll into Penn Station at Thirty-third Street and Seventh Avenue on the west side of the city. Madison Square Garden is next door. There are many subway connections and tons of taxis here; also, you're within walking distance of hostels in Chelsea. The Empire State Building is just a few blocks east. You'll see it. Trust us.

Extras: Cafe, lockers, laundry, fax service, television, grill, patio, Internet access ($), kitchen, free Wi-Fi

*O*f all the hostels (legal and otherwise) in New York, we've found that the Big Apple probably gets the best reviews from fellow hostellers. That's mostly because management knows exactly what their customers want, and they don't skimp giving it to them. It's obvious that time, money, and care went into this facility; it doesn't have that seat-of-the-pants feel that comes with a stay at most other Manhattan independent hostels.

The hostel is housed in a smart six-story building in the heart of Midtown. As a tourist, how could you ask for more? People pay hundreds of dollars for rooms with worse locations in the city. One block away from the hostel's front door is everything Times Square has to offer, from Broadway theaters to glitzy theme stores (Hershey's? Disney? Check. Check). The Square has cleaned up Its act significantly; long gone are the days of peep shows and pushers crowding Forty-second Street, because a little arm-twisting and a bunch of zoning lawsuits have pushed out much of the sleaze. It's a busy, busy place and very safe. Even at midnight there are usually plenty of crowds (and cops) walking the well-lit streets.

The hostel is tucked away on a quietish block that's buffered both from the Square and the somber suits over Rockefeller Center way. Radio City is a few blocks away; the Empire

Best bet for a bite:
Deli next door
Insiders' tip:
Half-price theater tickets at TKTS booth in Times Square
What hostellers say:
"Location is the best."
Gestalt:
Broadway bound
Safety: *A*
Hospitality: *B*
Cleanliness: *B*
Party index: 🎉🎉

State Building, about 10 blocks downtown—both easily walkable after your morning coffee. This would be a great base if you were only seeking proximity to New York's key tourist landmarks, but the facilities are better than they have to be.

It's not a big place—this is New York, after all. Hostellers sleep in dorm rooms that are about the size of walk-in closets, with two to four bunks per room and (hopefully) a window. There's just enough room to stand. Mattresses are firm and spacious, and the bathroom facilities are pretty good. All the dorm rooms are basically the same, no foam pads thrown onto the floor or such nonsense. The private rooms are pretty sweet, though they've sharply escalated in price over the past couple years. They've got queen beds, cable TV, in-room safes, and phones (free local calls!): just like a hotel. Bathrooms are shared, however. Families and small groups can rent their own four-bed dorm rooms on request. One thing we continue to notice here: It's cleaner than almost any other New York hostel. Kudos for that!

All the rooms are air-conditioned, too, which is key in summertime around here. You'll find a small kitchen downstairs, with the no-frills dining area doubling as common space. In the front of the hostel is a coffee shop serving NYC lunchtime staples, too. The place does lack a big interior common space, but that's only more incentive to get out on the town—which you will want to do. If you're really bent on socializing in-house, there's a backyard (!!) with seating right in the heart of the city, great in good weather for meeting world travelers. Pretty effin' cool.

How to Get There:

By airplane: From JFK, take bus to Grand Central Station or subway train to Forty-second Street. Exit at Eighth Avenue/Forty-second Street and walk uptown to Forty-fifth Street. Turn right and hostel is 1 1⁄2 blocks down on left.

From LaGuardia, take bus to Grand Central Station and walk west along Forty-fifth Street to hostel.

From Newark, use trains to Penn Station, then take cab or subway, or walk 12 blocks north (uptown) to Forty-fifth Street.

By car: Park in the cheap lot on Forty-second Street between Eighth and Ninth Avenues. Hostel is on Forty-fifth Street between Sixth and Seventh Avenues.

By train or bus: From Penn Station or Port Authority, walk uptown on Eighth Avenue to Forty-fifth Street and turn right. Hostel is 1½ blocks down on the left. From Grand Central, take subway shuttle (S train) or walk west to Times Square. Follow previous directions.

Chelsea International Hostel

251 West Twentieth Street, New York, NY 10011

(212) 647-0010

Fax: (212) 727-7289

E-mail: email@chelseahostel.com

Web site: www.chelseahostel.com

Rates: $28 per person; $80 for private room

Credit cards: AMEX, MC, VISA

Beds: 350

Private rooms: 20

Affiliation: None

Office hours: Twenty-four hours

Extras: Pizza nights, television, lockers ($), storage, coffee and tea, fax, Internet access ($), laundry

NOTE: Passport required at check-in

*W*ith the way Chelsea has expanded and shot upscale in recent years, it's nothing short of amazing that this hostel even still exists. The fact that it's getting better over time? Nothing short of a New York miracle.

The two fellows who started the place are an all–New York team if we ever saw one: The first time we ever visited, one was decked out in a New York Mets jersey, while the other proudly displayed his gold Rangers necklace. No fey Yankees pretenders or Islanders snobs here: These guys are New Yawk all the way, with all the accent, mannerisms, and expressions you'll find only here. Why did they start a hostel? Forget all that mumbo jumbo about world peace and bringing people together: These guys saw a void in the market and wanted in.

Whatever their motives, they are still doing a fine job of maintaining and improving their huge hostel—while keeping bed prices stable, which is just unheard of in New York, and especially here in Chelsea. Despite their beer-and-pretzels personalities, these folks have got themselves set up in the hippest residential section of town. Everybody wants to live around here; how they scored a building between Seventh and Eighth Avenues (across from a police station!) we'll never know, but the area looks a lot like what SoHo was after it was discovered but before mass commercialization took over. Chelsea is fashionable yet never faddy—a bit of flash and cash, with generous dashes of fashion design, gay culture, and Cuban food tossed into the mix. You can walk to any number of important city sights from here, but it's also a great place just to start a little local walking tour on a nice day.

The only trade-off is that you will live a bit like most New Yorkers do: in a pretty small space. Common space? Except for a seasonal courtyard (a mural-ed pleasure spot for socializing), don't count on finding much here. The dorm rooms themselves are narrow, too, though well-lit (big windows permit a flood of sunlight), with two bunk beds in each. Expect tight, slightly stuffy conditions. Couples can stay in rooms just slightly bigger than the double bed they hold (hmmmm, how *did* they get those things in there, anyway?). The hallways are also narrow, and the few bathrooms per-square-hosteller are not so commodious. Ditto for the kitchen facilities, but that's okay, actually: We recommend a stroll over to the wonderful Chelsea Market—staff can give you directions—for eats anyway. Management has provided a common dining area, though it looks more like a summer camp than a hip hangout. Most hostellers opt for the exterior courtyard instead of this space in good weather. Just get used to the squeeze for a couple days; plenty of locals live this way, and they spend most of their time enjoying the city instead of complaining about square footage. This is a clean, well-run, well-heated hostel, so you can handle it.

We've heard some complaints that staff are brusque. At times, some of them might be, and that sucks; but that's New York. Don't take it personally. Anyway, in New York it's all about location, location, location, and that's what you get here: a super-cool neighborhood at a good price that isn't rising ridiculously.

Best bet for a bite:
Chelsea Market
Insiders' tip:
Art galleries around Eleventh Avenue
What hostellers say:
"So who's got the cheapest mojito around here?"
Gestalt:
Chelsea morning
Safety: *A*
Hospitality: *B*
Cleanliness: *B*
Party index:

How to Get There:

By airplane: From JFK, take A train to Fourteenth Street. Walk north on Eighth Avenue 6 blocks to Twentieth Street and turn right. Walk down to #251.

From LaGuardia, take bus to Port Authority bus station and follow bus directions.

From Newark, take trains to Penn Station. Then walk south on Eighth Avenue 13 blocks to Twentieth Street, turn left, and walk to #251. Or take A, C, or E subway train to Twenty-third Street, walk 3 blocks to Twentieth Street, and follow directions above.

By bus: From Port Authority bus station, walk south on Eighth Avenue to Twentieth Street (about fifteen minutes). Turn left and walk down to #251.

By car: Look for parking down one of Chelsea's side streets. Cheap lot parking can be found around Eighth Street and Fourth Avenue. Hostel is on Twentieth Street between Seventh and Eighth Avenues.

By train: From Grand Central walk or take subway shuttle (about $2) to Times Square and transfer to the #1, #2, #3, or #9 (red line) downtown; go one stop to Penn Station. In Penn Station, go to Eighth Avenue exit, walk south on Eighth to Twentieth Street, turn left, and walk to #251.

The Gershwin Hotel

7 East Twenty-seventh Street , New York, NY 10016

(212) 545-8000

  Fax: (212) 684-5546

  Web site: www.gershwinhotel.com

  E-mail: askus@gershwinhotel.com

  Rates: $40–$45 per person; $109–$445 for private room

  Credit cards: AMEX, MC, VISA

  Beds: 150

  Private rooms: Yes

  Affiliation: None

  Office hours: Twenty-four hours

  Extras: Fax service, performance area, film screenings, rooftop garden, breakfast cafe, full bar, restaurant, Wi-Fi access ($)

*T*his ultraswanky joint not far from the Flat Iron district—an enclave of modeling agencies, clothing designers, and the like—is bidding to replace the legendary Chelsea Hotel as the next "upscale budget-designer hotel" where cool art types also happen to live. The problem is, it's not in a cool neighborhood: Madison Avenue (*especially* this stretch) is just boring, boring, boring. We'll give this to them: The Gershwin is trendy with a capital "T" (you've gotta love a place whose Web site is in both French and English). True to the claim of its press release, the Gershwin is "bold, daring, and much more than a place to stay." It's not perfect, but it *is* different from any other hostel in the city.

Anybody with even the remotest interest in pop art will be dazzled by the place, that's for sure. Everything in the hostel seems to be a work of art, from the groovy purple couches to the huge cubelike sculptures. High ceilings are cloaked in patterns and designs to intrigue the mind; in the lobby, we noted a Roy Lichtenstein influence. By the elevator you will find a trademark soup can signed by the man who iconicized the icon, Mr. Andy Warhol. Walls of the dormitories are covered with images and symbols, some of them making clear and obvious statements, others left to the imagination, all of it interesting to the eye. Hey, we're hostellers, expecting little more than a bed; to be surrounded by actual art is a real treat.

The owners are trying to make the Gershwin an event hotel, a sort of focal point for promising undiscovered and semidiscovered creative souls. Poetry readings and jazz jams have been regular features, as has an almost-too-cool-for-you wine bar, where conversations about chiaroscuro and meter abound. Film is also a big part of the Gershwin's identity: A regular series has attracted the likes of Abel Ferrara (*The Bad Lieutenant*) and Quentin Crisp (*The Naked Civil Servant*). Artists maintain a relationship with the hotel in the interest of keeping it a focal point of the New York arts scene, and an artists-in-residence program accommodates a few in-house by offering them shelter, work space, and a gallery in which to exhibit.

Where do hostellers fit into all this? Well, that's the problem. This place is more hotel than hostel. It doesn't hurt the aesthetic to have young international types milling around the place, but you might feel like an outsider amidst all the hipness, art, beauty,

Best bet for a bite:
Shake Shack (summer only) in Madison Square Park
Insiders' tip:
East Village is the punk New York
What hostellers say:
"Whatever shall I wear?"
Gestalt:
Hipper than thou
Safety: *A*
Hospitality: *B*
Cleanliness: *B*
Party index:

and money. The sleeping facilities are pretty standard, with smallish rooms, homemade wooden bunks, and somewhat rickety bathrooms. It could definitely be cleaner, as well. Hostellers have complained about overpaying for lower-floor dorms (private rooms are higher up, and nicer . . . and much more expensive), and of ambient noise leaking upward from the club at night. There is also no kitchen on the premises, although hostellers can eat very well near the hostel—there are enough cafes, plus chic spots on Park Avenue and curry houses on so-called Curry Hill too. Consenting adults may wish to check out the Museum of Sex, located on the same block as the hostel, and the Empire State Building is a stone's throw away—you surely can't miss it, glowing above you.

How to Get There:

By airplane: From JFK and LaGuardia, take bus (ask at ground transportation desk) to Grand Central Station. Exit at Madison Avenue and walk down to Twenty-seventh Street. Turn right and look for hostel on right. From JFK (alternate), take AirTrain ($5) to Jamaica station, then take A subway train to Thirty-fourth Street. Exit on Eighth Avenue and walk downtown to Twenty-seventh Street. Turn left and look for hostel on left after crossing Fifth Avenue.

From LaGuardia, take bus ($10 to $12) to Penn Station and follow train/bus directions.

From Newark, take AirTrain/Amtrak to Penn Station, then walk south to Twenty-seventh Street. Turn left and walk two blocks to hostel.

By car: Cheap lot on Forty-second between Eighth and Ninth. Hostel is on Twenty-seventh Street, just east of Fifth Avenue.

By train or bus: From Penn Station or Port Authority, walk along Eighth Avenue to Twenty-seventh Street and turn left. Hostel is between Fifth and Madison Avenues.

From Grand Central, walk or take subway shuttle (S train, about $2) to Times Square; transfer to #1, #2, #3, or #9 (red line) train headed downtown and continue one stop to Penn Station; follow previous directions.

 Attractive natural setting

 Ecologically aware hostel

 Superior kitchen facilities or cafe

 Offbeat or eccentric place

 Superior bathroom facilities

 Romantic private rooms

Comfortable beds

A particularly good value

Wheelchair-accessible

Good for business travelers

Especially well-suited for families

Good for active travelers

 Visual arts at hostel or nearby

 Music at hostel or nearby

Great hostel for skiers

Bar or pub at hostel or nearby

 Editors' choice: Among our very favorite hostels

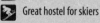 Key to Icons

International House

500 Riverside Drive, New York, NY 10027

(212) 316-8400

Web site: www.ihouse-nyc.org

Rates: $55 per person; $150–$160 for private room

Credit cards: MC, VISA

Season: May 15 to August 15

Beds: 500

Private rooms: Yes

Affiliation: None

Office hours: 9:00 a.m. to 5:00 p.m. (you must reserve at least one day in advance)

Extras: Cafeteria, pub, kitchen, gym, laundry, study rooms, television, DVDs, group programs, business services

---

NOTE: Open only to travelers over twenty-one with student ID

*T*he International House isn't really a hostel. Instead, it's a lavish housing facility that was established as part of a worldwide network of similar complexes intended to bring students from diverse cultures together for the sake of peace and understanding in cities around the world. The place opens its doors to students traveling through New York for a rate that is high by hostel standards, but a pittance considering the location and perks offered.

You can't ask for a more up-and-coming neighborhood from which to base your Manhattan exploration than the Morningside Heights district. Riverside Drive is home to an inspiring stretch of prewar architectural masterpieces overlooking the Hudson River; a day just spent strolling down this street would not be out of line. The heart of the community is Columbia University, New York's Ivy League pride, with its injection of intellectualism, sophistication . . . and cheap food. There are great clubs, bakeries, bookshops, and plenty of other great places to explore by foot around here—not to mention Central Park and a huge cathedral, both nearby.

The hostel overlooks a park on one side and the Hudson River on the other. High-rolling executives would dole out loads of dough for either view, yet some lucky hostellers do indeed snag bunks with that zillion-dollar view. Almost all the rooms here are singles—complete with desk, dresser, phone, and linens—though there are also a few larger rooms and suites, sort of pricey.

Everything's clean, friendly, and well-kept. But the place is so big that camaraderie among hostellers is hard to develop. There are lots of programs and activities in which to take part, but they're not scheduled to cater to hostellers' needs; they exist for the residents, and hostellers simply have the option of taking part. If you are looking to meet up with a museum-touring partner or club-hopping buddy, then you'll probably have better luck at a smaller hostel. Or by bringing someone from home. Other than that, this place is damn-near perfect.

Best bet for a bite:
Mike's Papaya, 110th and Broadway
Insiders' tip:
Find out who's in Grant's Tomb
What hostellers say:
"Wish I could live here."
Gestalt:
Global chillage
Safety: *A*
Hospitality: *B*
Cleanliness: *A*
Party index: 🎉🎉

How to Get There:

By airplane: From JFK, take A train ($2) to 125th Street (it's a long ride); walk west to Riverside Drive and 2½ blocks south to hostel.

From LaGuardia, take M60 bus ($2) to 120th Street and Broadway (bus operates 5:15 a.m. to midnight). Walk west 2 blocks to Riverside Drive, then walk uptown 2½ blocks to hostel.

From Newark Airport, take train to Penn Station, then take subway A train to 125th Street. Walk west to Riverside Drive and 2½ blocks south to hostel.

By bus: From Port Authority take #1 or #9 (red line) subway uptown to 125th Street. Walk west to Riverside Drive and 2½ blocks south to hostel.

By car: Hostel is uptown at Riverside Drive and 122nd Street. Parking is plentiful on Riverside. Otherwise park on a residential side street, or fork over the dough for lot parking.

By train: From Penn Station, take #1 or #9 (red line) subway uptown to 125th Street. Walk west to Riverside Drive and 2½ blocks south to hostel. From Grand Central, take subway to Times Square/Forty-second Street station and transfer to #1 or #9 (red line) uptown, then follow directions above.

Jazz on the Park Hostel ✳

36 West 106th Street, New York, NY 10012

(212) 932-1600

Fax: (212) 932-1700

Web site: www.jazzonthepark.com

Rates: $26–$33 per person; $75–$130 for private room

Credit cards: Yes

Beds: 150

Private rooms: Yes

Affiliation: None

Office hours: Twenty-four hours

Extras: Coffee bar, outdoor patio, Internet access ($), lounge, TV, laundry, barbecue, live music, breakfast, lockers

NOTE: Passport and out-of-state ID required.

*J*azz on the Park is located on the upper-Upper West Side of Manhattan, just next to Central Park and inches away from a newly hot Harlem. Here, travelers can theoretically enjoy a convenient home base. The hostel's located on the northwest side of the park, in a district sometimes being called SoHa (South of Harlem) by real estate types hoping to capitalize on the name's resemblance to SoHo—don't get the two confused or you'll wind up waaay downtown (in a cooler 'hood, though).

The hostel's two buildings are designed to resemble—surprise—a jazz club. Colorful string lights and murals decorate the high ceilings and concrete walls of the hostel's main gathering area, which houses a coffee bar, lounge, and outdoor patio. It's not quite as attractive as it sounds, but okay. Hostellers can catch live music here once a week, karaoke nights, and even the occasional barbecue.

But let's get to the crux of the matter, the physical condition and upkeep of the place. Rooms—in dorms ranging from four beds all the way up to fourteen-bed bunkrooms—are basic and super-tiny, with bright walls but a cramped feel. Some, especially in the annex building at night, even feel creepy. An included breakfast is a nice gesture but it's kinda measly, and staff seemed very short (or just incompetent). Cleanliness is severely lacking, too; we can even say that it's in decline since our last review, and that's saying something.

Hostellers appear to be a mix of Americans, internationals, and long-term residents—all of whom seemed to want to drink, regardless of nationality, so they didn't care much about whether it was clean. We can't recommend a stay here, but if you do stay, lock your stuff or take it with you.

At least the Upper West Side hosts a number of really great things to do: Columbia University and the massive Cathedral of St. John the Divine are both close by. Thirty blocks south is the terrific American Museum of Natural History (you know, where Ross on *Friends* worked). The Metropolitan Museum of Art and Guggenheim Museum also beckon. No stay at Jazz on the Park would be complete without exploring Central Park itself; keep in mind, while checking out some of its 843 acres, that every single inch of Central Park was man-made. Yes, really.

If you're walking away from the park—east of the hostel, in other words—be mindful of your surroundings. It's an okay neighborhood, but the blocks between Central Park West and Broadway could make cautious visitors uncomfortable. All in all, we think this is a good hostel, save the New Yawk attitude—although that's part of the quintessential New York experience, so if you can hack it, you will probably like this place.

Note that the hostel has also opened a slew of annex hostels in recent years, in the East Village, Harlem, and elsewhere. Check the Web site for details.

How to Get There:

By plane: From JFK, take A train ($2) to Thirty-fourth or Forty-second Street; switch to C train (no fee for transfer inside station) and continue uptown to 103rd Street station (a long ride), then walk 3 blocks north to 106th Street and turn left, continuing to hostel.

By bus: From Port Authority bus station, take C train ($2) to 103rd Street station, then walk 3 blocks north to 106th Street and turn left, continuing to hostel.

By car: Call hostel for the latest information on area garages. We don't recommend parking on the street.

By train: From Grand Central Station, take S train (shuttle, $2) to Times Square and transfer

---

Best bet for a bite:
Broadway's ethnic food
Insiders' tip:
Karaoke
What hostellers say:
"Hi, hotels.com? I need a room. Fast."
Gestalt:
Blue note
Safety: D
Hospitality: D
Cleanliness: D
Party index:

to B or C train; take train uptown to 103rd Street station, then walk 3 blocks north to 106th Street and turn left, continuing to hostel.

New York International Hostel ✳✳✳✳

891 Amsterdam Avenue, New York, NY 10025

(212) 932-2300

Fax: (212) 932-2574

E-mail: reserve@HInewyork.org

Web site: www.HInewyork.org

Rates: $32 per Hostelling International member; $150 for private room

Credit cards: AMEX, JCB, MC, VISA

Beds: 600

Private rooms: 7

Affiliation: Hostelling International

Office hours: Twenty-four hours

Extras: Coffee bar, laundry, air-conditioning, television, cafeteria, garden patio, game room, store, lockers, lectures, walking tours, Internet access ($), airport shuttle, kitchen, breakfast

*W*ell this is it; this hostel, among the largest hostels in the world, is the behemoth of a hostel that we are told almost sunk Hostelling International–America Youth Hostels financially. All that effort. All that money. All those facilities. All the perks. Everything you could ever want or need in a hostel building. All of it for a neighborhood that, we are sorry to say, is mediocre at best.

Amsterdam Avenue has its high and low points. This particular stretch of it is scraping bottom but on the upswing—Harlem has been rediscovered at last. It is by no means the most dangerous or most dismal section of town; it is simply the wrong part of town to have a hostel. While the hopping Upper West Side is just to the south and sophisticated Morningside Heights is to the north, the blocks that immediately surround the hostel are a drab, drab environs.

This is all too bad, because the hostel itself is astonishing. A hopping coffee bar and tremendous lounge with big-screen television offer great places to socialize. The outdoor courtyard, the location of summer barbecues and other social events, is the nicest of any Manhattan hostel. There is even a cafeteria that serves hot breakfast. Oh—and you can take care of all your travel needs at the stocked travel store and make arrangements for your stay in New York with the ever-helpful concierge. This is not to mention the good offerings in the way of walking tours and other outings arranged daily with the help of a corps of volunteers.

The dorm rooms vary in size. The biggest have ten beds and the smallest only four. (There are also a handful of coveted single rooms.) The more beds, the cheaper your rate. All rooms have high ceilings, big windows, and solid beds. The hostel kitchen and cafe both drew raves from happy hostellers. However, the echoey halls might keep light sleepers up a bit late.

Clean, safe, and close to the *Seinfeld* coffee shop . . . what more could you ask for? One gripe with the facility is the expected one: It's so big that it feels impersonal. One staffer acknowledged that there was room for improvement on that front. "We're trying very hard to improve our customer service," she insisted. But it's still hit or hiss. Keep trying!

Best bet for a bite:
On Broadway
Insiders' tip:
Cheap movie tickets at hostel
What hostellers say:
"Where the heck is the Statue of Liberty?"
Gestalt:
Melting pot
Safety: *B*
Hospitality: *C*
Cleanliness: *A*
Party index:

How to Get There:

By airplane: From JFK, take trains or bus to Penn Station. Then take #1 or #9 (red line) train to 103rd Street. Follow train directions. From LaGuardia, take bus to Penn Station and follow directions above. From Newark, take trains to Penn Station and follow directions above.

By car: Hostel is on corner of Amsterdam Avenue and 103rd Street. Call hostel for advice. Free parking on certain avenues overnight is possible from the 90s streets to the 100s, but check the area for safety and parking signs, and consider a garage.

By train or bus: From Grand Central, take S train ($2) or walk to Times Square, transfer to #1 or #9 (red line) train to 103rd Street. From 103rd Street Station, walk 1 block east to hostel on corner of Amsterdam Avenue.

From Penn Station or Port Authority bus station, take subway #1 or #9 (red line) to 103rd Street. Walk 1 block east to hostel.

Niagara Falls Hostel ✳✳✳

1101 Ferry Avenue, Niagara Falls, NY 14301

(716) 282-3700

Rates: $14 per Hostelling International member
Credit cards: None
Season: February 1 to December 15
Beds: 38
Private rooms: 2
Affiliation: Hostelling International
Office hours: 7:30 to 10:30 a.m.; 4:00 to midnight
Extras: Laundry, parking, storage, television, kitchen, playground, grill

*T*his hostel is a Georgian-style home with tons more character than its Canadian counterpart across the falls. It's still not without disadvantages, however; the worst one being a seedy neighborhood. If you had visions of Niagara Falls as an idyllic small town, this block may change your view. The 11:30 p.m. curfew and daytime lockout are also something you should consider before checking in; across the border there is no lockout and a 1:00 a.m. curfew.

What this place has going for it is a spunky energy. The common room is a feast for the senses, with plenty of interesting people and furniture. (Part of the room is covered in a wallpaper sure to induce hallucinations if stared at for too long.) Couch potatoes will be in hog heaven when they see the mega-size television set. Halfway up the original oak staircase is an open-air pseudo—common room where a small group of guests can listen to music or play cards. An interesting stained-glass window makes for more trippy lighting here, and the John F. Kennedy rug in the corner also adds to the effect.

On the flip side the dorms are pretty poor. Ditto the claustrophobic bathrooms. The aging metal bunks are practically piled on top of one another, and there is barely room to shower. The kitchen earns higher marks, but it's certainly nothing to write home about. The

Insiders' tip:
Canadian side is better
Gestalt:
True falls
Safety: *C*
Hospitality: *B*
Cleanliness: *B*
Party index: 🎉🎉🎉

crowd seems to be young here (mostly teenagers roamed the halls during our visit), but it's also more multicultural than at most American hostels. Many guests come from East Asia and Eastern Europe. On the upside, staff are friendly enough and facilities are clean.

And you can get out for a while. For a small fee, guests can take the hostel's two-hour sunset tour, a van ride along the Niagara River to the falls. Once there, you can stay on until darkness and see the water illuminated by colored lights.

How to Get There:

By airplane: From Buffalo airport, take #24 bus to Buffalo Transportation Center and change to #40 bus. Take to Niagara Falls bus terminal. Walk east on Niagara Street (away from river) 6 blocks to Memorial Parkway and turn left. Walk 1 block then turn right. Hostel is on right.
By bus: Greyhound stops in Buffalo. Take city bus to Niagara Falls. From bus station, walk east on Niagara Street (away from river) 6 blocks to Memorial Parkway, then turn left. Walk 1 block and turn right. Hostel is on right.
By car: Take Robert Moses Parkway into Fourth Street. Drive 4 blocks (pass under convention center) to Ferry Avenue, then go right. Hostel is 7 blocks down on right.
By train: Amtrak stops 3 miles from hostel. Call hostel for pickup or take cab.

Downing International Hostel

535 Oak Street, Syracuse, NY 13203–1609
(315) 472-5788

   Rates: $15 per Hostelling International member; $30 for private room
   E-mail: syracusehostel@yahoo.com
   Credit cards: None
   Beds: 35
   Private rooms: 5
   Affiliation: Hostelling International
   Office hours: 7:00 to 9:00 a.m.; 5:00 to 10:00 p.m. (to 11:00 p.m. Friday and Saturday)
   Extras: Laundry, storage, television, kitchen

Syracuse saw its glory days one hundred years ago, when it was responsible for one-seventh of the world's salt production. It probably wasn't much for tourism then, and it is still pretty bleak today. The hostel here has all the essentials you want, though, and serves as a fine stopping-off point for travelers in transit.

This is yet another of Hostelling International's turn-of-the-twentieth-century mansions with a stunning entranceway and a mediocre everything else. It was originally built as a private home by a leading salt trader and banker; among the house's most impressive attributes is a Victorian staircase, sliding gracefully around the front-hall entranceway. Adjoining this area is the quaint common room, designed like a typical American den. There's a fireplace, small paperback library, and a television. The plentiful seating is arranged, of course, to face the television.

Everything other than that, though, with the exception of a prominent front porch, is pretty drab. You'll want to spend as little time as possible in the damp, dark basement kitchen. The dining area seems to have been designed from the same concept many fast-food restaurants use; make it as unappealing as possible to promote turnover. Some of the dorm rooms and bathrooms are in poor condition, too. Arrive early to get yourself a suitable bed and proximity to one of the better bathrooms. (To its credit, this hostel does have an excellent guest-to-shower ratio.)

An eclectic variety of activities is available in the surrounding area: The Erie Canal Museum allows patrons to board a boat once used on America's controlled-water transportation link to the old western frontier. Visit the Salt Museum to catch a glimpse of an original boiling block used to turn salt water to salt. There is also always the option of taking in an event at Syracuse University, known as the "Beast of the East" thanks to its success in intercollegiate athletics. Volumes of informational pamphlets can be found in the kitchen.

The hostel is relatively central, and the neighborhood is pleasant enough. Be cautious, though, as Syracuse is full of strange surprises: A few blocks downhill from the hostel, for instance, lies nudie-bar central. You have been warned.

How to Get There:

By bus: Greyhound, Trailways, and Syracuse–Oswego Bus lines all stop downtown. Find Clinton Square at Salina Street and Erie Boulevard, cross to James Street (New York Highway 290), and walk 10 blocks west on James to Oak Street. Go left on Oak and walk 1 block to Highland Avenue. Hostel is on left corner. (Walk is about 1¼ miles, uphill.)

By car: Use exit 14 off Interstate 690 to Teall Avenue. Go north ¾ mile to left on James Street (New York Highway 290). Go 1 mile to right on Oak. Hostel is 1 block down on left.
By train: Amtrak stops in Syracuse. Take bus or taxi to hostel.

PENNSYLVANIA

Ironmaster's Mansion Hostel ✳✳✳✳

1212 Pine Grove Road, Gardners, PA 17324
(717) 486-7575
  Fax: (717) 486-7575
  E-mail: ironmastersmansion@pa.net
  Web site: www.hi-dvc.org
  Rates: $20–$22 per Hostelling International member
  Credit cards: MC, VISA
  Season: March to mid-December
  Beds: 46
  Private rooms: Yes
  Affiliation: Hostelling International
  Office hours: 7:30 to 9:30 a.m.; 5:00 to 10:00 p.m.
  Extras: Laundry, hot tub, hiking trails, kitchen, Internet access

*T*he grand Ironmaster's mansion has been the victim of revolving-door management and has seen the best—and worst—of managers in the past. However, with the current management, we hope (emphasis on hope) that things have improved. Because overall, we really like it for its supremely American location (near the Twirly Top ice cream parlor and peach orchards) and proximity to the great Appalachian Trail. We've had, we'll confess, some wildly different experiences at this unique place. The first time, it was like a dream: A pleasant manager asked us to remove our shoes, then ushered us into a soothing respite from a cold night and sold us a ton of supplies he'd stocked just for late-night starving travelers such as ourselves. Later he talked to us about hostelling and his genuine love of it. The second time, though, it was more like a nightmare. The fellow on duty clearly was annoyed (we were the only guests), and he refused to turn on the heat on a near-freezing night. Needless to say, we slept terribly.

Best bet for a bite:
Local orchards and diners
Insiders' tip:
Hike carefully during hunting season
What hostellers say:
"Thanks for the shower."
Gestalt:
Iron maiden
Hospitality: *B*
Cleanliness: *C*
Party index:

On our other visits we found the place somewhat rundown and cluttered. Perhaps it was a result of visiting during the very low season when hostel guests are scarce. It certainly didn't match our first visit. Then we came again, and it was fine.

There's clearly a different personality to this place, depending on who's working the desk and when you come. Regardless, it's certainly a gorgeous facility: set in the mountains, big and elegant. It really is a mansion, built for the local ironmaster back in 1827, and rumor has it the place was once an Underground Railroad stop (the manager should show you where the hiding place was said to be). Bunkrooms are standard but nice, and the big and bountiful kitchen is absolutely tops. Be aware that chores are enforced before checking out—at least they were when we stayed.

The only private room consists of four single beds partitioned from each other, each with reading light and table. Mattresses were fairly soft.

Want hiking? The Appalachian Trail passes right through the backyard, and hikers' grateful comments are scrawled throughout the guest book. Nature? There are deer all over the place, and you'll have to work not to see one. Biking, skiing, anything's possible. There's no denying the fab location of this hostel—just be prepared for anything.

How to Get There:

By car: Drive I-81 to Pennsylvania Highway 233 exit (Newtown), then drive south to Pine Grove Road. Hostel is near corner of Pine Grove and Highway 233; look for signs.

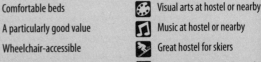

Tyler State Park Hostel ✺✺✺

Tyler State Park (P.O. Box 94), Newtown, PA 18940

(215) 968-0927

Fax: (215) 557-2100

E-mail: hityler@hi-dvc.org

Web site: www.hi-dvc.org

Rates: $18 per Hostelling International member

Credit cards: MC, VISA

Beds: 22

Private rooms: 1

Affiliation: Hostelling International

Season: Closed Thanksgiving and Christmas

Office hours: 7:00 to 9:00 a.m.; 6:00 to 11:00 p.m.

Extras: Fireplace, table tennis, kitchen, grill, television

*H*ere's a hostel that never lost sight of Hostelling International's original impetus: providing a means for groups of adolescents to experience new environments and cultures. This rustic outpost in the cornfields of Tyler State Park attracts scout groups by the hordes. In many ways it is the perfect place for them; the hostel is smack in the middle of 1,170 acres of park trails, yet only a hop, skip, and a jump from downtown Philly.

We're glad these kids are getting their fresh air. At the same time, however, we advise that if you wish to enjoy the same serenity that they are seeking, you come during the week when they aren't there. The dilemma then is that nobody may be there. Like other Pennsylvania hostels, this one's remote location often means that it is either full with a group or completely deserted.

What is now the hostel was once the annex to a millionaire philanthropist's country home. The dude had bought about twenty adjoining farms in the area to pursue his hobby of raising animals and working the fields (or at least having people do it for him). While his wife lived in a glitzy mansion elsewhere, this guy hung with the dogs and his dirty boots back at the farms so as not to soil the missus's house. The land went on to become the park, with fields and trails ideal for walking, horseback riding, and Nordic skiing, and what was his auxiliary cabin is now a quaint country hostel.

The building definitely has that Norman Rockwell feel, with creaky wood floors, a giant fireplace, and exposed wood beams—not to mention the faint smell of hickory. If you are looking for nighttime diversions, however, you won't find them here. While there is a television, there's no other place to go. It is tricky enough finding the rural hostel in the daytime; leaving and trying to come back after dark leaves you with a high probability of getting lost.

The remote location and lengthy weekday lockout (9:00 a.m. to 6:00 p.m. weekdays; none on weekends) make this a difficult hostel for those without transportation, especially during the winter, when darkness falls before 6:00 p.m. If you want to rough it, though, rides to and from downtown Philly can be arranged.

How to Get There:

By bus: Pickups from downtown Philadelphia possible. Call hostel for details. Or take R3 train from Philadelphia; change to SEPTA bus 130, continue to Bucks County Community College stop. Walk along Swamp Road to park, 1 mile.

By car: From Interstate 95, go 8 miles west on Pennsylvania Highway 332 and turn left on Richboro Road (also 332), then turn right on Pennsylvania Route 232 (also Second Street Pike) and proceed ½ mile. Turn right onto Twining Ford Road, an unpaved road, while continuing into park. Turn left at DO NOT ENTER SIGN onto White Pine Trail and keep right at fork. Turn left at stop sign onto Covered Bridge Trail and park past stop sign at bottom of hill.

By train: Pickups from downtown Philadelphia possible. Call hostel for details. Or follow bus directions.

PHILADELPHIA HOSTELS: A SUMMARY

	RATING	PROS	CONS	COST	PAGE
Apple Hostel	✹✹✹	staff; location	no parking	$29	p. 91
Chamounix Mansion Hostel	✹✹✹	kitchen; building	not central	$20–$23	p. 93

Apple Hostel ✸✸✸

32 South Bank Street, Philadelphia, PA 19106

(215) 922-0222

Fax: (215) 689-4555

E-mail: philly@applehostels.com

Web site: www.applehostels.com

Rates: $29 per person

Credit cards: None

Beds: 70

Private rooms: None

Affiliation: None

Office hours: Twenty-four hours

Extras: Laundry, television, air-conditioning, lockers, pool table, Internet access, kitchen

*A*n Apple Hostel in Philly? Fuggedaboudit! But it's true. This completely renovated nineteenth-century building is set smack in the middle of the City of Brotherly Love, in one of the nation's most historic neighborhoods. Just across the street from the hostel is Independence National Park, where you can relive the signing of the Declaration of Independence, see the Liberty Bell, and walk through some of the country's first official buildings. It's all free, too.

Beyond that you can get to almost every major cultural attraction in the city by foot from the hostel. The world-renowned Philadelphia Museum of Art is the longest haul, but only a thirty-minute walk on a nice day. Otherwise there is plenty of public transportation to go around.

Give us a cardboard box in this location, and we'd be thrilled, but this hostel is supreme. What we like best about the Apple is that it is as urban as it gets, while remaining incredibly warm and friendly. Seventy beds is

Best bet for a bite:
Geno's in South Philly, of course

Insiders' tip:
Film at visitors center

What hostellers say:
"I'm declarin' my independence. From bad hostels."

Gestalt:
Spirit of '76

Safety: *A*

Hospitality: *A*

Cleanliness: *A*

Party index: 🎉🎉🎉

a perfect size for such a place; unlike so many other urban hostels, this one does not operate as a quasi–budget hotel. Guests hang out together in the common room, and the manager gets to know all the hostellers well. Many folks take advantage of the nightly videos, interacting with one another as the show goes on. This was new for us because at other city hostels with movie nights, we regularly encountered guests sitting neatly in rows and remaining stoic throughout the show.

Another nice touch at the Apple is the unbelievably commodious kitchen. Even the cheap local diners can break the bank after a while, so it is nice to have a good kitchen to come home to in the middle of the city. You can spend your money at the movies or clubs instead of on bacon burgers. There are also great beds and bathroom facilities.

Bank Street itself is a bit suspect, only because it is a narrow alley with a few abandoned buildings. Not to worry, though, as the hostel is on the tail end of it, abutting busy Chestnut Street (the location of the national park visitors center). The only real setbacks hostellers must endure revolve around logistical issues. We're sorry to report that street parking is a nightmare in the area. You can avoid the headaches by pulling into one of the many area garages for big bucks. The other gripe we have is that there is an all-day lockout, which can be a hassle in a city hostel. Some may take issue with the curfew, but it was late enough—12:30 a.m. on weekdays and 1:00 a.m. on the weekend—not to bother us.

We digress: The long and short of it is that this is a great hostel we plan to come back to repeatedly. It most definitely serves as a model that other downtown city hostels should aspire toward.

How to Get There:

By airplane: Take R1 train to Market East stop. Follow Market Street toward Second Street, for about ten minutes to Bank Street. The hostel is on the right between Third and Second Streets.

By bus: From Greyhound and Peter Pan terminals, walk left for ten minutes down Market Street and turn right onto Bank Street between Third and Second Streets.

By car: Follow a map of Philadelphia to Independence National Park. Find parking in a garage near the visitors center on Chestnut and Third Streets. The hostel is between Second and Third Streets, off Chestnut Street toward Market Street.

By train: From Thirtieth Street Amtrak Station take Market Street subway to Second Street. The hostel is located ½ block toward Third Street.

Chamounix Mansion Hostel

Chamounix Drive, Philadelphia, PA 19131

(215) 878-3676

Fax: (215) 871-4313

E-mail: chamounix@philahostel.org

Web site: www.philahostel.org

Rates: $20–$23 per Hostelling International member

Credit cards: MC, VISA

Season: Mid-January to mid-December

Beds: 80

Private rooms: Vary; call for availability

Affiliation: Hostelling International

Office hours: 8:00 to 11:00 a.m.; 4:30 p.m. to midnight

Extras: Table tennis, tennis rackets, piano, lockers, grill, television, VCR, movies, kitchen, Internet access, bikes

*B*uilt back around 1899 by a merchant as a country retreat from the heat of the city, this mansion rests on a hill just outside central Philly. The city incorporated the mansion into surrounding Fairmount Park long ago, but it took a nonprofit group to rescue it from neglect. The group began leasing the home and maintaining it as a hostel in 1964.

It used to be great, but recent reports indicate things are falling off—putting this hostel in the "middle of the pack" category rather than the "outstanding" digs it used to provide. Dorms are as you'd expect; private rooms consist of four bunks in a room that can't be locked from the outside. (Third-floor rooms want for a bit of headspace, and the fire

Best bet for a bite:
Local grocer/pizza shop

Insiders' tip:
Biking to the art museum

What hostellers say:
"Used to be better."

Gestalt:
Philadelphia freedom

Safety: *B*

Hospitality: *B*

Cleanliness: *B*

Party index:

escape consists of a fold-up ladder or a 30-foot leap into the trees.) But, hey, there's some great period furniture in several drawing rooms. A carriage house has been renovated to accommodate groups, but it can be used for hostellers during peak season.

Management has traditionally been helpful to a fault—offering directions to local grub, history lessons, and free tennis rackets to use on the nearby courts—and genuinely pleased to have a hostel to share with the world, though, again, that has changed a bit lately. The Chamounix crew does deserve credit for keeping long office hours and adding thirty-five wheelchair-accessible bunks in an adjacent carriage house. The place is generally clean and has an extra-large kitchen, table tennis, and a piano. Wedged into a backstreet confusion of apartments, parks, and highways (police seem to make frequent drive-bys), it is tricky to find. Although the hostel isn't anywhere near downtown, there is a good bike trail that goes straight to the heart of the city. On weekends two nearby riverside roads are also closed to autos. That's why we applaud the hostel's addition of a few free bikes to its already generous offerings.

Our assessment now? Give the management high marks for a clean, extraordinarily well-run hostel. And the setting, ideal one hundred years ago—before urban blight and highway-building fever set in—is still pretty good.

How to Get There:
By airplane: Large airport in Philadelphia. Call hostel for transit route.
By bus: Greyhound stops downtown. Take #38 bus from Market Street to Ford, then walk 1 mile down Ford and left on Chamounix to end.
By car: Take Interstate 76 to exit 33 (City Avenue/U.S. Highway 1). Follow City to Belmont; make left at light onto Belmont Avenue, then another left onto Ford Road. Follow Ford 1 mile through tunnel to stop sign, bear left on Chamounix Drive. Hostel is at end of road.
By train: Call hostel for transit route.

Weisel Hostel ✷✷✷✷
7347 Richlandtown Road, Quakertown, PA 18951
(215) 536-8749
E-mail: weiselhostel@co.bucks.pa.us
Rates: $12–$15 per Hostelling International member
Credit cards: None
Beds: 20

Private rooms: 1
Affiliation: Hostelling International
Season: Closed Christmas Eve through New Year's Day
Office hours: 7:00 to 9:00 a.m.; 4:00 to 9:00 p.m.
Extras: Fireplace, television, storage, kitchen, laundry

*W*hat a striking appearance! Even if you've seen the pictures beforehand, your jaw still drops as you round the corner into the driveway of this century-old estate. Forget hostel standards; this mansion is an inspiring work of architecture by *any* standards. It's the stuff of which *Better Homes and Gardens* covers are made.

The house just came as a tag-on when Bucks County bought the encompassing 5,000 acres to form Nockamixon State Park. The bureaucrats didn't know what to do with the place, and that's where backpackers came in. A hostel was born.

Staff and hostellers lament that the house has become a bit sterile after being stripped of some of its original character to meet state and county regulations, but it's still a charming outpost. The staff has managed to infuse the hostel with a sort of countrified charm by installing swags and baskets around the kitchen and common space. The kitchen has two full stoves and great equipment for use, including a microwave. For a twenty-bed hostel there is a disproportionate amount of common space, and everything in the joint is clean. The huge tiled fireplace stands prominently in the exposed-beam lounge: It's a perfect place to commune.

Best bet for a bite:
Supermarkets in Quakertown
Insiders' tip:
Farmers' market on weekends
What hostellers say:
"I don't want to go back to the city."
Gestalt:
Penny-Weisel
Hospitality: *A*
Cleanliness: *A*
Party index:

The bunks are in good shape, too, so no need to worry about getting that sinking feeling. A family room provides more creature comforts than usual: pretty curtains, an alarm clock, and reading lights. The bulk of the guest list is composed of two main categories: adolescent groups and city folks abandoning ship for the weekend. You'll want to avoid crossing paths with the former, as the whole idea of Weisel is to get away from it all. It's a great retreat if you have been pounding the pavement in New York or Philadelphia and need some rest and relaxation between the grind of cities.

The park itself is perfect for unwinding, too, and offers a 1,450-acre lake. The surrounding area is chock-full of interesting cultural sites that provide a glimpse into old-time Pennsylvania, though a few attractions are clunkers, too. We were glad to discover the managers here were as wary of schmaltz as we are, eager to steer guests away from tourist traps toward more worthwhile areas. Among them is a local covered bridge tour you can take by car or bike. You'll be provided with a handy visitor's guide when you arrive.

Not to dampen the excitement, but don't forget where you are. There is a lockout and a strict curfew, and other regular hostel rules are enforced. Still, a great place.

How to Get There:

By car: From Pennsylvania Turnpike take exit 32 onto Pennsylvania Highway 663 to State Highway 313 east. Go 4 miles south of Quakertown on 313 then left onto Sterner Mill Road (at the Wagon Wheel Tavern). Then take immediate left onto Clymer Road. At stop sign take another left onto Richlandtown Road. Hostel is on right.

From Philadelphia: Take Pennsylvania Turnpike to exit 27, Willow Grove. Proceed north on Pennsylvania Highway 611 (toward Easton) and exit bypass at State Highway 313 (west). Stay on 313 until State Highway 563 north (Nockamixon State Park) and turn right. Drive about 1 mile to Sterner Mill Road. Turn left, then take an immediate right onto Richlandtown Road. Follow to hostel.

South

Page numbers follow hostel names

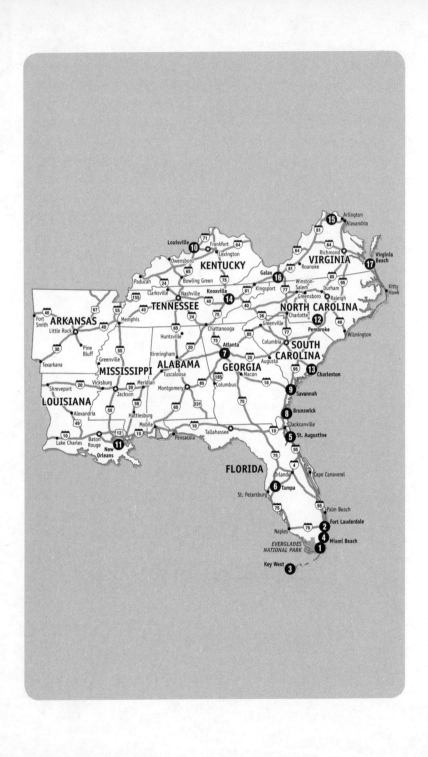

TENNESSEE

VIRGINIA

FLORIDA

Everglades International Hostel ✳✳✳

20 SW Second Avenue, Florida City (Homestead), FL 33034

(305) 248-1122; (800) 372-3874

Fax: (305) 245-7622

E-mail: gladeshostel@hotmail.com

Web site: www.evergladeshostel.com

Rates: $22–$25 per person; $60–$65 for private room

Credit cards: AMEX, DISC, MC, VISA

Beds: 45

Private/family rooms: 2

Affiliation: None

Office hours: 9:00 a.m. to 9:00 p.m.

Extras: Meals, grill, gazebo, canoe rentals, bike rentals, laundry, free pickups, Internet access, kitchen, DVD player, TV room, hammock, Everglades tours

*T*his Boho-type place could be a rising star, but upkeep and a way laid-back attitude seem like they could be derailing the hostel's promise. An offshoot project from those same folks who built the funky, woodsy, and winning Hostel in the Forest (see Brunswick, Georgia later in this chapter), it's of a similar ilk: democratic and socially conscious. Which don't always equal "perfectly clean," but hey.

By the way, it's important to note that this hostel is not actually located in the Everglades, though it's pretty close, on the outskirts of Homestead—an ethnically diverse city south of Miami that was leveled by Hurricane Andrew but has been busily rebuilding itself ever since. The neighborhood here is Hispanic in character, lending an interesting tinge to things.

Improvements are ongoing. What were once apartments housing transient workers are now all dedicated to the hostel. Dorms are mostly six- and seven-bedded. They have added a number of features, including free Internet access, a twenty-four-hour kitchen house, a hammock, a television room with a mondo TV and DVD player, and a laundry. The lawn is full of trees, and there's a screened-in gazebo for lounging around. Check ahead, though, because even in summer's sopping heat and humidity, this place gets crowded.

The hostel staff gives great tips on what to see and do in the Everglades or en route to the hostel. This is actually pretty central to south Florida's attractions; the best options besides the 'Glades include Biscayne National Park, Coral Castle, Key Largo, or, heck, the rest of the Keys. The same staff will also rent you a canoe to strap on top of your car and see the swamp creatures up close and personal. Or book an Everglades tour directly with the hostel.

Best bet for a bite:
Rosita's for Mexican
Insiders' tip:
Robert Is Here (fruit stand)
What hostellers say:
"Here, gator, gator . . ."
Gestalt:
Made in the 'Glades
Hospitality: *B*
Cleanliness: *C*
Party index:

Food? Check out all the U-pick farms in the area for getting your cheap breakfast. Bring burgers and charcoal to use the hostel barbecue. Or, as at the Georgia hostel, enjoy staff-prepared common meals for a small charge—the best way to get to know your fellow hostellers in a hurry.

How to Get There:

By airplane: From Miami airport, take J bus to Douglas Road and Metrorail Station. Pick up Metrorail and bus transfers and take Metrorail South to Dadeland Mall South. Take Bus 34 or Bus 38 to Southwest 344th Street and Southwest Second Avenue in Florida City. Hostel is on the right.

By bus: From Homestead Greyhound station, call hostel for pickup.

By car: From Miami, take the Florida Turnpike Extension toll highway south to its ending point in Homestead. Turn onto State Road 997. At Southwest 344th Street (Palm Drive), turn right at Chevron gas station. Go 1½ blocks to Mexican restaurant. Hostel is just before gazebo.

From Tampa, drive Interstate 75 south approximately 170 miles to Naples, then exit just before Alligator Alley toll road onto Route 41 (the Tamiami Trail). Continue east on Route 41 approximately 90 miles to S.R. 997. Turn right onto 997 and drive south through Homestead. At Southwest 344th Street (Palm Drive), turn right at Chevron gas station. Go 1½ blocks to Mexican restaurant. Hostel is just before gazebo.

Backpackers Beach Hostel ✸✸✸✸

2115 North Ocean Boulevard, Fort Lauderdale, FL 33305

(954) 567-7275

Fax: (954) 567-9697

E-mail: info@fortlauderdalehostel.com

Web site: www.fortlauderdalehostel.com

Rates: $20–$22 per person; $55 for private room

Credit cards: MC, VISA

Beds: 35

Private rooms: Yes

Affiliation: None

Office hours: 10:00 a.m. to 4:00 p.m.; 6:00 p.m. to midnight

Extras: Pickups, free parking, lockers, Internet access, grill, free local calls, pool table, laundry, television, shop

---

This hostel in Fort Laud opened a couple years back, and it seems to be delivering on its promise of a hassle-free bed and a pleasant experience. Good reports keep coming up. With both private rooms and bunks in a variety of accoms (mostly motel rooms and four- to six-bedded, dormlike apartments), the place comes bearing a boatload of free goodies: cable TV, free parking in a lot, lockers, Internet access, a gas grill for your grilling pleasure, free local calls, a pool table, laundry (okay, that's not free), a small hostel shop, a kitchen for cookin'... they'll even pick you up if they can during working hours at the local airport, bus terminal, or Amtrak station. There's no curfew, either—you can come and go anytime.

A few hostellers here have carped afterward about a seemingly uneven office-hours policy. The hostel's office is actually open for most of the day and until midnight, but apparently the staff don't always keep those hours. Whatev. All in all, repeated snooping confirms that Fort Laud finally has a second good hostel—make that, a bona fide excellent hostel.

Tip: In addition to the directions below, also inquire about the Tri-Rail Shuttle, which sometimes offers free pickups and dropoffs to the hostel neighborhood at certain times. Call (954) 567-7275 for more info.

Best bet for a bite:
Las Olas, probably
Gestalt:
"Laud don't slow me down"
Safety: A
Hospitality: A
Cleanliness: B
Party index:

How to Get There:

By airplane: From Fort Lauderdale airport, take city bus #1 north on U.S. Highway 1 to Broward Central Terminal. Transfer to #11 bus and take to corner of North Ocean Boulevard (Route A1A) and NE Twenty-first Street. Hostel is across the street.

By bus: Greyhound stops in Fort Lauderdale. From bus station, walk 4 blocks southwest or take bus #1 to Broward Central Terminal. Take #1 bus to corner of North Ocean Boulevard (Route A1A) and NE Twenty-first Street. Hostel is across street.

By car: From I-95, take exit 95 (Sunrise Boulevard). Follow Sunrise Boulevard east toward beach to end; turn left onto North Ocean Boulevard (also called Route A1A) and continue to NE Twenty-first Street. Hostel is on left, at northwest corner.

By train: Amtrak stops in Fort Lauderdale. From station, take free Tri-Rail Shuttle (city bus #55) or bus #22 to Broward Central Terminal. Change to #11 bus and continue to North Ocean Boulevard (Route A1A) and NE Twenty-first Street. Hostel is at corner.

Floyd's International Youth Hostel and Crew House ✻✻✻

Fort Lauderdale, FL · Call for address

(954) 462-0631

Fax: (954) 462-6881
E-mail: info@floridahostel.com
Web site: www.floridahostel.com
Rates: $25 per person; $40 for private room
Credit cards: MC, VISA
Beds: 40
Private rooms: Yes
Affiliation: None
Office hours: 8 a.m. to noon; 5:00 to 8:00 p.m.
Extras: Free food, free phones, free laundry, free fax receiving, television, DVDs, free pickup, free parking, free high-speed Internet access, kitchen

---

Floyd Creamer, a former boat hand who hostelled extensively during his earlier years, began Fort Lauderdale's best hostel with the idea of doing something different. "I liked the idea of creating a place from scratch," he told us, "so I created a hostel from scratch."

What he created is a cross between a college dorm room, a nonstop picnic, and your first apartment. His hostel consists of five apartment units in three buildings, all of which include four bunk beds, a kitchen, a bathroom, and a common living room with a television. Very homey, but also very much a communal living situation. In fact, there are no private accommodations here at all (except in summer), so you'd better like company.

The focal point of Floyd's isn't really the apartments, though, but the outdoor common space. Beneath shrubs sprouting red flowers practically year-round, a very international crowd hangs out in a mellow groove, eating and drinking at a series of central tables. The gardens here are great, with palm trees and flowers.

The hostel management throws in lots of free services for your money: laundry, fax receiving, and local phone calls, to name a few. They dole out free (if basic) foodstuffs, too—as many boxes of cornflakes, packages of spaghetti, pots of rice or mac 'n' cheese, and cups of tea as you can consume. They pick up arriving hostellers at no charge, and even refund a hosteller's money if the hosteller pays for a week but leaves earlier: almost unheard-of in this business.

On the disciplinary side, Creamer screens guests by phone before booking them in, prefers a passport to secure a bed, and makes no bones about kicking out guests for suspected drug use, loud noise, refusal to do the dishes, or even just plain antisocial behavior. A few hostellers complained that he was too quick to criticize or give 'em the hook, but in general guests don't seem to mind his gentle prodding.

This hostel certainly isn't located in the most interesting neighborhood of Fort Lauderdale, although it isn't too terribly far from the water, either. If you're looking for adventure, this can be a great hostel to visit: The area is known as the yachting capital of the world, and offers of boat work in exotic places frequently are the star attractions of the hostel bulletin board. The hostel also dispenses information on SCUBA courses and cheap dive trips.

Creamer is a decent guy who'll help you find work or just a good hostelling experience, and—all things considered—he runs a decent place.

How to Get There:

By airplane: Call hostel for transit route from Fort Lauderdale airport.
By bus: Call hostel for transit route from station.
By car: Call hostel for directions.

Sea Shell Hostel

718 South Street, Key West, FL 33040
(305) 296-5719; (800) 909-4776 (U.S. only)
Fax: (305) 296-0672
E-mail: kwssm@bellsouth.net
Web site: www.keywesthostel.com
Rates: $34 per person
Credit cards: MC, VISA
Beds: 92
Private rooms: 14
Affiliation: None
Office hours: 9:30 a.m. to 9:00 p.m.
Extras: Kitchen, meals, television, VCR, library, pool table, bike rentals

---

*W*arning: This hostel does not take advance reservations except by fax (and even then it's iffy), so be prepared with a backup plan.

First the good news: The Sea Shell is by far your cheapest lodging choice in Key West, particularly in the winter. A hotel could easily cost you way more than $100 during January or February, while this place charges around $30 per (dorm-room) head, an incredible deal. There's more good news for the budget traveler: the cheapo breakfasts here. Yes, for just a couple bucks you can get a meal, once again a serious savings on this tourist town's going rates.

Best bet for a bite:
Blue Heaven fruit market/diner
Insiders' tip:
Try in-line skating around town
Gestalt:
Off-key
Hospitality: *F*
Cleanliness: *F*
Party index: 🎉🎉🎉🎉

Here's the flip side, though: This place sucks. Really. We've gotten such discouraging reports from hostellers who have stayed here that we cannot possibly recommend you stay, and this situation has not changed an iota in the ten years we've been filtering through reviews. It's a crazy scene, busy and crowded. The facilities aren't as cared-for as they should be, and the staff are downright rude. One staffer told a hosteller that he could "sleep at Denny's" (a twenty-four-hour restaurant) since the hostel had no space available because of their no-reservations policy.

At least the place is geared toward fun; no matter what the weather's doing (it'll probably be either sunny and warm, windy and warm, or raining hard and warm), there's something to do both inside and outside. Among the attractions: a television and VCR, grill, pool table, and video games. Bike rentals are available, too, for those who want to explore the Conch Republic in the local fashion.

The town itself, of course, is legendary for its attractions: Sloppy Joe's, the bar where writer Ernest Hemingway threw 'em back, the Hemingway House, and the southernmost point in the continental United States (a meaningless spot, to be sure, especially if you happen to hail from Hawaii). If Key West has lost much ground to commercialization, it's still the finest place we know to catch a sunset. Each evening a carnival of locals, performers, and sun-struck tourists collect to watch the day's departure and to celebrate it in grand style. The Old Town, which is more southern-fried than strip-mall, is also still a fine place to go walking.

Our verdict: Come to this hostel if you're looking for sun, fun, bad attitude, and a party with other young travelers from the world over (and if you don't value sleep or immaculate rooms so much as a good bar conversation). Stay somewhere (anywhere) else, though, if you're looking for peace, quiet, and the best management.

How to Get There:

By bus: Greyhound stops in Key West. Call hostel for free pickup.
By car: Drive U.S. Highway 1 south to downtown Key West; turn left on Simonton Street, drive 4 blocks, then turn left onto South Street. Drive 2 more blocks. Hostel is on right.

Key to Icons

Attractive natural setting	Comfortable beds	Visual arts at hostel or nearby
Ecologically aware hostel	A particularly good value	Music at hostel or nearby
Superior kitchen facilities or cafe	Wheelchair-accessible	Great hostel for skiers
Offbeat or eccentric place	Good for business travelers	Bar or pub at hostel or nearby
Superior bathroom facilities	Especially well-suited for families	Editors' choice: Among our very favorite hostels
Romantic private rooms	Good for active travelers	

MIAMI BEACH HOSTELS: A SUMMARY

	RATING	PROS	CONS	COST	PAGE
Tropics Hostel	✳✳✳	pool	slacker crowd	$24–$34	p. 113
Clay Hotel International	✳✳✴	atmo	kitchen	$17–$26	p. 107
Miami Beach Int'l Travellers	✳✳	lobby	upkeep	$19–$26	p. 109
South Beach International	✳✴	bar	condition	$11–$17	p. 111

Clay Hotel International Hostel ✳✳✴

1438 Washington Avenue, Miami Beach, FL 33139

(305) 534-2988; (800) 379-2529

Fax: (305) 673-0346

E-mail: info@clayhotel.com

Web site: www.clayhotel.com

Rates: $17–$26 per person; $60–$145 for private room

Credit cards: JCB, MC, VISA

Beds: 200

Private rooms: 120

Private bathrooms: 120

Affiliation: None

Office hours: Twenty-four hours

Extras: Laundry, patio, discounts, movie nights, Internet access, kitchen

*Y*ou've just been deposited in Miami Beach for the first time in your life. You want to get some history, you want fun and sun, you want a glimpse of your favorite celebrities, but most of all you want a nice place to stay. Oh yeah, and you don't want to spend a mint. So what are you gonna do? You're gonna stay at the Clay Hotel, probably.

We've always been struck by this hostel's amazing location, on a cute side street off a main drag and a few blocks from the beaches, as well as its usually knowledgeable staff. This is all the more remarkable because the front desk is constantly busier than a beehive that's just been kicked over. Yet the staff is multilingual, a necessity in Miami and a bonus for European travelers. This hostel attracts an extremely Latin American clientele, we noticed, along with the usual folks from Germany, Down Under, the British Isles, Texas, and so forth.

Want history? This building has got tons of it: both good and bad. Al Capone once ran gambling operations out of the pink stucco hotel, which unwinds along half a city block, but it was badly crumbling by the time New York native Linda Polansky bought it in 1979 and converted it to hostel rooms. She made the decision after meeting a couple of Swiss backpackers.

"The way they described it, it sounded like a camp for travelers. I had slept in bunk beds for ten years in Connecticut, so I knew what that was like," recalled Polansky, who worked with locals to help revitalize the Art Deco district from a formerly crime-ridden area to the hip address in Florida. The corner where the hostel sits is so cool, in fact, that *Miami Vice* shot some scenes here, as did the director of the film *The Specialist* (with Sly Stallone and James Woods facing off).

Plants in the lobby, good bulletin boards, paddle fans, refrigerators in the rooms, and lots of common space make the traveler feel more at home than usual. The pink interior stucco walls are retouched periodically, and rooms are standard but good enough, with each four- to eight-bed dorm including a small fridge and private bathroom.

Many of the private rooms are nicer, though it really depends where you are placed and in which building. All come with dressers and mirrors, and some also include television sets and private bathrooms. A special few come with balcony views of a side street that jumps (sometimes too loudly) with piped-in Latin music, bleating car alarms, and other street symphonies that are part of the South Beach experience. (Note: If you're a light sleeper, do *not* request a streetside room.) Some rooms are flimsy, others are borderline luxurious; this is a big hotel, so it's a bit of a crap shoot. But if you don't like your room or it's not as clean as you expected or paid for, try the front desk—they might help relocate you.

As we note, it's not perfect here. Some rooms are cleaner than others. The kitchen is

Best bet for a bite:
Fruit markets along Washington
Insiders' tip:
Avenue gets noisy on weekend nights
What hostellers say:
"Cute location."
Gestalt:
Smart Deco
Safety: *B*
Hospitality: *B*
Cleanliness: *C*
Party index: 🎉🎉🎉🎉

disappointingly small and underequipped, as it has been for a long time. If it's sunny out, that isn't a problem; there's plenty of enclosed courtyard space covered with umbrellas here to escape the crowds inside the hostel, and plenty of cheap eats outside, too. If it's raining, though, you'll get soaking wet walking out to the kitchen (accessible through a gate down the street) and probably jostled by a throng of hostellers glued to the television set, too. Meh.

Luckily you can walk outdoors and buy almost anything you could want—from freshly harvested mangoes and juicy shakes (across Washington Avenue; ask at the stalls) to pricey bistro food. Miami has, quite simply, the best fruit in America, and it's sold everywhere. Many hostellers also hang out in the local coffee shops—there are several within a stone's throw of the hostel—or you might stumble across local ice cream, a Kosher-Cuban bakery (only in Miami), a grocery store with a great cheap deli. Suffice to say that you probably won't be cooking much while you're staying here anyway.

How to Get There:

By airplane: Large airport near Miami (twenty minutes). Take J bus to downtown Miami, change to C bus and get off at corner of Washington Avenue and Española Way.

By bus: Greyhound stops in Miami. From station, take C bus to corner of Washington Avenue and Española Way between Thirteenth and Fourteenth Streets.

By car: From I-95 exit east and cross bridge to Florida Highway A1A. Drive south to Española Way. Hostel is on the corner of Washington Avenue and Española Way.

By train: Amtrak stops in Miami. From station, take L bus to corner of Washington Avenue and Española Way.

Miami Beach International Travellers Hostel

236 Ninth Street, Miami Beach, FL 33139

(305) 534-0268

    Web site: www.hostelmiamibeach.com

    Rates: $19–$26 per person; $79–$99 for private room

    Credit cards: MC, VISA

    Beds: 77

    Private rooms: 12

    Private bathrooms: 12

    Affiliation: None

Office hours: Twenty-four hours

Extras: Laundry, pool table, fax, television, VCR, library, bike rentals, tours, kitchen, free meals

NOTE: Passport required of Americans in dormitories.

This hostel, tucked on a little side street but still close to all the Art Deco action Miami Beach has to offer, is a mixed bag. The location is amazing, yes. And the place tries to embody the best ideals of a small European hotel at rock-bottom hostelling prices.

Unfortunately, it doesn't.

Entering the lobby, you immediately notice fancy tilework and wicker furniture, lamps, plants, prints, a bright pastel pink SoBe color scheme. So far, so good. Outdoor seating is another nice touch, with speakers piping music out there for easy listening. The international slacker crowd here seems to appreciate the effort as they congregate and smoke.

The simple dorms come four beds to a room, and they seem big enough but sparsely furnished. This is where the trouble starts. Management controls the air conditioners and only turns 'em on at night; that can be a problem, but the real issue is with hygiene. These dorms aren't clean, either. At all. And the staff doesn't seem all that concerned about it—pretty useless mostly. Why should they care? *They* don't have to sleep here. (Well, some of them look like they did, actually.) Anyway, the private rooms are lightly furnished with old furniture, big with small desks and private bathrooms: again, nothing fancy, and despite regular housekeeping we noted crawling critters.

Best bet for a bite:
Puerto Sagua
What hostellers say:
"Où se trouve la plage?"
Gestalt:
So-so SoBe
Safety: *B*
Hospitality: *C*
Cleanliness: *F*
Party index:

Downstairs in the basement are a kitchen and dining room, which, despite lingering smells, are fairly well-equipped. There are several stoves, microwaves, and cubbyholes for storing food. A pool table, stamp machine, foosball unit, television/ VCR combo (you need to get keys to it at the front desk), and small laundry also share this basement space with the kitchen. But the hostellers we met weren't really motivated to cook; they were mostly interested in partying. Anyway, the hostel advertises free breakfast, lunch, *and* dinner, so check that out if you really intend to stay.

This isn't the hippest neighborhood on the beach, though it's not terrible. The neighbors are down-to-earth businesses, for the most part. Some nightclubs and Latin food joints are close at hand. You can walk to the beach or Ocean Drive in a short time without getting winded, and that's really all people seem to care about here. Ownership says they've tried to make this place a friendly, homey joint. Unfortunately, it's still a party pad, not clean enough, and not staffed by people with skills. Oh well. We'll pass, for now.

How to Get There:

By airplane: Large airport near Miami (twenty minutes). Take J bus to downtown Miami, change to C bus, and get off on Washington Avenue.

By bus: Greyhound stops in Miami. From station, take C bus to corner of Washington and Ninth.

By car: From I-95, exit east and cross bridge to Florida Highway A1A (Collins Avenue). Turn onto Ninth Street.

By train: Amtrak stops in Miami. From station, take L bus to Washington Avenue.

South Beach Hostel ✳✸

235 Washington Avenue, Miami Beach, FL 33139
(305) 672-2137

E-mail: info@thesouthbeachhostel.com
Web site: www.thesouthbeachhostel.com
Rates: $11–$17 per person; $48–$56 for private room
Credit cards: DISC, AMEX, MC, VISA
Private rooms: Yes
Affiliation: None
Office hours: Twenty-four hours
Extras: Free breakfast, bar, Internet access, free phone calls, grill, kitchen, lockers, television, pool tables, free airport shuttle

---

In theory, this *could* be a good hostel. It has a superior central location 2 blocks from the beach, friendly staff (sometimes a little too friendly), tons of amenities. A free (worth $35) ride from the airport, free Internet access, free breakfast, free long-distance phone access (are we dreaming?); pool tables; and a thoroughly social atmo that would not be

out of place in a hostel in Prague, Munich, or Berlin. How, you might wonder, could such a place possibly go wrong?

Well, it can. And does. Check out how it bills itself, for starters: "The only South Beach hostel with a full liquor bar." And they do buck-fifty Buds during happy hour. Okayyyy . . . but we just wanted a clean bed.

Nope, we didn't find it here. The place is sometimes dirty and in a state of disrepair. Dorm rooms contain four, six, eight, or even (gulp) fourteen bunks. The private rooms each have a full-size bed for two people, but their bathrooms are shared. Cleanliness and maintenance don't seem to factor into the equation at all—rooms were dirty, plumbing and fixtures were *still* falling apart when we came through—so if it's high on *your* list too, look elsewhere in town.

If you're seeking a super-social place, on the other hand, this might be the place for you. That bar sure is popular! (New management took over this hostel as we were going to press, by the way; they have vowed to improve the place's condition. We'll see.)

How to Get There:

By airplane: Hostel maintains free shuttle. Call hostel for details.

By bus: Greyhound stops in Miami (two stations). From NE Tenth Street station, walk 2 blocks to NE Second Avenue and take K bus ("Diplomat" or "Haulover") to Miami Beach; get off at Fifth Street and Washington Avenue. From NW Twenty-seventh Street station, walk 1 block west to Le Jeune Road (Twenty-seventh Street and Forty-second Avenue); take bus marked "J BEACH" to Forty-first Street and Sheridan Avenue, then transfer to M bus. Get off at Second Street and Washington Avenue. Hostel is across street.

By car: Take I-95 south to 395 east; this will take you over the bay on the MacArthur Causeway. As you come off the ramp you will be on Fifth Street heading east. Continue in that direction for ½ mile and take a right on Washington Avenue. The hostel is located between Second and Third Streets at 235 Washington Avenue.

By train: Amtrak stops in Miami. From station, take taxi to hostel or L bus to Lincoln Road; transfer to Electrowave shuttle bus heading south, get off at Second Street and Washington Avenue.

Tropics Hostel

1550 Collins Avenue, Miami Beach, FL 33139
(305) 531-0361

Fax: (305) 531-8676
Web site: www.tropicshotel.com
E-mail: email@tropicshotel.com
Rates: $24–$34 per person; $59–$150 for private room
Credit cards: None
Beds: 130
Private rooms: 48
Affiliation: None
Office hours: Twenty-four hours
Extras: Grill, pool, television, laundry, air-conditioning, kitchen

Tropics, a grand-looking Art Deco hotel that has been partly converted into a hostel right on the main South Beach hotel strip, is probably one of the best indy hostels in the South (in a field of very weak contenders)—less a crash pad than a place to relax and meet fun travelers from the world over. On the other hand, we don't always like the scruffiness of the crowd. That seems a tiny complaint, though.

Dorms come just four beds to a room, so there's no crush at bathroom time. The private rooms (actually hotel rooms!) are especially stylish, among the nicest you can get in a hostel, and obviously you pay more for those—but the price is not out of line. Each private room includes a bed or two, coffee table, dresser, television, phone for free local calls, and a big closet. Other nice touches include bathroom fixtures a step above standard hotel-issue design, shower curtains that are clean enough, even recycled toilet paper. Cleanliness in the common areas and kitchens appears to have slipped a bit in recent years, but it's still better than at least two of the other three hostels in town.

> **Best bet for a bite:**
> Cuban diners on Collins
> **Insiders' tip:**
> Local shuttle bus
> **What hostellers say:**
> "Great private rooms."
> **Gestalt:**
> Hot Tropic
> **Safety:** C
> **Hospitality:** C
> **Cleanliness:** C
> **Party index:**

The kitchen, believe it or not, is actually outdoors. This really is tropical-style living, isn't it? Under a tarp-covered patio, shielded from most of the elements, you cook with a single gas range or on the grill. We felt this kitchen was too small and sparsely outfitted, but you can't beat the view: It's surrounded with lush tropical plants, beside a sparkling, roomy swimming pool.

The main activities here seem to be lounging in deck chairs around the pool, sitting on the front veranda watching the scene (more lounge chairs), hanging with fellow hostellers in the spacious lobby, or shooting pool in a ground-floor pool room. There are no mandatory chores. There's no curfew. There's a laundry. The well-regarded Bass Museum is nearby. Be aware that prices are a lot higher during high season, from the third week of December to the beginning of April, but otherwise we like this place well enough.

How to Get There:
By airplane: Large airport in Miami. From airport, take J bus to Forty-first Street and Alton Road; change to C bus, take to Lincoln and Collins. Hostel is 1 block south on Collins on left.
By bus: Greyhound stops in Miami. From station, take C or S bus to Lincoln and Collins. Hostel is 1 block south on Collins on left.
By car: Cross causeway and turn onto Collins Avenue (Florida Highway A1A). Hostel is between Fifteenth and Sixteenth Streets on west side.
By train: Amtrak stops in Miami. From station, take L bus to Lincoln and Collins. Hostel is 1 block south on Collins on left.

Pirate Haus Inn & Hostel
32 Treasury Street, St. Augustine, FL 32084
(904) 808-1999; (877) 466-3864

Rates: $20 per person; $60–110 for private room
Beds: 31
Private rooms: 5
Affiliation: None
Office hours: 8:00 to 10:00 a.m.; 5:00 to 10:00 p.m.
Extras: Lockers, deck, laundry, bike rentals, Internet access, tour discounts, parking, kitchen, barbecue, breakfast, TV room

---

*T*his totally pirate-themed hostel has always been a legendary source of cheap bunks in northern Florida, and several recent changes in management have only lifted the place back to its former glory—maybe even beyond it.

The latest owner, known variously as Peg-Leg Tom or Captain Conrad (is this two guys? or the same guy?), really goes to town on the pirate thing—that will either amuse or annoy you—and while prices have risen in recent years and the place is now more of an inn than a hostel, it's still well worth a look.

Several former dormitories have been transformed into great family/couples rooms, each with private bathrooms, tubs, refrigerators, and lockers. They can hold up to four people each, and some can be used as overflow dorms when the place is heavy on individual hostellers and light on the families. Sure, they cost a little more, but they're worth it. And check out the wild theme rooms: a Jane-and-Tarzany jungle room, a tropical fish room (think Nemo), a tree room, a map room, and—of course—the obligatory pirate room, complete with ship-like touches and a skull-and-crossbones motif in the bathroom. Okayyyy. All have ceiling fans and air-conditioning, and some have mini-fridges, as well. The six- to eight-bedded dorms for hims and hers are equally good, if a bit tighter on space. Newer paint, newer rugs, plenty of heat—it all adds up to good sleeping quarters, we say.

The small kitchen has a washing machine (yes, it works), the rooftop patio features a grill, and there's Internet access and a pay phone. Best of all, a bend-over-backward-to-help staff keeps things friendly, low-key, and interesting. They even make pancakes each morning, for free, for hungry hostellers.

St. Augustine's a little gem of a city, overrun by tourists at times, to be sure, but still mighty interesting: This was the oldest city in the nation, after all, founded by Spaniards and later captured by the British. Fortunately for you, the hostel is only steps from the action. Start out at the Castillo (castle), a star-shaped Spanish fortress across the road. Then move on to the Spanish Village Quarter, a Williamsburg-style historic re-creation with a carpenter, blacksmith, weaver, and other interpreters demonstrating by example what eighteenth-century life was like in the fortified town.

Just west of the hostel, another set of buildings is the legacy of oil and railroad man

Best bet for a bite:
Free pancakes!
Insiders' tip:
Bike along the beach
What hostellers say:
"Avast, ye maties!!"
Gestalt:
Fountain of youth
Hospitality: *A*
Cleanliness: *A*
Party index: 🎉🎉

Henry Flagler, who single-handedly built this town to prominence in the late 1800s. Among Flagler's key contributions were several hotels and a beautiful church (built as a memorial to his daughter); most of his property is now part of Flagler College, and you can usually tour the buildings.

For fun, head a few miles west to Route A1A and several sets of good beaches and parks. Surf shops, souvenir stands, and bars provide further distraction.

How to Get There:

By airplane: Large airport in Jacksonville (one hour away). Call hostel for transit route.
By car: Drive I-95 to St. Augustine exit; follow signs to Florida Highway A1A and drive downtown. Turn right at central plaza, then immediately right again onto Charlotte. Park on Charlotte and walk up Treasury; hostel is on right.

Gram's Place ✳✳✳✳

3109 North Ola Avenue, Tampa, FL 33603
(813) 221-0596
  E-mail: gramspl@aol.com
  Web site: www.grams-inn-tampa.com
  Rates: $23–$25 per person; $60 for private room
  Beds: 18
  Private rooms: Yes
  Private bathrooms: Yes
  Affiliation: None
  Extras: Kitchen, hot tub, piano, television

---

*T*his place is an oasis in Florida, a combo B&B and hostel—named for prescient, too-young-deceased alt-country rocker Gram Parsons (born in Florida)—and sometimes it's hard to tell where one begins and the other ends. But there's no doubt that hostellers love the place, particularly musical hostellers: If you're the type to noodle away on a guitar for hours, this place is practically heaven.

The place consists of six private rooms (half with private baths, half with shared baths) and then one slightly bigger dorm room kitted out as a simulated rail car on the "Gram Central

Railroad." Get it? It's all Gram, all the time here. That's not all: There's also a "Gram Straat," a simulation of where Parsons would've lived in the Netherlands—um, had he been Dutch, that is. Which he wasn't. Anyway. Most of the rooms here are named after types of music— folk, rock and roll, jazz, blues, and so forth. Walls are lined with instruments, music CDs and tapes in each room reflect the room's theme, as do the windows. Cool. These rooms are clean and furnished with iron-framed beds that are probably similar to the ones in your bedroom at home. Only rooms with private baths are eligible for the free continental breakfast or use of the kitchen, though; hostellers must fend for themselves.

On the upside, the rooms with shared bath are in the main house, which is the central gathering point, home to a piano, fireplace, jukebox, and television room. There's a BYOB bar, and owner Mark Holland keeps the music going here, of course—he might even talk you into jamming with him, if you're so inclined. The Adventure Room, a separate free-standing structure, contains a loft bed that sleeps two, plus a sofa and skylight; though small, it's best for families. Note that you have to go outside to use an outdoor shower and toilet (yes, really!) or over to the main house for facilities. (There's a hot tub outside, as well.)

Two of the six private rooms actually have bunk beds (single on top, double below), so a single traveler might end up sharing the room with a couple decamped in the double beds. The hostel section is in the "train," which looks just like one (but isn't—we think). This section has its own bathroom, shared amongst six bunks; cable television with DVD player; and a stereo. There's not much privacy: You simply curtain off your bunk, and that's it, just like on a shared sleeper car of a train. There is an outlet next to each bunk, which theoretically allows one to charge a laptop, but that might be a bit tricky in such close quarters.

Overall, hostellers just love this place. The owner's friendliness, the cleanliness and centrality (central Tampa and the vaunted Ybor City neighborhood are just minutes away by car or cab), the Boho vibe, and constant tunes knocked us out. Only potential pitfall? They give discounts for "extended stays," which in theory is cool but can lead to the dreaded "long-termer's disease," i.e., somebody basically living in the hostel. There's a fine line between artist-in-residence and transient ne'er-do-well, and let's hope Gram's doesn't allow guests to cross it. We've also heard a few mixed reports about upkeep. Probably it's best suited for single or couple travelers inclined toward music, rather than older folks or families.

How to Get There:

By bus: Greyhound stops in Tampa. From station, walk west on Polk Street to Morgan Street, turn right, continue north 4 blocks to Marion Transit Center. Catch bus #1 (Florida Avenue); ask bus driver to stop at first bus stop after Floribraska Avenue (at Plymouth Street). Turn left on Plymouth Street and continue 3 blocks to Ola Avenue. At gate, dial #22 on phone. Call ahead if arriving after 2 p.m.

By car: From St. Petersburg or I-75, take I-275 to exit #46B (Martin Luther King Boulevard). Bear right and continue west through three lights to Highland Avenue. Continue 2 more blocks to North Ola Avenue, turn left (south) and continue to corner of West Plymouth Street. Entrance is first gate from corner on West Plymouth Street. Park on Plymouth Street.

From Orlando, take I-4 west. Just past Ybor City exit, get into right lane and take I-275 north. Then take first exit (#46B, Martin Luther King Boulevard). Bear right and continue west through three lights to Highland Avenue. Continue 2 more blocks to North Ola Avenue, turn left (south) and continue to corner of West Plymouth Street. Entrance is first gate from corner on West Plymouth Street. Park on Plymouth Street.

By train: Amtrak stops in Tampa. From station, walk west on Polk Street to Morgan Street, turn right, continue north 4 blocks to Marion Transit Center. Catch bus #1 (Florida Avenue); ask bus driver to stop at first bus stop after Floribraska Avenue (at Plymouth Street). Turn left on Plymouth Street and continue 3 blocks to Ola Avenue. At gate, dial #22 on phone. Call ahead if arriving after 2 p.m.

GEORGIA

Atlanta Hostel ✸✸

223 Ponce de Leon Avenue, Atlanta, GA 30308
(404) 875-9449; (800) 473-9449

   Web site: www.hostel-atlanta.com
   Rates: $25 per person
   Credit cards: MC, VISA
   Beds: 100
   Private rooms: 3
   Affiliation: None
   Office hours: 8:00 a.m. to noon; 5:00 p.m. to midnight
   Extras: Parking ($), kitchen, games, pool table, free coffee and doughnuts, Internet access, television

*T*he best and worst thing about the Atlanta Hostel may be its location: Easily accessible by most forms of public transportation, this historically significant building is also close to cultural points of the city. On the other hand, the 'hood is edgy at best. And the hostel? More dodgy and doddering than edgy; time, wear and tear, neglect, and issues with cleanliness and staff friendliness pervade here, as they have for years. At least the bottom floor has a socializing space where guests can play pool or watch TV; outside, guests gather on comfy couches but there's not a whole lot to do in the area once the sun sets. Catch a cab to Buckhead or Virginia-Highland for some real fun.

As we said, this hostel is located right downtown, and hostellers often complain they don't feel safe in the vicinity at night. You're closest to the city's big underground shopping mall (ho-hum), the World of Coke (big deal), and the Sweet Auburn neighborhood where Martin Luther King Jr. grew up

> **Best bet for a bite:**
> *Mary Mac's Tea Room*
> **Insiders' tip:**
> *Virginia-Highland neighborhood is cool*
> **What hostellers say:**
> *"Ain't nothin' but a thang."*
> **Gestalt:**
> *Home of the Braves*
> **Safety:** *C*
> **Hospitality:** *D*
> **Cleanliness:** *D*
> **Party index:** 🎉

and preached (much more interesting). Lots of eats are around, too. We'd opt for Mary Mac's Tea Room (which has moved around the city a few times, so check on its status) or the Beautiful Restaurant, a cafeteria in Dr. King's old neck of the woods. Entertainment? The grand old Fox Theater is close at hand. Atlanta's city parks make a nice day outing, too, especially in spring, when the white of dogwood blossoms and the pink of azaleas reign.

Atlanta is flat-out fantastic as a vacation. But we'd have to recommend a chain motel on I-285 over this place.

How to Get There:
By airplane: Large airport nearby. Take MARTA to North Avenue stop. See directions below.
By bus: Greyhound stops in Atlanta. Take MARTA to North Avenue stop. Walk 4 blocks east to corner of Myrtle and Ponce de Leon.
By car: Take I-75 or 85 to Tenth Street exit. Go east on Tenth, then turn right onto Myrtle Street, and follow it to U.S. Highway 78. Hostel is at corner.
By train: Amtrak stops in Atlanta. Take MARTA to North Avenue stop. See above directions.

Hostel in the Forest ✹✹✹✹

8901 U.S. Highway 82 West (P.O. Box 1496), Brunswick, GA 31521
(912) 264-9738

Web site: www.foresthostel.com
E-mail: foresthostelinfo@gmail.com
Rates: $15 per person (plus one-time fee of $5)
Credit cards: None
Beds: 40
Private rooms: 9
Affiliation: None
Office hours: 10:00 a.m. to 8:00 p.m.
Extras: Treehouses, laundry, kitchen, pond, pool, library, pool table, art room, piano, guitar, DJ spinning tables, labyrinth, meditation/yoga classes, some meals included

---

*T*he road to the hostel may be long and very bumpy, but once you navigate it, you will be amazed at the intriguing place upon which you have happened; truly, this is among the most unique hostels we've encountered in our world travels. (Be warned, however, that the road in is sometimes pocked with potholes so big and deep that you might not touch bottom.) Drive slowly and carefully, 'cause you wouldn't want to miss the Hostel in the Forest due to a flat tire.

Once you make it to the hostel, you'll witness a testament both to the power of one man's dream and the inventiveness of subsequent creative additions by staff and visitors alike. Tom Dennard, the local lawyer and writer who purchased this ninety-acre tract of Georgia pinelands back in the early 1970s,

Best bet for a bite:
Communal kitchen suppers
Insiders' tip:
Driftwood Beach on Jekyll Island
What hostellers say:
"Teaberry gum, anyone?"
Gestalt:
Brunswick stew
Hospitality: *A*
Cleanliness: *C*
Party index: 🎉🎉🎉

built two wooden geodesic domes, and subsequent volunteers took it from there. Some rooms have three single beds. The roundish dorms in the two-story bunkhouse are spacious, earthy, and airy, with sturdy handmade bunks, loft beds, and even some hammocks. The infamous treehouses are actually a series of little cabins on stilts. We can see why hostellers rave about them: First, you climb a ladder edged with string lights to the entrance of your treehouse. Once inside, you're astonished by the double bed, light, paddle fan, and—best of all—huge plate-glass window opening onto your own private view of the woods. Light one of the candles and admire the trinkets and artwork other hostellers have thoughtfully left behind for you. This is a true love nest; bring your own hostelling honey.

The common room, kitchen, and large front porch are wonderful places to exchange travel tales with some of the coolest characters you'll ever meet; eccentric, artsy-crunchy people are drawn to this place. The common room features a piano, guitar, chess set, and a written history of the hostel; be sure to relax on one of the comfy couches and read a bit about your new discovery. Dinner is the defining hostel event; each guest is asked to either help cook or clean. After you stand in the circle of hostellers and tell everyone what you're thankful for (getting there alive?), take your dinner outside to the delightful screened-in eating room. Bring lots of bug spray; mosquitoes love to chomp on visitors year-round at night. Also be sure to visit the other wonderful features in the main cluster of domes: Indulge your creative side in the art room, your book-nerdish side in the amazing library, or check out the DJ spinning tables (singular in U.S. hostels). Take a break from your book to look up and admire the huge mural painted by one particularly inspired Brazilian guest, too.

Beyond these structures the rest of the grounds are practically a New Age dream. Boardwalked paths lead through the woods to a natural swimming pool (no chemicals here, of course), pond, and a glass meditation house. You shower beneath outdoor, solar-powered water with organic soap. You discover chicken coops, blueberry fields, vegetable gardens that still produce in January, and flower gardens. It's essential that you walk through the labyrinth to fully experience the care with which the staff (all volunteers) maintain the grounds.

The bathrooms use ecologically sound composting toilets and outdoor showers. There are very few showers and toilets per hosteller, but this doesn't seem to be a problem for most who find this laid-back hippie haven . . . which leads to this: The hostel also allows folks to pee on the grounds (literally), which might be of concern to hygiene-conscious readers. Then again, it might be no big deal: This *is* the forest, after all.

In short, if you love the woods and communal attitudes, make every effort to get here. If you're a romantic, so much the better; for those of that inclination, this place is a real find.

How to Get There:

By bus: Greyhound stops in Brunswick. Call hostel for free pickup, but give them a couple of hours' notice.

By car: Access road is very rough. Drive I-95 to exit 6; drive west 2 miles on U.S. Highway 82. Look for triangular reflector on right; take next left, make U-turn, and drive east to hostel entrance (easy to miss). Follow rutted dirt road 1 mile to the parking lot.

Savannah International Hostel ✴✴✴✴

304 East Hall Street, Savannah, GA 31401
(912) 236-7744

> **Rates:** $23 per person; $45–$85 for private room
> **Credit cards:** None
> **Season:** March to November
> **Beds:** 18
> **Private rooms:** 4
> **Affiliation:** None
> **Office hours:** 7:00 to 11:00 a.m.; 5:00 to 11:00 p.m.
> **Extras:** Foosball, television, pickups (sometimes), Internet access, kitchen, bike rentals

NOTE: This hostel has undergone a partial conversion into a pensione-style bed-and-breakfast, and it might not be offering shared bunks (among strangers) anymore by the time you read this. Please check in advance.

It's impossible to fault the location of this hostel. Set smack in the middle of Savannah's justly famous historic district, the building is only a short walk from living history on all four sides. Housed in one of those gorgeous old antebellum mansions you see only in the movies, it's a fine place to crash, though a little small to hang around in all day long. That's fine, because there's so much to see in Savannah and the nearby beaches of Tybee Island that you won't feel like staying in anyway. (Also, the noon to 5 p.m. lockout policy will force you—in a good way—to get out and see the city.)

Savannah crooner Johnny Mercer's uncle once lived in this house, and the singer himself lived just a few doors away. Breathtaking homes are everywhere. Inside, the hostel's bunks are well-distributed in high-ceilinged (and thus well-ventilated) rooms. Paddle fans and air-conditioning do their best to try and keep the air moving around when it gets hot and sticky, which it does often. Couples can rent one of several nice private rooms—one has a comfy bed and a little balcony overlooking the street—and there's a carriage house in back offering even more privacy. Beautiful hardwood floors, tall ceilings, and big windows all contribute to the southern feel of the building. Note that the tiny kitchen can get crowded at peak times. It's a nice spot to share breakfast stories, but fixing dinner can get a little tricky as backpackers queue up for stove space. Manager Brian Sherman has thoughtfully covered tables with maps that have led to many conversations starting with either "This is where I live" or "I've been here and here." Comfortable futons that pull out as beds flank the common area, providing excellent reading areas. Need food? There's a supermarket located right across the street—unusual for a hostel—so finding eats won't be a problem if you're allergic to restaurant tabs. Sherman also supplies morning doughnuts to get you jump-started.

Once you're up and at 'em, Sherman often recommends a walk around the city for starters—and he's absolutely right. There aren't many finer walking cities in all of America than this one. A series of twenty public squares focus the city's architecture (and horticulture) into public green spaces with distinctive personalities. You might try a self-made tour built around the best-selling novel *Midnight in the Garden of Good and Evil*. Or you could investigate the various museums (several great small ones), cemeteries, historic spots, pubs, and eateries sprinkled throughout the downtown. Or walk all the way to the river and browse through the shops that occupy a former cotton market. We won't give away all Savannah's secrets; go find 'em yourself, armed with a good pair of walking shoes. With a car you can also reach a good beach on Tybee Island 20 miles away or one of several other parks that showcase the coast's unique ecology.

After dark Sherman sometimes wanders upstairs to encourage a game of foosball or air hockey. He also gives directions around town and occasional rides to the airport or wherever. Don't push his buttons, though—not a good idea. There's no guest telephone, but there's a pay phone at the supermarket.

One tip: There's nearly always room at the inn here, but it's possible you won't be able to find a bed around St. Patrick's Day, when tourists descend on the flowery city in droves for a huge parade—the nation's second-largest after New York City's. Book well ahead for that event. Girl Scouts also very occasionally make pilgrimages from all over the nation. (The founder's home and headquarters are just a block or two away.) The hostel's crowd is friendly and quiet at night, even on that infamous St. Patrick's Day weekend—possibly the only refuge in town from the drunken debauchery (think green beer and vomit) that characterizes this annual celebration.

And one more serious warning: The hostel itself is very secure, but this area of Savannah has experienced a few crime problems in recent years. Don't set out alone from the hostel on foot at night, stay in well-lit areas, and you should be fine.

Our verdict? This hostel provides a good and affordable base to explore a great tourist town.

How to Get There:

By airplane: Small airport 7 miles away. Call hostel for transit route.

By bus: Greyhound stops downtown. Call hostel for pickup or bus route.

By car: Drive I-95 to Savannah; take exit for Interstate 16 east, then exit on Montgomery Street. Go right on Liberty Street, right on Abercorn, and left on Hall. Hostel is at corner of Hall and Lincoln.

By train: Amtrak stops in Savannah; call hostel for shuttle bus details

KENTUCKY

Emily Boone Guest Home

102 Pope Street, Louisville, KY 40206

(502) 585-3430

E-mail: emilyboone@aol.com

Rates: $10 per person

Credit cards: None

Beds: 3

Private rooms: None

Affiliation: None

Office hours: Vary; call

Extras: Laundry, bike rental, dog, kitchen

*E*mily Boone doesn't offer hostellers a decent bed. It's your only hostel option in Louisville, but good luck trying to get a spot there. It's not so much that this place fills up as it is that Boone is regularly out of town and is tough to reach. Add to that the fact that she won't give anybody a reservation until meeting with her in person, and you have a frustrating situation. Advance planning and perseverance, however, just might get you in with Boone and her very large Irish wolfhound that runs roughshod. Oh, and expect to do an unpleasant chore in the morning on your way out.

The hostel—which is in her garage (yes! really!)—has a separate entrance and its own bathroom and kitchen. However, the accommodations are depressing and uncomfortable, with cratelike beds, not enough heat, and aging furnishings and linens. There is a small yard in the back with a garden and a floodwall to prevent the roaring Ohio from overtaking the house, but it still tries anyway. Ceilings here are high, yet the place still manages to always seem cluttered with posters, artwork, notices, and gosh-knows-what-else.

Best bet for a bite:
Farmers' market nearby

Insiders' tip:
Check out the falls of the Ohio

Gestalt:
Boone's Farm

Safety: *B*

Hospitality: *D*

Cleanliness: *C*

Party index:

So if you've really got to stay, get outside. Horse racing, college basketball games, and whiskey drinking are the three activities of choice in Louisville (but don't bring that whiskey into the hostel!). We suggest Churchill Downs for the horses and advance reservations for the ball games. Bardstown has all the nightlife you'll possibly want and need. Just try not to book a night here when you do.

How to Get There:
By bus: Take #19 Muhammad Ali bus line and walk 1 block to hostel.

LOUISIANA

India House Backpacker's Hostel
124 South Lopez Street, New Orleans, LA 70119
(504) 821-1904
> **E-mail:** info@indiahousehostel.com
> **Web site:** www.indiahousehostel.com
> **Rates:** $17–$20 per person; $45 for private room (all rates higher during **festivals**)
> **Credit cards:** MC, VISA
> **Beds:** 120
> **Private rooms:** 6
> **Affiliation:** None
> **Office hours:** Twenty-four hours
> **Extras:** Television, laundry, pool, meals (sometimes), grill, off-street parking, Internet access, kitchen, swimming pool, free Wi-Fi

*F*irst off, kudos for rebuilding this hostel and reopening it in the wake of Hurricane Katrina. That, in and of itself, is a *major* accomplishment. And yes: India House is indeed a place to have a jumpin' time if you're hostelling in New Orleans. What it lacks in facilities it tries to make up for in pure fun.

It only partly succeeds, though.

The layout is groovy and laid-back . . . too laid-back, some say. The founders once ran a floating hostel in Amsterdam, so what else would you expect? Indescribable murals snake up the walls. Parachutes hang from the ceiling in the main common room that contains a too-well-loved television, which tends to attract plenty of long-term guests. An outdoor backyard area has been constructed to maximize group fun, which usually consists of drinking beer and smoking late into the night. The facilities include an in-ground swimming pool known as the "Indian Ocean," good for hot summer days. The hostel kitchen is roomy, clean, and well-equipped.

Upstairs six- to eight-bed dorms occupy nooks and crannies of a lovable old house. Bunks are packed somewhat tightly, and we've heard plenty of complaints about cleanliness; if you value clean beds, look elsewhere perhaps, though there's not much to pick from in NoLa at the moment. There's a laundry on site. As for private rooms, the owners have constructed a mini-bayou area complete with tropical fish, turtles, native flora, and cabins that actually resemble Cajun fishing shacks. Sadly, though, Sid and Nancy (caimans, a smaller version of a 'gator) no longer partake in the festivities.

Now on to the negatives. It's one big free-for-all during the big party that's Mardi Gras and during the Jazz Festival—but it's also a party year-round. Well, that's not a negative necessarily, but if you're traveling with a family, consider a hotel instead. And there is a real clique-ishness that has developed, as out-of-work hostellers become long-term guests become hostel employees . . . basically, there are people living here, and if you get in their way, they don't like it. Hey, dudes, listen up and listen carefully: We paid for *our* beds. Don't give *us* attitude . . . or we'll kick your asses next time. Hopefully the attitude problem will disappear in time, 'cause it is a really fun place, but we wouldn't necessarily bet on it.

One plus is the India House's location in the Mid-City neighborhood of New Orleans. This area, never touted in tourist guides and located far from both the French Quarter and Garden District, is a locals' kind of place: Lots of exotic restaurants with more reasonable prices than the downtown stuff, a big city park, and the New Orleans Museum of Art are all within hailing distance. A few blocks east of the hostel, Esplanade Avenue takes center stage as an up-and-coming neighborhood sprinkled with brightly painted shotgun-style houses, cozy and low-priced restaurants, and a natural foods store. There's a streetcar directly to the French Quarter (note: it stops running by 11 p.m.; then you'll need a cab to or from the city).

On a side street often littered with the remains of smashed car windshields, this area doesn't look at first like a safe place to rest. The owner reports, though, that neighbors recognize backpackers and will kindly point them in the right direction toward the hostel if they look lost. Moonlighting cops are said to work the local bars for extra cash, adding security, and twenty-four-hour drug stores on the main drag right around the corner from the hostel keep a bit of foot traffic going. You're probably unlikely to come to bodily harm here; just keep an eye out.

All in all, this isn't a terrible place to stay, and it is cheap. But perfectly clean, or perfectly welcoming to non-partiers, it is not. This place is probably best for the sort of traveler who'll happily trade sparkling and spacious accommodations for a six-pack.

Best bet for a bite:
Mid-City Lanes Rock'N'Bowl
Insiders' tip:
WWOZ 90.7 radio
What hostellers say:
"Don't touch my beer."
Gestalt:
Jambalaya
Safety: *C*
Hospitality: *C*
Cleanliness: *D*
Party index:

How to Get There:

By airplane: Large airport in New Orleans.
Take taxi or downtown bus to Tulane and South Lopez. Walk left to number 124.
By bus: Greyhound stops in New Orleans. Take #41, #42, or #43 toward the cemeteries. Stop at Lopez and Canal and turn left, then follow to hostel.
By car: Take Interstate 10 to Carollton Avenue or Tulane Avenue exit. Drive east on Carollton to Canal, then south on Canal to Lopez; go right on Lopez. Hostel is less than 1 block on left. Or go south on Tulane to Jefferson Davis Parkway, turn left, follow parkway to Canal and turn right. Follow to Lopez and turn right; hostel is less than 1 block on left.
By train: Amtrak stops in New Orleans. Take bus #41, #42, or #43 toward the cemeteries. Stop at Lopez and Canal. Turn left onto Lopez and follow to hostel.

Key to Icons

Attractive natural setting	Comfortable beds	Visual arts at hostel or nearby
Ecologically aware hostel	A particularly good value	Music at hostel or nearby
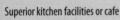 Superior kitchen facilities or cafe	Wheelchair-accessible	Great hostel for skiers
Offbeat or eccentric place	Good for business travelers	Bar or pub at hostel or nearby
Superior bathroom facilities	Especially well-suited for families	Editors' choice: Among our very favorite hostels
Romantic private rooms	Good for active travelers	

NORTH CAROLINA

Pembroke Youth Hostel ❋❋❋

c/o Baptist Student Center, UNC-Pembroke, Pembroke, NC 28372

(910) 521-8777

Fax: (910) 521–7166

E-mail: pembrokehostel@carolina.net

Rates: $12–$15 per Hostelling International member

Credit cards: None

Beds: 8

Private rooms: 3

Affiliation: Hostelling International

Office hours: 8:00 a.m. to 10:00 p.m.

Extras: Kitchen, big-screen television, video games, table tennis, foosball, laundry

*T*he Pembroke Youth Hostel isn't the kind of place you'd normally find or need to find; tucked in a small college town 20 miles inland from I-95, it might be Hostelling International's least-visited hostel.

Yet a stay here is a unique experience because you're sure to interact with members of the Lumbee Indian tribe, a local tribe that, instead of seeking federal recognition status and a reservation, has chosen to live in town like Caucasian residents. (Legend has it, by the way, that this light-skinned tribe is partly descended from the lost Roanoke colony.)

We're getting ahead of ourselves, though. Although it's located on the campus of the University of North Carolina at Pembroke, this hostel is actually owned and maintained by North Carolina's Baptist Student Ministry. There aren't many actual bunks, which is fine because few travelers find the place. For those odd times when a crowd is at hand, there's a bit of a strange

Best bet for a bite:
Down the back roads by the river

What hostellers say:
"Amen."

Gestalt:
Blind faith

Hospitality: *A*

Cleanliness: *A*

Party index: 🎉

setup: A back room with a pull-out couch is pressed into duty; a big television room becomes a slumber party. But most of the rooms are fine.

The biggest drawback here? Just one: There's almost nothing to do in the tiny town once you're here, just rest from the monotony of I-95 and those campy South of the Border billboards. The house stocks video and action games (foosball, table tennis), so that's one option. Or you can do like local southerners do: Take a seat on one of the wooden rockers on the shaded front porch, sip a cold drink, and try to beat the scorching lowland heat. Best of all, bend someone's ear about the Lumbee. Failing at these, you might nose around Pembroke looking for southern cooking.

Oh, yes, one more thing. The building is owned by a Baptist group, so there will be occasional religious classes or meetings taking place, usually on Tuesdays, we've heard. Don't feel you must participate. Just know it might happen.

How to Get There:
By car: Drive I-95 to exit 17; travel east 10 miles to Pembroke, then go right at third light. As college approaches on left, watch carefully on right for building and hard-to-see driveway to hostel.

SOUTH CAROLINA

The NotSo Hostel
156 Spring Street, Charleston, SC 29403
(843) 722-8383
> **Web site:** www.notsohostel.com
> **E-mail:** charlestonhostel@hotmail.com
> **Rates:** $21 per night; $60 for private room
> **Credit cards:** None
> **Beds:** 18
> **Private rooms:** 1
> **Affiliation:** None
> **Office hours:** 8:00 to 10:00 a.m.; 5:00 to 10:00 p.m.
> **Extras:** Kitchen, lockers, laundry, bike rentals, VCR, TV room, free Internet access, free breakfast, pickups, free parking, hammock, porch, games, campground

*T*his cutely named place ("not-so-hostile". . . get it??), in a big, 150-year-old white house with a red tin roof, fills a much-needed gap after several other budget accommodations in beautiful Charleston closed up shop in recent years. Young owner Claire Cunningham, a local South Carolinian, has created a wonderful environment for getting to know both the city and fellow hostellers. If there's any quibble, it's that the great popularity of the place is making it hard to keep clean—something we've noticed here a few times already. If you crave spic 'n' span, you might give it a pass.

Otherwise, though, management does most things right. Accommodations in the double-porched home range from rooms with just two bunks to bigger rooms of four or more beds. Outside, the porch is festooned with wicker chairs for lounging, there's a hammock, and the big backyard is shaded by palmetto trees and features both a vegetable garden and assorted feline interlopers. There's a small game room with plenty o' games. Can things get more relaxing? (If cruising the 'net is your idea of relaxing, there's free high-speed access here, too.)

The kitchen is stocked with the basics, like flour and oil, for cooking. Amazingly, linens are free—this is unusual in the hostelling world—and they've got a coin laundry for doing the wash. They'll rent you a bike, too, which is a boon in this gorgeous town. See as much of it as you can: It's as lovely a city as America possesses. Other big positives include a free breakfast (you make your own waffles in a machine, and coffee and tea are provided), no charge for parking, and lockers; bring your own padlock for those. There's an eco-ethic and a sunny vibe throughout.

We found this place quite friendly and comfortable, enjoying a potluck dinner on New Year's Day with the other hostellers. Despite the fact that some of the guests were long-termers when we visited, the atmosphere was good and Claire was super-friendly. The dorms are a bit small, but they sport comfortable mattresses.

Needless to say, Charleston is just crammed full of stuff to do. Check with the staff for tips. You can eat well, sightsee well, and get back at night for a song. It's really a city that shouldn't be missed, full of historic gardens, quaint homes, and cafes.

Best bet for a bite:
Wali's Fish Supreme
Insiders' tip:
Visit Fort Sumter
What hostellers say:
"Wow!"
Gestalt:
Doin' the Charleston
Safety: *B*
Hospitality: *A*
Cleanliness: *C*
Party index:

This hostel started with ten beds, now has eighteen, and is still growing. Check in to see how it's going. Prices like this can't be beat in a tourist town like Charleston, so book now.

How to Get There:
By bus: Bus depot in downtown Charleston. Call hostel for pickup.
By car: From Interstate 26, take King Street exit, turn right on King Street, and continue 4 blocks to Spring Street, then turn right.

From U.S. Highway 17 South, cross high bridge and take King Street exit; turn right onto King Street, then make second right onto Spring Street and continue 5 blocks to hostel on right.

From U.S. 17 North, cross bridge into city and take Cannon Street exit. Make second left onto Ashley Avenue, then first left onto Spring Street. Continue 1 block to hostel on right.
By train: Amtrak station in downtown Charleston. Call hostel for pickup.

TENNESSEE

Knoxville Hostel ✳✳✳✳
404 East Fourth Avenue, Knoxville, TN 37917
No phone
> **Rates:** $17 per person
> **Credit cards:** None
> **Beds:** 10
> **Private rooms:** None
> **Affiliation:** None
> **Season:** Year-round except closed Thanksgiving weekend and Christmas through New Year's
> **Office hours:** 7:30 a.m. to 4:00 p.m.
> **Extras:** Kitchen, free laundry, pickups, TV room, library, free Internet access, free breakfast, shuttle to Great Smoky Mountains

NOTE: This hostel has no phone; it is only bookable online, using reservations services.

*T*his hostel is tiny, and Knoxville's not exactly your top destination in the world, but friendly owner Al *more* than makes up for it with his friendliness. Visiting this hostel is like coming home. The place has two dorms—six and four beds, respectively—and a lot of space; there's a homey kitchen with all you need to cook up a little meal; and the free laundry and free Internet access are just cherries on the cake. You can eat your meal in the living room while others watch ballgames on the tube in the TV room.

Best bet for a bite:
Ott's Pit for BBQ
Insiders' tip:
Learn the words to "Rocky Top"
Gestalt:
Opportunity Knoxville
Safety: *A*
Hospitality: *A*
Cleanliness: *A*

There is, however, some noise from the interstate. (On the up side, it's just a short walk from the city's Greyhound station.)

Unfortunately, there's not a whole lot to do in Knoxville itself—it's an uninspiring place, save for the University of Tennessee campus nearby. If you love college football, you'll *love* that aspect. But there is one *great* reason to stay here: to visit the nearby Great Smoky Mountains, whose boundaries enclose some of America's prettiest big rockpiles. Al owns a transport organization that runs shuttles out to the Smokies, so it's easy to get a lift (for a fee). Spring and fall are especially beautiful in the mountains. One other drawback to this hostel is its surrounding neighborhood, which is very quiet. It's a long walk to the nearest supermarket, though the city center is pretty close.

How to Get There:
By bus: Greyhound stops in Knoxville. From bus depot, walk along Central Avenue to East Fourth Avenue, turn right, and continue 3 blocks to hostel on right.
By car: Take Interstate 40 to Knoxville, exit at James White Parkway, and take first exit right onto Summit Hill; turn right on Central Avenue, continue over railroad tracks and beneath interstate, and turn right onto East Fourth Avenue. Hostel is on right.

VIRGINIA

Bear's Den Trail Center and Hostel   ✹✹✹✹

18393 Blueridge Mountain Road, Bluemont, VA 20135

(540) 554-8708

E-mail: info@bearsdencenter.org

Web site: www.bearsdencenter.org

Rates: $15–$21 per person (children $10); $55–$75 for private room (kids extra)

Credit cards: MC, VISA

Season: Closed January and Christmas Day

Beds: 26

Private rooms: 3

Affiliation: None

Office hours: 8:00 to 9:30 a.m.; 5:00 to 9:30 p.m.

Extras: Laundry, store, fireplace, library, kitchen

*T*his beautifully restored stone lodge in the Blue Ridge Mountains is only 60 miles from Washington, D.C., but you'd never know it. Set back in the woods a mere 150 yards from the Appalachian Trail, this picturesque hostel is a nature lover's dream come true. Seldom does one find such serenity so close to a major metropolis.

Dr. Hurin Lawson built the lodge back in 1933, utilizing the work of a few incredibly gifted local masons. It became a retreat spot for rich folks from the city looking to escape the summer heat, and back then the train came through town to bring them here. It is easy to understand the allure of the place. Location aside, the building itself is a remarkable piece of work, blending in perfectly with the bucolic environment. It looks as if it belongs there.

The inside is equally remarkable, with a grand common area chock-full of hearty wood furniture. High ceilings and French doors are among the luxuries of this spotless respite. It is also worth noting that this room is acoustically divine. Lawson's wife was an opera singer, and he had it built to suit her needs. Today singing groups visit the lodge every now and then for country excursions. The kitchen is all class, with every cooking supply you could possibly need, and then there is the stately stone dining room. The two big single-sex dorm rooms are decent as well, though the small beds are on the stiff side.

Since it's right off the 2,158-mile-long Appalachian Trail, that means lots of through-hikers. You couldn't ask for a better lot of hostellers. Most of these folks have been sleeping in a tent for months and eating little more than oats; they are delighted to have a bed and have lots of good stories to tell. About half the guests on a typical night are hikers.

A place to party, the Bear's Den is not. The doors (and the gates to the driveway, too!) lock at 10:00 p.m. sharp, and you must be on your way by 9:30 the next morning. There is a day-use area in the basement that is open all day for people needing a spot to chill. The hostel has a surprisingly good store where they sell a bunch of food staples (for example, pasta, eggs, frozen pizza, and ice cream) and dispense hiking information.

The area's major attraction is, of course, the Bear's Den Rocks. During the Civil War, scouts used the amazing panorama offered at these rocks to view enemy troop movements below. Don't leave the area without catching a sunset there. Bicycling is also big because that old train line that used to come out from Washington is now a rail-trail. Cyclists can go from Mt. Vernon all the way to Purcellville (6 miles east of the hostel) on a path paved just for them.

Best bet for a bite:
All-night supermarket in Purcellville
Insiders' tip:
Tubing the Shenandoah River
What hostellers say:
"I can see for miles and miles and miles."
Gestalt:
Happy Trails
Hospitality: *A*
Cleanliness: *A*
Party index:

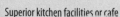
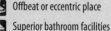

How to Get There:

By bus: Call hostel for schedule and pickup information.

By car: From Interstate 81, take Virginia Highway 7 east for 20 miles to State Highway 601 South; turn right. Go ½ mile and turn right at first driveway. Look for green mailbox that says BEARS DEN.

Blue Ridge Mountains Hostel

214507 Blue Ridge Mountains , R.R. 2, Box 449, Galax, VA 24333

(276) 236-4962

Rates: $22 per Hostelling International member

Credit cards: None

Season: April to October

Beds: 20

Private rooms: Yes

Affiliation: Hostelling International

Office hours: 7:00 to 9:30 a.m.; 5:00 to 10:00 p.m.

Extras: Recreational barn, board games, musical instruments, jam sessions, kitchen, laundry

---

Best bet for a bite:
Um . . .
Insiders' tip:
Love the view!
What hostellers say:
"I can see for miles."
Gestalt:
Fiddle heads
Hospitality: *A*
Cleanliness: *A*
Party index:

*W*ay up in the mountains of southwestern Virginia, just a bit off the winding Blue Ridge Parkway, lies a pretty nice hostel—a place with a grand view off the back deck down the mountains that is every bit as lovely as you'd expect from such a location. And the hostel remains as friendly and well-kept as it has ever been.

Alex Koji and his wife, Lois, bought this house in the 1980s, then added hostel rooms in an upstairs addition in 1988. It's well-equipped; the kitchen even has a dishwasher, for goodness' sake. A separate cottage on the grounds serves as a family room or overflow dorm, as well, sleeping up to four for a better-than-B&B price.

Besides the twenty-eight acres of grounds, you get the run of much of the hosts' house, too, and this is a real treat; in particular, there's a great music room featuring a piano, dulcimer, and lots of other instruments. Know how to play? Then you're welcome to them. As an added bonus, we're told, the hostel hosts a mountain jam session every other Friday.

Should you be so inclined, there's plenty to do in the surrounding area. There's a hiking area a few miles down the road, and a longer trail for serious trail-heads. The local hamlets are silly during summer and fall with various festivals, demonstrations, and fiddle music, including the annual Fiddler's Convention. There's always the Blue Ridge Parkway itself, which is perhaps America's greatest scenic drive, especially in fall, when the leaf colors are turning.

How to Get There:
By car: From Interstate 77 or I-81, take exit 100 to North Carolina Highway 89 and follow road to Blue Ridge Parkway; turn onto parkway and drive north about 1$\frac{1}{10}$ miles. At Milepost 214.5, turn into entrance with iron gate (watch carefully for hostel sign). Hostel is at end of road.

Angie's Guest Cottage ✳✳✳✳
302 Twenty-fourth Street, Virginia Beach, VA 23451
(757) 491-1830

> **Fax:** (757) 428-8087
> **Web site:** www.angiescottage.com
> **Rates:** $15–$20 per Hostelling International member; $48–$60 for private room
> **Credit cards:** None
> **Season:** April 1 to October 1 (sometimes open March and October)
> **Beds:** 34
> **Private rooms:** 2
> **Affiliation:** Hostelling International
> **Office hours:** 10:00 a.m. to 9:00 p.m.
> **Extras:** Grills, clothesline, sundeck, parking, kitchen, lockers

---

*A*ngie's Guest Cottage might be a block from a rowdy beach, but think again before you reach for a six-pack: Owner Barbara Yates runs her hostel tighter than a drum, banning booze and kicking out the unruly with the efficiency of a drill sergeant. Yates, a world traveler who borrows good ideas from hostels in Europe, runs a bed-and-breakfast in part of the hostel building. She hopes eventually to convert the entire place into hostel bunks.

Yates, who has a reputation for hiring talented managers, has managed to establish one of the East Coast's better hostels, and it's just 100 yards from the cool Atlantic. People rave about this one, despite the so-so beach town.

The crowd here is quite young and international. Families don't seem to visit much, and with good reason; you sleep in tidy coed dorms, in bunks packed as close together as sardines. That's great if you like up-close contact with young folks from all over Europe and don't mind navigating a cheerful sea of backpacks, water bottles, beach paperbacks, and the like. (It's not so great if you treasure your privacy. There aren't any family rooms, either, although a 2002 merger with an adjacent motel has helped change all that.) Anyway, private rooms are usually available in the bed-and-breakfast portion; you can choose to skip breakfast for a lower rate. Rates are higher in the busy summer months.

This place is surprisingly clean. There's an open-air kitchen, a well-loved grill, picnic tables to hang out at, and a super-friendly attitude pervading the hostel. Even the no-nonsense rules are posted everywhere just to keep folks informed. There's no air-conditioning, but good ceiling fans keep the air circulating. The hostel also gives you a permit good for free on-street parking in a town where you can't park in many places if you're not a resident. (It will cost you a deposit, but you get it back when you check out.)

Attractions? It's the beach, stupid, and bars when the beach closes down. There's not much else to do here but drink, surf, tan, and ogle. Virginia Beach itself is a sometimes-seedy beach town, sided by a military base—there have been some scary incidents involving women who were drinking alone in local bars—but the hostel itself is quite safe. The managers use combination locks and stern warnings to combat unwelcome visitors. So far there haven't been any problems, and we highly recommend this hostel.

How to Get There:

By airplane: Take airport shuttle from Norfolk airport (runs twenty-four hours), or call hostel for bus route.

By bus: Greyhound stops in town. Call a cab for ride (long walk).

By car: Take U.S. Highway 64 to Virginia Beach–Norfolk Expressway into town; go left on Arctic at light and right on Twenty-fourth Street to hostel.

By train: Amtrak stops in town. Walk 5 blocks north to Twenty-fourth, go left to hostel.

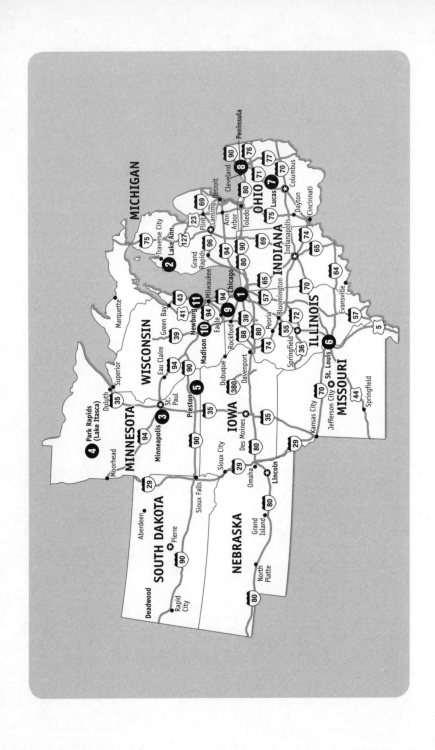

Midwest

Page numbers follow hostel names

ILLINOIS

Arlington House International Hostel & Hotel

616 West Arlington Place, Chicago, IL 60614

(773) 929-5380; (800) 467-8355

Fax: (773) 665-5485

E-mail: arlingtonhouse@earthlink.net

Web site: www.arlingtonhouse.com

Rates: $31–$33 per person; $65–$79 for private room

Credit cards: MC, VISA

Beds: 335

Private rooms: 100

Private bathrooms: 15

Affiliation: None

Office hours: Twenty-four hours

Extras: Coffee, laundry, foosball, television, kitchen, Internet access, storage

*T*his renovated old-folks home with a bunch of bunks crammed in the basement clearly doesn't attract hostellers by offering stellar facilities. The downtown Hostelling International–affiliated complex is cleaner, brighter, and more comfortable in every way. This place is the pits. It's weird. Rowdy hostellers and tired nursing home patients used to make an odd mix when the hostel was housed inside a retirement facility. (It no longer is, thank goodness.) At least one guest had commented that the strangeness of it all reminded him of Stephen

King's *The Shining*. Loud twentysomethings raced in and out of the hostel through the night, drinking from bottles covered in paper bags. Meanwhile, confused residents sat in front of televisions, barely moving. Some got lost roaming the hallways and asked hostellers for directions back to their rooms. While we're glad that this merging of worlds has ceased, we have to wonder sometimes if the place has actually gone *downhill* since then, rather than uphill.

Some rooms here are incredibly tiny and stuffy (don't come in the summer unless you are bringing ice with you). Private rooms in particular are about the minimum possible size of a "room," and that includes the bathrooms. Rooms are kitted out with aging bunks or beat-up twin beds. Upkeep is minimal to nonexistent, and staff continue their indifferent ways.

At least the location is good. Arlington House is located in the center of Lincoln Park, easily Chicago's most happening neighborhood. Pockets of cute brownstone apartment buildings are surrounded by a wide array of nightclubs, bars, and coffee shops. Downtown's museums are only an eight-minute subway ride away, but the inviting trance of Lincoln Park can easily keep you there your entire stay. The hostel is snuggled neatly among several classy residential buildings on a safe, quiet block. Get out (and stay out) as much as possible.

Best bet for a bite:
Bourgeois Pig cafe
Insiders' tip:
Two-fer deals at nearby art movie theater
What hostellers say:
"Where'd Grandpa go?"
Gestalt:
Chicago hopeless
Safety: *C*
Hospitality: *D*
Cleanliness: *F*
Party index: 🎉🎉🎉

How to Get There:

By airplane: From O'Hare, take Congress/Douglas A or B El train (get a transfer) from lower level of airport to Logan Square. Take #76 bus east on Diversey and get off at Clark Street. Walk south 3 blocks to Arlington Place, turn right and walk 1¼ blocks to hostel.

From Midway, take Orange Midway El train to Clark and Lake. Cross platform and take Ravenswood North Line to Fullerton. Walk east on Fullerton to Orchard, then walk 1 block north to hostel.

By bus: Greyhound stops in Chicago. From station, take #60 bus east on Harrison to Dearborn. Change to #22 or #36 bus to Roslyn. Cross street to Arlington Place and walk west 1¼ blocks to hostel.

By car: Take Lake Shore Drive (U.S. Highway 41) to Fullerton exit; go 4 blocks to right on Orchard Street. Arlington Place is immediately on right; hostel is down block, on left.

By train: Amtrak stops in Chicago. From station take any bus east on Jackson to Dearborn. Change to #22 or #36 bus to Roslyn. Cross street to Arlington Place and walk west 1¼ blocks to hostel.

Fat Johnnie's Last Resort Home Hostel

2822 West Thirty-eighth Place, Chicago, IL 60632

(773) 254-0836

> **Rates:** $15 per person
> **Credit cards:** None
> **Beds:** 10
> **Private rooms:** None
> **Affiliation:** None
> **Office hours:** Vary; call
> **Extras:** Television, VCR, movies, laundry

---

*W*e'd come here *only* as a last resort—well, maybe not even then. It's basically a few mattresses piled on top of heaps and heaps of junk. No effort at cleaning appears to have been made for quite a while. We once arrived at 2:00 p.m. to find a man sleeping in the hallway who looked like he'd been there a few days. The neighborhood is run-down and out of the way, and at least a fifteen-minute walk to the subway.

Yet the owner somehow remains aloofly chipper in the midst of it all, and he's the lone selling point—if chipperness in the face of decline can be called a positive. The dude sometimes distributes maps of the city with the "dangerous area crossed out" (funny how they happen to coincide with "ethnic" neighborhoods, though) and hangs with hostellers at a local blues bar like a man who's forever pursuing his own childhood.

Um, okay. But maybe he ought to spend more time working on what they call the "physical plant"?

Best bet for a bite:
Superdawg hot dog stands
Gestalt:
Lost resort
Safety: *D*
Hospitality: *C*
Cleanliness: *F*
Party index: 🎉🎉🎉

How to Get There:
Call hostel for directions.

Hostelling International-Chicago Hostel

24 East Congress Parkway, Chicago, IL 60605

(312) 360-0300

Fax: (312) 360-0313

E-mail: reserve@hichicago.org

Web site: www.hichicago.org

Rates: $27 per Hostelling International member

Credit cards: MC, VISA

Beds: 250

Private rooms: None

Affiliation: Hostelling International

Office hours: Twenty-four hours

Extras: Laundry, lockers, Internet access, kitchen, library, television, DVD player

The great city of Chicago is blessed with a suitably great hostel that took the place of several makeshift hostels that previously tried to fill a huge need for year-round beds.

Hostel guests give kudos to this shining facility, which—even if it is a bit sterile—has a super-friendly staff who go out of their way to help travelers. There are tons of amenities here, like Internet access and twenty-four-hour access to your room. The kitchen is large and well-equipped, and there's a library and television room with DVD player. It's a viable option for travelers of all stripes—including families, backpackers, and businesspeople.

Our only gripes? As it's located right downtown in the business district, the area surrounding the place tends to get very deserted at night—and that means you've gotta be extra careful walking or even taking public transit. Look sharp. And the wear and tear of hostellers is beginning to tell on this place; cleanliness and upkeep have dipped a bit recently. Also, some hostellers don't like the institutional, warehouse feel

Best bet for a bite:
Deep-dish pizza
What hostellers say:
"Finally!"
Gestalt:
Sweet home Chicago
Safety: *C*
Hospitality: *A*
Cleanliness: *A*
Party index: 🎉🎉

of the place. That's a fair assessment. But it's so much better than any other hostel in Chicago that you should stay here anyway.

How to Get There:

By airplane: From O'Hare Airport, take Blue Line train to LaSalle. Walk 3 blocks east on Congress Parkway to hostel.

From Midway Airport, take Orange Line train to library at State and Van Buren. Follow State Street south 1 block, turn left at Congress Parkway, and continue 1 block to hostel.

By bus: From Greyhound bus station walk north on Jefferson 3 blocks to Jackson; take #7 bus to Congress Plaza and continue 2 blocks west to hostel.

By car: Take Congress to State Street and go left on State. Continue for 2 blocks to Jackson and turn right onto Jackson, then go 1 block to Wabash. Take a right on Wabash and go 2 blocks to Congress (unload car on Wabash because you can't stop on East Congress Parkway).

By train: From Amtrak station, take #1 bus to Congress and Wabash stop.'

MICHIGAN

Adventurers Lodge Hostel ✹✹✹✹✹

18701 Barber Road, Lake Ann, MI 49650

(231) 275-2000

Fax: (231) 275-2000

E-mail: adventurers@coslink.net

Web site: www.coslink.net/personal/advnture

Rates: $16 per person; double $45–$50

Credit cards: None

Beds: 12

Private/family rooms: 2

Private bathrooms: 2

Affiliation: None

Office hours: 8:00 a.m. to noon; 4:00 to 8:00 p.m.

Extras: Canoes, paddleboats, hot tub, television, fireplace, free breakfast, deck, fishing gear, kitchen, grill

*P*eople kept telling us to see this place, and we gotta admit it's a good pick. Rarely do you get this much value for your dollar—lots of freebies in a ranch-style building nicely set on a quiet, wooded little lake. And prices have actually dropped in the past two years! The only hassle is getting here; you kinda need a car.

They've got one double B&B–style room with a full bath and queen bed, plus two good-size bunkrooms that sleep eight hostellers apiece. Each room has its own private bathroom and there's yet another one for common use. That's it, all kept clean and comfortable, as though you were in the owners' home. Which you are.

A great breakfast is included with the bed for no charge, and check out all the stuff you can use for free—canoes, paddleboats, recreation room, kitchen, reading room, and fishing tackle. And wait. Don't make up your mind yet. There's a hot tub, too.

It's not far to the pleasures surrounding Traverse City, including Sleeping Bear Dunes National Lakeshore, full of great beaches, plus other lakes, ski and golf resorts, and wineries.

Go to Traverse City for culture. As they'll tell you at the front desk, the little town of Lake Ann isn't super-exciting but has a great little general store where you can get anything from a loaf of bread to a haircut. Now that's America!

How to Get There:
By bus: Call hostel for transit route.
By car: Hostel is midway between U.S. 31 and M 72, just north of the village of Lake Ann; go ¼ mile west of County Road 667 on Barber Road.
By train: Call hostel for transit route.

 Attractive natural setting
 Ecologically aware hostel
 Superior kitchen facilities or cafe
 Offbeat or eccentric place
 Superior bathroom facilities
 Romantic private rooms

Comfortable beds
A particularly good value
Wheelchair-accessible
Good for business travelers
Especially well-suited for families
Good for active travelers

 Visual arts at hostel or nearby
 Music at hostel or nearby
 Great hostel for skiers
 Bar or pub at hostel or nearby
Editors' choice: Among our very favorite hostels

Key to Icons

MINNESOTA

Minneapolis International Hostel

2400 Stevens Avenue South, Minneapolis, MN 55404

(612) 522-5000; (800) 250-3315

Fax: (612) 872-8510

Web site: www.minneapolishostel.com

Rates: $25–$31 per person; $56–$95 for private room

Credit cards: AMEX, MC, VISA

Beds: 55

Private rooms: 5

Affiliation: None

Office hours: 8:00 a.m. to midnight

Extras: Television, VCR, DVD player, kitchen, fireplace, secured storage, guest phone (free)

*T*he former City of Lakes Hostel has changed ownership, names, and a whole lot more. We truly miss this hostel's founder, the late, great Pete Schmit. We can never drink a Hacker-Pschorr again without thinking of him. Luckily, this hostel mostly retains the cool feel of his place and now includes ornate furniture, cozy nooks, and a couple more rooms. Keep going through the maze of beauty that is this house and find a manager, because these have got to be some of the friendliest hostel managers on the planet, and their hostel is a lot of fun.

Even with the obvious things—recommendations for good local restaurants, activities, and the like—they've created a big map of the local city blocks to help you map out a route to great nearby tacos, sprouts, or beers. Under a mile away is a place to rent bikes, a real bonus because Minneapolis is surrounded by one of the country's finest urban bike trails. (They include a scenic loop that rolls 20 miles through green lawns and gardens and around three small lakes.) Or you can bike shorter stretches of the hostel path. The resident cat keeps things interesting, too.

Bunkroom quarters (four rooms of four to five beds each, two of seven and eight beds, and one of sixteen beds) can get tight in summer, and so can the otherwise well-furnished kitchen. Thank goodness for a neat back porch with lots of comfy lounging chairs. In the winter guests gather in the lounge, light a fire, and watch a movie on the entertainment system. The private rooms—three singles and two doubles—are better and can alleviate the crush if you're traveling as a couple or family. As for upkeep, the managers clean fastidiously (though the hostel's young crowd sometimes undoes their work in a hurry).

Safety isn't really a concern as long as you remember that this is an urban hostel; it's a block or so from a couple downtrodden neighborhoods. The management reserves a

Best bet for a bite:
Black Forest Inn (German)
Insiders' tip:
Museum is free every day
What hostellers say:
"Great location."
Gestalt:
Art attack
Safety: *A*
Hospitality: *B*
Cleanliness: *C*
Party index: 🎉🎉🎉🎉

few off-street parking spots out back for the nervous folks willing to spend five bucks for peace of mind. Otherwise, don't leave valuables in plain sight in your car, and you'll be all right.

On the upside, the downtown location sits directly across the street from a fantastic art museum, the Minneapolis Institute of Arts. Want to stand 6 inches from a van Gogh, a couple Monets, a Warhol? A thirty-second walk gets you there, and it's all free. A host of ethnic restaurants, as well as Minneapolis's compact downtown, are also very close at hand.

This is hostelling at its European-style best: an active, fun place where the managers work overtime to make the experience as pleasant as possible. Pete would be proud.

How to Get There:

By airplane: Large airport in city. From airport, take #7 bus to Nicollet Avenue; change to #10, #17, or #18 bus south to Twenty-fourth Street. Walk 2 blocks east to corner of Twenty-fourth and Stevens Avenue. Or take taxi to hostel.

By bus: Greyhound stops in Minneapolis. Walk 3 blocks to Nicollet Avenue; take #10, #17, or #18 bus south to Twenty-fourth Street. Walk 2 blocks east to corner of Stevens Avenue. Or take taxi to hostel.

By car: Call hostel for directions.

By train: Amtrak stops in St. Paul. From station, take #16 bus west to Nicollet Avenue; change to #10, #17, or #18 bus south to Twenty-fourth Street. Walk 2 blocks east to corner of Stevens Avenue. Or take taxi to hostel.

Mississippi Headwaters Hostel ✳✳✳✴

27910 Forest Lane, Park Rapids (Lake Itasca), MN 56470

(218) 266-3415

Fax: (218) 266-3415
E-mail: mhhostel@himinnesota.org
Web site: www.himinnesota.org
Rates: $20 per Hostelling International member
Credit cards: None
Season: January to mid-March and May to October
Beds: 31
Private rooms: 6
Affiliation: Hostelling International
Office hours: 8:00 to 10:00 a.m.; 5:00 to 10 p.m.
Extras: Laundry, game room, grills, library, canoe rental, bike trails, kitchen

*T*his hostel in northwestern Minnesota is hard to get to but well worth the trouble. It lies within one of Minnesota's oldest and most beautiful state parks, which is home to the lake that marks the source of the Mississippi. (The park also includes a virgin pine forest, Native American historic sites, and a number of stone-and-wood structures that can be rented for lodging.)

You're here for the hostel, though, right? Well, it's a beauty. Formerly a log cabin that housed the headquarters for the park, it is kept immaculate by the staff. The interior features such modern amenities as wheelchair-accessibility, a fully equipped kitchen, day-use room, and a very comfortable living room with a fireplace.

Outdoors enthusiasts will find this place heavenly: There's biking (on paved bike trails), hiking (more than 30 miles of trails), canoeing, fishing, camping, snowshoeing, and cross-country skiing, to name a few pursuits here.

> **Best bet for a bite:**
> *Foraging and rummaging*
> **What hostellers say:**
> *"Let's go hiking."*
> **Gestalt:**
> *Land o' lakes*
> **Hospitality:** *B*
> **Cleanliness:** *A*
> **Party index:** 🎉

How to Get There:

By car: Take U.S. Route 71 to Lake Itasca State Park entrance ($4 entry fee required). Follow signs to hostel.

Lanesboro Old Barn Resort Hostel

Route 3 (Box 57), Preston, MN 55965
(507) 467-2512; (800) 552-2512

Fax: (507) 467-2382
Web site: www.barnresort.com
E-mail: info@barnresort.com
Rates: $23–$25 per person; $44–$50 for private room
Season: April to Mid-November
Beds: 53
Private rooms: 1
Affiliation: None
Office hours: 9:00 a.m. to 9:00 p.m.
Extras: Laundry, kitchen, bike rentals, pool, golf course, driving range, volleyball court

---

*A*ttached to a big campground, the Preston hostel consists of four carpeted rooms in the basement of a converted barn. The one private room is in the "milk house" and has two twin beds. The "bunkhouse" has the usual—restroom and shower facilities, a kitchenette, and a common room complete with a television. Bicyclists use this place a lot, thanks to the 40-mile trail that runs nearby and a handy local repair shop. Other attractive features include no lockout or curfew, a heated swimming pool, a new golf course, and an on-premises restaurant that features all-American fare, from prime rib to sandwiches. Don't want to spend so much

Best bet for a bite:
On-premises grub
Insiders' tip:
Golf here now
What hostellers say:
"You betcha!"
Hospitality: *B*
Cleanliness: *C*
Party index:

on eats? There's a camp store here, too. Some hostellers over the years have complained that the manager was a bit unfriendly, though most have no problem with him.

How to Get There:
By car: Call hostel for directions.

MISSOURI

Huckleberry Finn Youth Hostel
190408 South Twelfth Street, St. Louis, MO 63104
(314) 241-0076

> **Web site:** www.huckfinnhostel.com
> **E-mail:** info@huckfinnhostel.com
> **Rates:** $25 per person
> **Credit cards:** AMEX, DISC, MC, VISA
> **Season:** February 1 to December 24
> **Beds:** 44
> **Private rooms:** 1
> **Affiliation:** None
> **Office hours:** 8:00 to 10:00 a.m.; 6:00 to 11:00 p.m.
> **Extras:** Lockers, kitchen, television, parking

*T*his place is located on the edge of a dodgy city neighborhood in downtown St. Louis and allows hostellers to use the facilities all day long. Hostellers who have stayed here give it mixed reviews; some didn't like the uneasiness that comes with being in a dodgy neck of the woods. But others disagree and claim that the area, with pubs and restaurants, is perfectly okay—especially the nearby historic Soulard district—and that the manager/owners are friendly and accommodating. We give it a mixed recommendation.

The hostel is fairly close to downtown, however, with what that offers—Cardinals baseball, Rams football, and (of course) a trip up the Arch. And in the Soulard you'll also find a number of well-preserved architectural gems as you amble through the neighborhood.

How to Get There:

By airplane: Large airport in St. Louis. From airport, take Metro to downtown Union Station exit. Walk to Market Street (through station), then take taxi to hostel.

By bus: Greyhound stops in St. Louis. Take taxi to hostel.

By car: Call hostel for directions.

By train: Amtrak stops in St. Louis. Take taxi to hostel.

Best bet for a bite:
Ted Drewes Frozen Custard
Insiders' tip:
Zoo is free!
Gestalt:
Huck U
Safety: *C*
Hospitality: *B*
Cleanliness: *D*
Party index:

OHIO

Malabar Farm Hostel

3954 Bromfield Road, Lucas, OH 44842

(419) 892-2055

> **Fax:** (419) 892-3055
> **E-mail:** MalabarFarm@hiusa.org
> **Rates:** $20 per Hostelling International member
> **Credit cards:** None
> **Season:** Mid-January to mid-December
> **Beds:** 19
> **Private rooms:** 1
> **Affiliation:** Hostelling International
> **Season:** Mid-January to mid-December, Thursday through Sunday only
> **Office hours:** 7:00 to 10:00 a.m.; 5:00 to 10:00 p.m.
> **Extras:** Laundry, kitchen, garden

NOTE: This hostel is open Thursday through Sunday only.

*W*e have come to this place expecting big things, but it has sometimes disappointed us a little.

The hostel, which sits on attractive grounds in a state park, is best known for formerly housing Pulitzer Prize–winning writer Louis Bromfield. Despite three or four different levels, though, it can feel crowded at peak times. Bathrooms were spotless, we'll note; the kitchen was adequate. Strangely, it is no longer open seven days per week—instead you can only stay on a weekend.

There isn't a whole lot to do in the immediate area, either; the park sometimes hosts interpretive programs where you can learn about traditional Ohio farming methods, but that's about it. It's a long haul down a winding road to civilization (drive carefully at night), and even that doesn't offer much: just some fast-food franchises and truck stops. Stop in a real town well beforehand and pick up everything you'll need to fix supper, unless you're feeling flush. In that case, you might try the Malabar Inn just up the road, a classy restored stagecoach inn built in 1820. It's open from May through October.

Better yet, call up the road to the hostel in Peninsula (see next entry) about a room.

Best bet for a bite:
Malabar Farm Restaurant
Insiders' tip:
It's not far to Peninsula
What hostellers say:
"Loosen up, willya?"
Gestalt:
Farm team
Hospitality: *C*
Cleanliness: *A*
Party index:

How to Get There:

By car: Take Interstate 71 to exit 169; turn left (north) onto Ohio Highway 13 for less than ¼ mile, then turn away from interstate onto Hanley Road. Go 2 miles, then turn right at four-way stop onto Little Washington Road. Go ¼ mile, bear left onto Pleasant Valley Road; go 6 miles, turn right onto Bromfield. Hostel is on right.

Stanford House Hostel ✴✴✴✴❂
6093 Stanford Road, Peninsula, OH 44264
(330) 467-8711
  Fax: (330) 467-8711
  E-mail: StanfordHostel@windstream.net
  Rates: $15 per Hostelling International member
  Credit cards: None

Season: Closed Tuesday evening through Thursday morning, January through March
Beds: 33
Private rooms: 1
Affiliation: Hostelling International
Office hours: 8:00 to 10:00 a.m.; 5:00 to 10:00 p.m.
Extras: Piano, hiking trails, laundry, table tennis, kitchen

*O*nce the farmhouse of the Cuyahoga River valley's earliest settlers, Stanford House has got lots going for it: a nice location amidst maple trees, great facilities, cheerful staff, quiet, and a much-needed dose of interesting travelers passing through its creaky doors and floors.

We've seen our share of hostel kitchens that wouldn't pass muster with the local health department, but the kitchen here is dressed to impress. You'll find every cooking implement you need logically located, and there's enough elbow room to whip up a tasty meal for the masses. Hostellers here actually scour their pots and pans after cooking with them and do chores in the morning before heading out. The dorm rooms, albeit small, do provide comfy beds (there are three to six beds or bunk beds per room) replete with army-issue wool blankets and double mattresses.

You're locked out all day, but there's a lot to do around here. First there's the little historically correct village of Peninsula nearby, where you can sip a pint of ale, nose through antiques, and otherwise imagine what it must have been like during the river's heyday. Just get back before the 11:00 p.m. curfew.

Better still, the Cuyahoga Valley National Park stretches north and south from the hostel: a 22-mile belt of protected greenery carved out of that netherland between Akron and Cleveland. It might not sound like much, but it is: A canal towpath across the street allows for great cycling (you can rent the two-wheelers right in Peninsula), walking, or even horseback

Best bet for a bite:
Winking Lizard Tavern
Insiders' tip:
Beware of deer
What hostellers say:
"Know any Pete Seeger tunes?"
Gestalt:
Way to go, Ohio
Hospitality: *B*
Cleanliness: *A*
Party index:

riding for those who are so inclined. Waterfalls, historic areas, and drives to Cleveland are among the other interesting activities with which you could fill your daytime hours.

How to Get There:
By car: Take Interstate 271 to exit 12, then turn east on Ohio Highway 303 and left on Riverview. Just after downtown, turn right on Boston Mills. Then turn north on Stanford Road in less than a mile.

WISCONSIN

Eagle Home Hostel
Call for address
Eagle, WI 53119
(608) 931-2201
> **Fax:** (262) 495-8455
> **E-mail:** eagle@hostellingwisconsin.org
> **Rates:** $25 per Hostelling International member
> **Beds:** 10
> **Credit cards:** None
> **Affiliation:** Hostelling International
> **Office hours:** Vary; call
> **Extras:** Kitchen

*T*his little home hostel within range of the Milwaukee 'burbs sits within one of the Midwest's unappreciated natural gems: the lovely Kettle Moraine State Forest, a region of hills, lakes, and fish. (How did this landscape get here? Ice, ice, baby—the last great glaciers scoured out these ponds and green hills.)

This is a "home hostel," which means you're bunking down beneath someone's actual roof—in this case, the two-story brick home of J. P. and Miki Herman. Be respectful. These owners offer a kitchen, a deck overlooking woods, and an area where you can make a campfire. There's also a real live (okay, it's not actually alive) hammock out back. Pretty cool.

The hostel is very close to the mega (for these parts) tourist attraction known as Old World Wisconsin, a sort of living history museum of rural life replete with old and reconstructed buildings, staff dressed in old-world attire, baseball played by guys with handlebar moustaches (we hope), and farming demonstrations. No word on whether Bernie Brewer stops by now and again to distribute free brats. Probably not. But still, you might want to give it a look.

Milwaukee isn't far off, and there's a great country diner called the Elegant Farmer nearby, too. This is definitely worth a visit if you're into real Americana.

How to Get There:
By car: Contact hostel for directions.

Madison Hostel

141 South Butler Street, Madison, WI 53703
(608) 441-0144
   E-mail: madisonhostel@yahoo.com
   Web site: madisonhostel.org
   Rates: $22 per Hostelling International member; $44 for private room
   Credit cards: MC, VISA
   Beds: 28
   Private/family rooms: 4
   Affiliation: Hostelling International
   Office hours: 8:00 a.m. to 9:00 p.m.
   Extras: Laundry, Internet access, lockers, kitchen

*M*adison's hostel has been around since about 1998, but it was originally a summer-only affair operating out of some University of Wisconsin dormitory buildings. Each year its status was very up in the air.

Things are looking up, though. The hostel now has its own building and is open year-round, attesting to the popularity of this cool Midwestern outpost. It's located in an older building resembling a college fraternity building—but without the *Animal House*–like

ambience—near Madison's cool downtown. For fun, check out State Street's ethnic food kiosks or the grid of streets surrounding the capitol building, where you're sure to find used CDs, cool bars, and the like.

From mid-August to the end of May, there is a lockout between 11:00 a.m. and 5:00 p.m. The hostel is open twenty-four hours from June to mid-August. Also take note of the parking situation; you could get a ticket if you park on the street and don't feed the meter early in the morning. Ask at the desk about your best options.

How to Get There:

By airplane: If you arrive on a weekday, you can take the #24 bus to the North Transfer Point. From there take either the #2 or #4 bus and exit at Capital Square. Walk to King Street and follow to corner of Wilson, King, and South Butler Streets. Turn left on South Butler to hostel.

By bus: From Badger Bus Depot, walk along West Washington Street to Capitol building and walk around Capitol Square. Take a right on King Street. Or, from University of Wisconsin Memorial Union, walk to State Street and take bus to Capitol Square. Get off at Main or Pinckney Street. Continue down King Street until you reach South Butler.

By car: From I-90 or 94, exit at Route 30. Follow East Washington Street and exit at State Capitol; continue about 3 blocks to South Butler Street and turn left to hostel.

By train: Contact hostel for transit details.

Wellspring Hostel ✹✹✹

4382 Hickory Road (P.O. Box 72), Newburg, WI 53060
(262) 675-6755

E-mail: wellspring@hnet.net
Rates: $20 per Hostelling International member; $40 for single room
Credit cards: MC, VISA
Season: Closed Easter, Thanksgiving, and Christmas
Beds: 5
Private rooms: None

Affiliation: Hostelling International
Office hours: 9:00 a.m. to 9:00 p.m.
Extras: Laundry, kitchen, television, garden

*T*his is probably one of the most pastoral hostels you can visit in the United States, and it comes as a special pleasure after a day spent, say, fighting the traffic in and around Chicago or Milwaukee.

Wellspring serves as a communal educational center most of the time, teaching folks how to raise organic herbs and the like. Hostel staffers live on the grounds of a farm. This is back-road America, so not many hostellers find their way here (though a number of cyclists do; it's a popular part of the state for wheelmen and -women). As a result, the facilities get away with being pretty basic: It's just one big floor covered with mattresses and beds, plus use of the manager's well-equipped kitchen, a basement common room, and showers in a separate building. There's an extremely high level of environmental awareness here, reflected in the magazines and chitchat.

What do you do when you're visiting? Not a whole heck of a lot, except maybe stare at the town chapel sticking up from the corn-fields, watch the mist lifting from the little river that runs through town, bike the country roads, or maybe check out one of the little taverns that dot the countryside.

All in all, this is an extremely quiet place. Bring something to do or you're sure to get caught up in a conversation about the New Agey doings on site. Unless you're into that. Then you'll be in nirvana.

> **Best bet for a bite:**
> *Tavern grub in town*
> **What hostellers say:**
> *"Odd but endearing."*
> **Gestalt:**
> *Dairy nice*
> **Hospitality:** *B*
> **Cleanliness:** *A*
> **Party index:**

How to Get There:

By airplane: Airport in Milwaukee. Call hostel for transit route.
By bus: Call hostel for transit route.
By car: Take Interstate 43 to Wisconsin Highway 33 exit; follow Highway 33 to Newburg, then bear right onto Main Street, cross bridge, go right on Hickory Road, make right onto gravel road ½ mile later.
By train: Amtrak stops in Milwaukee (thirty minutes). Call hostel for transit route.

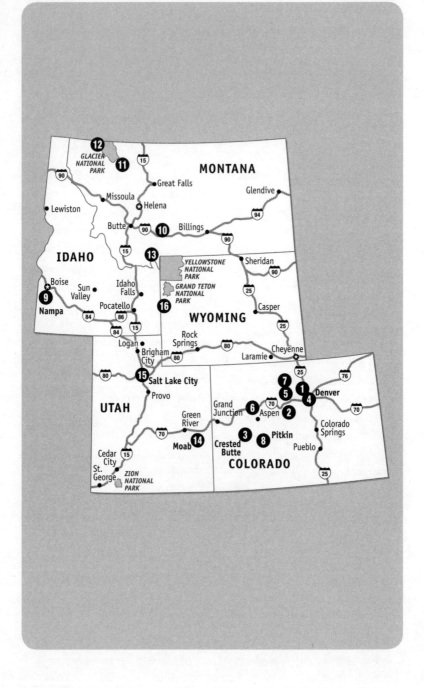

The Rockies

Page numbers follow hostel names

COLORADO

Boulder International Hostel

1107 Twelfth Street (P.O. Box 1705), Boulder, CO 80306

(303) 442-0522

> **Fax:** (303) 442-0523
>
> **E-mail:** reservations@boulderhostel.com
>
> **Web site:** www.boulderhostel.com
>
> **Rates:** $17 per person; $35–$40 for private room
>
> **Credit cards:** AMEX, MC, VISA
>
> **Beds:** 300
>
> **Private rooms:** 20
>
> **Affiliation:** None
>
> **Office hours:** 8:00 a.m. to 11:00 p.m.
>
> **Extras:** Laundry, kitchen, fireplace, television, Internet access

This hodgepodge hostel consists of a mashup of buildings, all in decent shape and safe, though there's no guessing in what type of atmosphere you'll land upon arrival. Possibilities run the gamut from noisy college boarding house (students rent monthly in the hostel) to quiet apartment units.

You're most likely to stay in the busy main building, a massive old sorority house with a prominent front porch and grand lounge area. Most guests pass their time in the common areas because the rooms are decorated only with white walls. All of the hostel's thirteen buildings are located in a great neighborhood, just a couple blocks from both the university and downtown. There is an extensive bike path network in the city. Part of the path passes about 2 blocks from the hostel. The area is usually bustling with trendy students toting hacky sacks and Rasta bags.

The hostel fits in well with Boulder's laid-back, liberal way of life. This is a city where smoking a cigarette in a restaurant could land you in jail, while the punishment for possession of pot is just a $50 fine (or something like that; we could be exaggerating a tad). The two most popular activities among locals seem to be hiking and defying authority. The former is easily accessible by a city bus system that will get you to the area's 5,500 acres of mountain parks. Rock climbing is also king here, and there are plenty of opportunities to hook up with a local group to do so. (Anti-authority types can head for a downtown coffee shop to commiserate about the Bush years: easiest way to find a friend fast around here, hands-down.)

Surprisingly for a hostel tucked right into a frat-house neighborhood—and if you don't believe us, just try staying here on a Friday night and ignoring the thump and throb of dance beats from keg parties, we dare ya—it's pretty well-kept, clean enough most nights and friendly enough, too. It won't get into the Hostel Hall of Fame (were there such a mythical place, we mean), but it's better than average, and that's saying something given the college-kid vibe.

Getting a reservation at this hostel can be a bit of a hassle, though. Management will only accept a night's cash deposit to guarantee a bed, and they like to get a look at prospective guests in person before giving an honest assessment of room availability. There is almost always a place to stay, but there is no assurance it will be in a quiet area.

How to Get There:

By airplane: From Denver airport take Skyride bus to Boulder. Get off at Pleasant Street stop, walk west across Broadway on Pleasant to Twelfth Street. Turn left and go south 2 blocks on Twelfth; hostel is on northwest corner of Twelfth and College.

By bus: Ride Greyhound or Trailways to Denver, then take A or B bus to Boulder. Keep luggage with you. Get off at Pleasant Street stop, walk west across Broadway on Pleasant to Twelfth Street. Turn left and go south 2 blocks on Twelfth; hostel is on northwest corner of Twelfth and College.

By car: From Denver take U.S. Highway 36 to Boulder; exit left on Baseline Road, then turn right onto Broadway, and follow into town. Go left on College; hostel is 2 blocks farther on right.

From Estes Park, take Highway 36 to Colorado Highway 93 to Broadway. Drive past Pearl Street Mall and City Hall to university area. Take right on College; hostel is 2 blocks on right at corner with Twelfth.

Fireside Inn Hostel ✸✸✸

114 North French Street (P.O. Box 2252), Breckenridge, CO 80424

(970) 453-6456

Fax: (970) 547-0023

E-mail: fireside@colorado.net

Web site: www.firesideinn.com

Rates: $28–$43 per person; $66–$190 for private room

Credit cards: DISC, MC, VISA

Season: Open all year except first three weeks in May

Beds: 12

Private rooms: 4

Affiliation: None

Office hours: 8:00 a.m. to 8:00 p.m.

Extras: Breakfast, television, VCR, hot tub, lockers, ski shuttle, kitchen, bike storage, Internet access, garden

*H*ere's a place for those who refuse to give up the luxuries of a resort ski vacation— hot tub, expensive restaurants, country breakfast, boutiques, local nightlife—but are willing to share a room to save a couple of bucks. Even those savings, mind you, are never going to make Breckenridge affordable in the winter; lift ticket prices alone are enough to put you in the poorhouse.

Nevertheless, this comfy Victorian inn is your most economical downtown lodging option that has a modicum of civility. Hostellers are relegated to one of four tiny dorm rooms with two bunks in each or to a large attic where one double and eight twin beds crowd around a center bathroom. No frills here, but it's clean. The lavish parlor is the designated hangout for all, with period furniture and a huge television. The hostel's biggest selling point, however, is a superior Jacuzzi room.

Because the dorms are rather cramped, you should really consider a private room at the Fireside, if you have the dough; it has some of the nicest Breckenridge has to offer, and some of the best hostel private rooms in the nation. Trouble is, they cost as much as $190 a night. The Brandywine Suite, for instance, sleeps four in two rooms with a bathroom, fridge, cable television, VCR, plus its own entrance to the hot tub. It has antique brass beds, an oak dresser, and a walk-in closet. The smaller Hunter's Room also sleeps up to four in a spiffy red-and-green forest motif with excellent views of the ski mountain. Then there's the Sweetheart's Room . . . well, you get the point.

Only 2 blocks from Main Street, the hostel's location is prime. Unfortunately, downtown is getting more plastic with each passing year. Bits and pieces of the original mining town flavor still exist, but you have to look hard for them amid T-shirt and fudge shops. Breckenridge has been a popular ski resort for a while now, and that means no end in sight for the development—and price gouging—except a recession. Which we're having. But still. A hosteller's best asset here is the free year-round shuttle that will take you to most of the excellent ski areas and other major attractions of Summit County.

The Fireside has no lockout or curfew, drawing a slightly more raucous crowd than you might have expected at first glance. This is particularly true in the off-season, when the hostel offers weekly rates to ski bums in withdrawal, er, transition.

Best bet for a bite:
Fatty's Pizza downtown
Insiders' tip:
Arapaho's got the most/best snow
Gestalt:
Ski school
Hospitality: *B*
Cleanliness: *A*
Party index:

How to Get There:

By airplane: From Denver airport, take Resort Express shuttle or use public transport to reach Greyhound station, then catch a bus to Silverthorne and free Summit Stage bus to Breckenridge. Hostel is at corner of Wellington and French.

By bus: Greyhound stops in Silverthorne. Take free shuttle to Main and Wellington in Breckenridge. Walk 2 blocks east on Wellington (uphill) to French Street. Hostel is on corner.

By car: Take Interstate 70 to exit 203; go south on Colorado Highway 9. In Breckenridge look for Wellington Road. Take Wellington 2 blocks to hostel at corner of Wellington and French.

 Attractive natural setting

Ecologically aware hostel

 Superior kitchen facilities or cafe

 Offbeat or eccentric place

 Superior bathroom facilities

 Romantic private rooms

Comfortable beds

A particularly good value

Wheelchair-accessible

Good for business travelers

Especially well-suited for families

Good for active travelers

Visual arts at hostel or nearby

 Music at hostel or nearby

 Great hostel for skiers

 Bar or pub at hostel or nearby

Editors' choice: Among our very favorite hostels

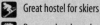 *Key to Icons*

Crested Butte International Hostel

615 Teocalli Avenue (P.O. Box 1332), Crested Butte, CO 81224

(970) 349-0588; (888) 389-0588

Fax: (970) 349-0586

E-mail: hostel@crestedbutte.net

Web site: www.crestedbuttehostel.com

Rates: $25–$38 per person; $65–$110 for private room

Credit cards: DISC, MC, VISA

Beds: 52

Private/family rooms: 5

Affiliation: None

Office hours: 7:30 a.m. to 9:00 p.m. (mid-December to first week of April, and June through August); 8:00 a.m. to noon, 4:00 to 8:00 p.m. (rest of year)

Extras: Laundry, kitchen, information desk, lockers, fireplace, television, VCR, breakfast, dinner, Internet access

*Y*es, folks, it's yet another Hostelling International hostel located in a small Colorado town with drop-dead views. This one's in a beautiful building in Crested Butte—a speck of a town set in the rugged west-central region of the state, an area rife with those bright alpine wildflowers that make Colorado such a nice place in spring and summer. There are plenty of rock formations around here, too, if you're a rock-head.

Rooms here come in configurations of four, six, and eight beds apiece; each is equipped with storage drawers, desk, and chair, and all are said to have wonderful views. (Come when they're not too busy— summer, perhaps?—and you might get a private room.)

The common room includes a fireplace, small library, games, and an informa-

Best bet for a bite:
Meal plan
Insiders' tip:
Music festivals in summer
What hostellers say:
"It's a Rocky Mountain high."
Gestalt:
Real Butte
Hospitality: *A*
Cleanliness: *B*
Party index:

tion desk as well as the usual TV/VCR combo. This hostel also offers a meal plan—sit-down dinners, takeout lunches, and continental breakfasts for a small charge. Nice touch.

Okay, so you've made it here. What to do next? The quaint little town itself was founded on coal mining, but today folks come mostly to ski at a local resort. (Mountain biking, hiking, fishing, rafting, and music occupy the summers.) Skiers will be especially happy to learn the hostel is just a half-minute's walk from the nearest bus stop—where a free shuttle can whisk you to a ski area 3 miles away. There's lots of storage on the hostel premises for skis, bikes, and luggage, too—did you expect anything less? Sometimes they even offer package rates including ski tickets.

How to Get There:

By bus: Greyhound stops in Gunnison. Contact hostel for transit details.

By car: From Denver take I-70 West to the Copper Mountain/Leadville exit or take 285 South to Buena Vista. Follow either to Poncha Springs. Turn right on Highway 50 and travel west to Gunnison. Follow Highway 135 right to Crested Butte. The hostel is located 3 blocks north of Elk Avenue on Teocalli Avenue.

DENVER HOSTELS: A SUMMARY					
	RATING	PROS	CONS	COST	PAGE
Hostel of the Rockies	✳✳✳	trying	shady area	$24	p. 169
Melbourne International Hotel & Hostel	✳✳	cheap	unfriendly; poor location	$16–$28	p. 171
Denver International Youth Hostel	✳	beatnik crowd	unclean	$11	p. 167

Denver International Youth Hostel ✳

630 East Sixteenth Avenue, Denver, CO 80201

(303) 832-9996

> **E-mail:** denver@youthhostels.com
>
> **Rates:** $11 per person
>
> **Credit cards:** None
>
> **Beds:** 190
>
> **Private rooms:** None

Affiliation: None

Office hours: 8:00 to 10:00 a.m.; 5:00 to 10:00 p.m.

Extras: Laundry, television, lockers, free food (sometimes), organ, barbecue, kitchen

*S*orry, this place just is not cutting it. The cramped quarters at the hostel could use a mop or three, but that's not happening anytime soon. Still, while it's obviously not the headquarters of Mr. Clean, this hostel is a decent information exchange for the spontaneous traveler. Other than that, we really cannot recommend it.

The building has the sagging yet loved look of a condemned complex revived by innovative squatters. Engaging murals, a spunky two-tiered organ, and piles of paperbacks rule the place alongside general disorder. Tired chairs and ashtrays sit on the extended fire escape that serves as a popular sunporch; guests often relax here, overlooking a parking lot filled with newly acquired junk cars they'll use to get into the mountains, then sell a few weeks later for whatever they can get. Keep in mind, however, that while international travel is celebrated here, foreigners do *not* make up the majority of guests. One manager spoke of rent rather than daily rates and told us the facility also operated as a halfway house of sorts. He also had to "evict" someone for smoking crack. Enough said. (That's not really surprising once you get a look at the 'hood: Tattered tenements and sex shops are the neighbors, though luckily so is a police station.)

Grimy dorms here are divided by sex, with as many as ten beds squeezed tightly into each room. Each dorm has its own bathroom and a disorderly small kitchen. In the basement is another community kitchen where a variety of free items can be scavenged. Exactly what can be found depends on what didn't sell at the supermarket that week; the manager collects those items and distributes them to food banks. Whatever the food banks don't want? *That* goes to the hostellers. Processed cheese spread and yogurt are good examples.

The free-spirited traveler without cash or plans will feel right at home here.

Best bet for a bite:
On the pedestrian mall

Insiders' tip:
Catch a concert at Red Rocks Amphitheater—at night

What hostellers say:
"Laundry? Huh? What's that?"

Gestalt:
Rocky Mountain low

Safety: *C*

Hospitality: *B*

Cleanliness: *F*

Party index: 🎉🎉🎉🎉

Others might be a bit out of their element . . . especially those who like soap and hate bugs. Everyone else should love it, though.

How to Get There:

By airplane: From Denver airport take RTD bus to Colfax. At Colfax change to #15 bus westbound and get off at Washington Street. Hostel is 1 block north at intersection of Washington and Sixteenth.

By bus: Greyhound stops in Denver. From station walk east on Seventeenth Street, then 3 blocks to Market Street. Go 1 block south (right) to Market Street bus station. Take free bus to the end of Sixteenth (at Broadway), then walk east 6 blocks on Sixteenth Avenue to intersection with Washington. Hostel is on right corner.

By car: Take Interstate 25 to Colfax exit. Drive east on Colfax until Washington Street. Go left on Washington to Sixteenth Avenue. Hostel is on left corner at Washington and Colfax.

By train: Call hostel for directions.

Hostel of the Rockies

1717 Race Street, Denver, CO 80206
(303) 861-7777

   Fax: (720) 429-4722
   E-mail: reservations@innkeeperrockies.com
   Web site: www.innkeeperrockies.com
   Rates: $24 per person; $30–$35 for private room
   Credit cards: MC, VISA
   Beds: 50
   Private rooms: 4
   Affiliation: None
   Office hours: 7:30 a.m. to 2:00 p.m.; 6:00 to 10:00 p.m.
   Extras: Kitchen, television, VCR, games, laundry, lockers, Internet access

---

*A*lso known as Innkeeper of the Rockies, this Denver entry replaces the former Hostel of the Rocky Mountains, which frankly had devolved into almost flophouse digs, home to transients aplenty. Current owner Linda Lankford pledges vast improvements to her 1905 apartment building–turned-hostel, and she's won half the battle. Let's see if she can improve it even further.

Dorms are carved out of retrofitted former apartments, and contain bunks of two, four, six, or eight beds per dorm, most with Coleman airbeds. The common area contains the hostel kitchen, as well as a TV with VCR, bookshelves, games, and a coin-op laundry. Most, but not all, of the dorms have private bathrooms. Three of the dorms also have outdoor decks, while the backyard is stocked with tables, picnic areas, and a big grill. (Volleyball and horseshoes might one day sweeten the deal further.) Though these dorms are fine, there are also four private rooms in a nearby inn operated by the same owner, full-, queen-, and king-bedded rooms that differ in character: One has a sunporch and airbed lounging area, for instance. All four of the private rooms share one bathroom and a kitchen.

The hostel is ramping up social activities, such as barbecues. There are also plenty of things to do in Denver when you're alive: a Museum of Nature and Science, a zoo, botanic gardens, shopping, Old West ambience, the capitol of Colorado, and so forth. Just bear in mind you'll need to get a transit pass for this, as some of these lie a fair piece from the hostel. However, on the upside, loads of restaurants are within walking distance of your digs, and a huge city park and golf course is also within a half-dozen blocks.

Our verdict? A good start in a town that desperately needed a good hostel. Now let's see the place get cleaner. This hostel just might overcome its Rocky past one day and really take off.

How to Get There:

By airplane: From Denver International Airport, take AT (Skyride) bus to Colfax Avenue, then transfer to #15 bus and get off at Race Street. Walk 2⅓ blocks north to hostel. Or take AF (Skyride) bus to 17th and Market Streets, transfer to #20 bus eastbound, and get off at Race Street; hostel is ⅓ block north.

By bus: Greyhound stops in Denver. Take #15 local bus from city center, eastbound on Colfax. Get off at Race Street, walk 1⅓ blocks north to hostel. Or take #20 local bus eastbound, get off at Race Street and walk across street to hostel.

By car: From the center of town (Broadway and Colfax, next to Colorado State Capitol

Building), go east 19 blocks to Race Street and turn left. Continue 2½ more blocks to hostel at #1717.

By train: Amtrak stops in Denver. Walk to corner of Wazee and 16th, catch Free Mall Shuttle, exit at Lawrence, then catch #20 local bus eastbound. Get off at Race Street and walk 1⅓ blocks north to hostel.

Melbourne International Hotel & Hostel

607 Twenty-second Street, Denver, CO 80205

(303) 292-6386

E-mail: info@denverhostel.com

Web site: www.denverhostel.com

Rates: $16–$28 per person; $39–$44 for private room

Credit cards: MC, VISA

Beds: 47

Private rooms: 12

Affiliation: None

Office hours: 7:00 a.m. to 10:00 p.m.

Extras: Kitchen, laundry, storage, deli, free Wi-Fi

---

*M*any hostellers are turned off by the Melbourne's neighborhood, which is one of Denver's worst. Others complain that the staff has a tendency toward downright nastiness. Then there is the hot steam from the Laundromat below that turns the place into a sauna at times . . . and the bus station right across the street that brings noise early each morning and packs of bus travelers to the sidewalks out front in the evening. Still, the physical accommodations themselves are the nicest hostel digs in town, and in that respect it puts the other Denver hostels to shame.

A multitude of ceiling fans rotating above dark red carpets sets a saloon tone. Add stucco walls, dark landscape paintings, a few velvet couches, and a row of old wooden desks with swivel chairs set along a seemingly endless hallway, and you're getting the picture. The four- to six-bed dorm rooms are true to the owner's proclamation: "nothing elaborate but sparkling clean and well-maintained." Unfortunately, he can't do anything about loudmouths on the street or the light rail line visible from hostel windows (again, early-morning

Best bet for a bite:
Deli here
Insiders' tip:
Bring earplugs
Gestalt:
Buckin' Bronco
Safety: *C*
Hospitality: *D*
Cleanliness: *B*
Party index:

noise); this place can get a bit loud, in case you hadn't figured that out already. But the rooms all have high ceilings, plenty of open floor space, quaint bamboo shades, and a fridge. They are all secured by a lockable metal gate door to allow circulation during the day to fight the Laundromat's steam, a feature hostellers complain creates a jail-like atmosphere. Refuge can be sought outside in the inspiring patio around which a garden sprouts.

Neighborhood and staff aside, the Melbourne is not bad. Yet those first two elements undeniably make or break a place like this. Supporters claim an increased police presence and changes in staff schedules are helping work out the hostel's "kinks," but we're not convinced it has happened. Not yet.

How to Get There:

By airplane: Large airport in Denver. Call hostel for transit route.

By bus: Greyhound stops in Denver. Call hostel for transit route.

By car: Take I-70 to Denver, exit at I-25 south and take exit 213 to Park Avenue West. Follow signs to Downtown and Coors Field. At Coors Field (on left) street becomes Twenty-second Street; follow Twenty-second to Welton Street.

By train: Amtrak stops in Denver. Call hostel for transit route.

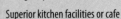 Attractive natural setting

 Ecologically aware hostel

 Superior kitchen facilities or cafe

 Offbeat or eccentric place

 Superior bathroom facilities

 Romantic private rooms

Comfortable beds

A particularly good value

Wheelchair-accessible

Good for business travelers

Especially well-suited for families

Good for active travelers

 Visual arts at hostel or nearby

 Music at hostel or nearby

 Great hostel for skiers

 Bar or pub at hostel or nearby

 Editors' choice: Among our very favorite hostels

The Rocky Mountain Inn & Hostel

15 CR 72 (P.O. Box 600), Fraser, CO 80442

(970) 726-8256; (866) 467-8351

E-mail: info@therockymountaininn.com
Web site: www.therockymountaininn.com
Rates: $19–$38 per person; doubles $59–$219
Credit cards: AMEX, DC, DISC, MC, VISA
Beds: 38
Private/family rooms: 6
Affiliation: None
Office hours: 8:30 a.m. to 10:00 p.m.
Extras: Kitchen, laundry, DVD player, Internet access, fireplace, breakfast, shuttle

*J*ust 2 miles from the ski town of Winter Park, the Rocky Mountain Inn is a combination B&B and hostel. It's a great place, though an inn first and foremost—which means it's obviously best for families, couples, and those who love to ski. But even backpacking bums will get a kick out of the really nice kitchen, laundry, fridges in the rooms, and bike storage area. (The view of 12,800-foot Byer's Peak ain't bad, either.) As we've said, the six big family rooms are nice, if pricey—they're basically hotel rooms, some with king-size beds! The dorms themselves ain't bad, though, with two to seven beds apiece.

> **Best bet for a bite:**
> *De Antonio's (pizza)*
> **What hostellers say:**
> *"Rocky! Rocky! Rocky!"*
> **Gestalt:**
> *Fraser first*
> **Hospitality:** *A*
> **Cleanliness:** *A*
> **Party index:** 🎉🎉🎉

The hostel's just 2 blocks from the local bus and train stations, and once you're here there are tons of outdoor options in the surrounding area: skiing, mountain biking, golfing, hiking, and more. Just remember that prices are higher in winter, which is prime season here.

How to Get There:

By bus: Hostel is 2 blocks from bus depot.

By car: Take Highway 40 to town of Fraser. At stoplight (the only one on Highway 40) turn west. Take immediate right into hostel parking lot.

By train: Hostel is 2 blocks from train station.

Glenwood Springs Hostel ✶✶✶✶

1021 Grand Avenue, Glenwood Springs, CO 81601

(970) 945-8545; (800) 946-7835 (U.S. only)

E-mail: info@hostelcolorado.com

Web site: www.hostelcolorado.com

Rates: $16–$25 per person; $33–$58 for private room

Credit cards: AMEX, MC, VISA

Beds: 42

Private rooms: 5

Affiliation: None

Office hours: 8:00 to 10:00 a.m.; 4:00 to 10:00 p.m.

Extras: Laundry, meditation room, records, ski packages, shuttle, bike rentals, Internet access, kitchen

---

*G*lenwood Springs Hostel owner and guru Gary Grillo stood in front of the beaten-down house marked by a psychedelic hostel sign and tried to describe a typical guest. Not an easy task. "Athletes" and "people who are into making things" were all that came to his mind. On the porch a twosome with dreadlocks and Rasta caps smoked their morning cigarettes and listened. They were preparing for another rigorous day of mountain biking, followed by another rigorous night of drinking.

If this one-of-a-kind hostel resembles anything, it's the house on a college campus where all the artsy folks reside: home to the best parties and the best conversations.

In the lower kitchen of the hostel (there are two kitchens, both decent, one with a cute checkerboard floor), two women try to reach consensus on the spirituality of organic produce. Above them a guest is beating the resident African drum to the tune of an eclectic jazz selection spinning on the turntable. "I prefer music over TV. It brings people together,"

Grillo said. His passion is reflected by the amazing record collection that resides in milk crates on the common-room floor. His (primitive but not bad) artwork hangs on the walls and works to motivate guests to pick up free art supplies and create something. The paperback exchange, offering the likes of Noam Chomsky and Umberto Eco, is among the most impressive in a hostel we've seen. Guitars are inevitably lying about for the playing; woodstoves are fired up and waiting for chats.

Make no mistake about it, this is still a hippie hostel. If you seek order and convention, you're not going to find it here.

It follows, then, that the rooming arrangements are a bit unconventional. The "custom" dorm rooms have two bunk beds shoved so close together that it is unwise for more than one person to stand at once. The other option is larger dorms with a disorderly slumber-party feel. The lounge and meditation rooms, however, are quite comfy and a lot of fun.

Glenwood Springs is a perfect spot for this hostel. It's right off I-70, the only artery cutting right through Colorado's Rockies. The town offers a multitude of interesting activities, such as the communal therapeutic hot springs pool or Yampah Vapor Caves "in the mountain" natural sauna. The outdoor sporting options in the mountains are limitless, too. Guests rave about trips offered through the hostel to awe-inspiring Fulford Cave and whitewater rafting in the historic canyon. A paved bike path offers a scenic ride to great hiking trails. Winter attracts skiers with easy access to world-famous Aspen: Ski packages are available (that's a lift ticket plus a night's stay!), and there's a ski shuttle to the hills. A more local and affordable option is to ski Sunlight, with its fifty-odd runs and a 2,000-foot vertical drop. The managers have thoughtfully worked out discount lift tickets and entrance to the hot springs for their guests.

It's also worth noting that this hostel is your best bet for affordable lodging if you want to spend a few days gallivanting around the glitzy streets of Aspen (which is 40 or more miles away, by the way) but don't have the bucks—and who does, these days?—to bed down there.

How to Get There:

By bus: Greyhound stops in Glenwood Springs. From station on Sixth walk 2 blocks away from I-70 to footbridge (next to castle and hot springs pool). Cross bridge and walk up Grand to Tenth; hostel is on right.

By car: Take I-70 to Glenwood Springs exit; follow signs to Colorado Highway 82, go to Grand. Hostel is on left, between Tenth and Eleventh.

By train: Amtrak stops in Glenwood Springs. Leave station at exit directly opposite river and walk left to Grand. Walk up Grand to Tenth; hostel is on right.

Shadowcliff Hostel � ✺✺✺✺

405 Summerland Park Road (P.O. Box 658), Grand Lake, CO 80447

(970) 627-9220

> **Fax:** (970) 627-9220
> **Rates:** $15 per person; $30 for private room
> **Credit cards:** None
> **Season:** Late May to early October
> **Beds:** 14
> **Private rooms:** 4
> **Affiliation:** None
> **Office hours:** 8:00 a.m. to 9:00 p.m.
> **Extras:** Piano, fireplace, meals, chapel, kitchen

"Gentleness, reflection, unhurriedness, acceptance, and transcendence" are the words Shadowcliff's owners use to describe their hilltop lodge overlooking Grand Lake. Spend a night here, and you'll see what they mean. The balcony provides a lake view that is so peaceful you'll think you've left civilization behind. Add to that the soothing sound of North Inlet Stream gushing below, and you have a setting of unparalleled serenity in the hostel world.

Shadowcliff, however, gets mixed reviews from hostellers because it is a mixed-use facility, oriented mainly toward religious groups. The lodge was built as a dedicated hostel in the peace-love era by 500 volunteers from seventy-two countries—when has *that* happened lately? They worked for several years in four-week increments, hauling logs up the mountain one by one. The hostel never saw enough traffic to make it financially, and now hostellers take a backseat to other guests and are stuffed into two small dorm rooms on the top floor, with a claustrophobic kitchen that's good for little more than heating up soup.

Whining aside, it's undoubtedly as sweet a deal as they come, especially given the view. Hostellers have free rein over the lodge and grounds, including access to many luxurious facilities that are here thanks to the higher-paying guests. These include a sprawling common room resembling the parlor of a grand European

Best bet for a bite:
Downhill on the main drag
Insiders' tip:
Window beds have soothing river sounds
What hostellers say:
"Relaxing."
Gestalt:
Mountain spirits
Hospitality: *B*
Cleanliness: *B*
Party index: 🎉

hunting lodge. Heck, we'll overlook those normal dorms and the puny kitchen. Because this property is beautiful.

Shadowcliff is located on the opposite side of Rocky Mountain National Park from the dry-side Estes Park; its owners like to call it the "wetter better side" because numerous lakes provide ample fishing, boating, and swimming opportunities. The area sees fewer visitors because it is farther away from a major population center and inaccessible by public transportation. This has its advantages in terms of less company on the hiking trails (although solitude is not hard to come by on either side of the park) and a smaller, more rustic town. A bunch of trailheads are within walking distance of the hostel, and a feed-in to the Bikecentennial Trail is nearby, too.

Young raucous types looking to meet their match might want to pass Shadowcliff up; it's a quiet hideaway more fitting for the spiritual sort. It's as congenial as can be, but not overly social; couples and families seeking seclusion in the forest will do well here.

How to Get There:
By car: Take U.S. Highway 34 to Grand Lake. Enter town and go left at the triangle park fork. Drive ⅔ mile on West Portal Road to Shadowcliff sign. Go left uphill to hostel.

Pitkin Hotel and Hostel ✶✶✶✺

329 Main Street (P.O. Box 164), Pitkin, CO 81214

(970) 641-2757

E-mail: joanpitkin@webtv.net

Web site: www.pitkincolorado.com/Hotel

Rates: $15–$20 per person

Credit cards: None

Season: June to September

Beds: 20

Private rooms: 3

Affiliation: None

Office hours: 8:00 a.m. to 10:00 p.m.

Extras: Piano, television, storage, pool table, laundry, kitchenette

NOTE: This hostel is considering closing its doors. Check ahead before arriving.

*T*he wood-carved sign hanging in front of the Pitkin Hotel and Hostel states simply, A STEP BACK IN TIME. Nothing could be closer to the truth. The historic building probably hasn't changed much since it was built a century ago when Pitkin was a booming mining town. Therein lies its charm; Pitkin is one of the few remaining former mining towns in the state that has been scarcely altered by the ills of development and sees little in the way of pesky tourists.

Believe it or not, the focal point of town is actually the hostel, a prominent two-story white-stone building with a sprawling second-story side balcony and large windows dressed smartly in lace curtains. Inside wooden fans rotate slowly from a high ceiling that's decorated with antique moldings. Wood rocking chairs with plush cushions are arranged in various spots, amid a series of interesting collector's items such as the antique tools hanging from the wall or old-fashioned bottles piled in a corner. The huge dorm room is an interesting work of carpentry, with about twenty mattresses connected head-to-toe on top of a double-decker wood structure around the perimeter of the room. (Worry not, personal space isn't an issue as only a half-dozen or so hostellers trek out to Pitkin each week.) In the center sits a common area and pool table.

Pitkin was settled in 1878, a few years after a prospector discovered $50,000 worth of gold in the area. By 1880 there were more than 1,800 residents in town, and Pitkin held the title as Colorado's fourth-largest city, with seventy-five new miners arriving daily. Then the town collapsed as rapidly as it grew—the mines emptied, and only 500 people were left by 1884. Today there are fewer than one hundred year-round residents, although a few hundred easygoing summer residents make the trek out here each year to escape contemporary society. There's a general store, a gas station, a couple of feed joints, and a lot of history.

The only way to comprehend the hostel's unique character is to experience it. One newspaper reporter described it as "equal parts hotel, museum, library, hunting lodge, New Age commune, and grandmother's house in the woods." Owner JoAn Bannister woke the building from a long rest with her meditation group in 1981 and turned it into a commune, but that failed after six months. Thus the spiritual hostel/hotel. Resident caretaker Marty—a rugged, gruff mountain type—offers massages in between chopping wood, and several Pitkin residents are trained in New Age healing.

If the spiritual element doesn't interest you, don't be discouraged. There are a thousand more great reasons to visit the area. You can take a scenic mountain bike ride up to the Alpine Tunnel (elevation 11,523 feet), the first train passageway blasted through the Continental Divide. Nearby are a number of ghost towns, all with interesting stories. There are, of course, the many offerings of the unspoiled Gunnison National Forest, too.

For a real treat visit the hostel in winter when the town empties to only the hardcore year-rounders. After a peaceful day of snowshoeing or Nordic skiing on the forest's many paths, you can curl up next to wood-burning stoves with a selection from the generous bookcase. Just make sure to buy your food before turning onto County Road 76.

Best bet for a bite:
Cafe next door
Insiders' tip:
Bring your mountain bike
What hostellers say:
"Keep this place a secret!"
Gestalt:
Pitkin and grinnin'
Hospitality: *A*
Cleanliness: *B*
Party index: 🎉🎉

How to Get There:
By car: Take U.S. Highway 50 west from Gunnison 11 miles to County Road 76 and turn left. Drive for 16 miles, passing hamlet of Ohio, and hostel is on left just after entering Pitkin (look for two-story stone building).

IDAHO

Nampa Hostel ✳✳✳

17322 Can Ada Road, Nampa, ID 83687

(208) 467-6858

E-mail: mail@hostelboise.com

Web site: www.hostelboise.com

Rates: $19–$35 per person; $40 for private room

Credit cards: MC, VISA

Season: March to January

Beds: 11

Private/family rooms: 1

Affiliation: None

Office hours: 7:00 to 10:00 a.m.; 5:00 to 10:30 p.m.

Extras: Free Internet access, meals ($), laundry, storage area, free local calls, grill, patio, linens ($), kitchen

Idaho's newest hostel is right in the heart of the state, where you can participate in lots of outdoor activities ranging from hiking and biking to whitewater rafting and skiing. It's well-kept, friendly, and reasonably clean. We can definitely recommend it.

Snake River, site of a famous daredevil motorcycle stunt—and some serious bends and cliffs—is nearby. More important, though, the hostel is also within shouting distance (okay, more like 15 miles) of downtown Boise, where there's lots more culture (as much as can be expected in Idaho).

The management here was associated with another hostel in Idaho that

Best bet for a bite:
Arctic Circle (burgers)

Insiders' tip:
"Nampa" means "pick up girls" (but only in Japanese)

What hostellers say:
"Idaho, Alaska."

Gestalt:
Boise zone

Hospitality: *A*

Cleanliness: *C*

Party index: 🎉🎉🎉

closed a few years back; they seem to be enthusiastic about this hostel. You'll find a quiet, small-town/suburban ambience here: Staff claim that you can even have fun watching the grass grow, though we're a little dubious about that.

If you plan on arriving at night and want to cook, bring enough food for dinner since grocery stores near the hostel close early, leaving you with dreadfully overprocessed and expensive food from a convenience store. However, the hostel stocks a few canned goods if you can't make it to the store. Contact the hostel for its lockout policy.

How to Get There:

By bus: Contact hostel for transit details.

By car: Take exit 38 off of Interstate 84, just east of Nampa (12 miles west of Boise). Drive approximately 2 miles straight north on the Can Ada Road. Look for hostel sign on the right side of the road.

MONTANA

Bozeman Backpackers Hostel ✳✳✳

405 West Olive Street, Bozeman, MT 59715

(406) 586-4659

> **E-mail:** bozeman4hostel@yahoo.com
> **Web site:** www.bozemanbackpackershostel.com
> **Rates:** $20 per person; $42 for private room
> **Credit cards:** None
> **Beds:** 16
> **Private rooms:** 2
> **Affiliation:** None
> **Office hours:** Vary; call
> **Extras:** Kitchen

*A*n astonishing number of Australians seem to find their way to Bozeman's hostel; this phenomenon is possibly attributed to the Aussie heritage of one of the managers. This hostel has changed hands (to another Aussie, don't worry), but we've been assured that the laid-back vibe is still the "driving force" of the hostel.

Located on a quiet residential street not far from the local university, it consists of a few rather basic bunkrooms upstairs. Downstairs the kitchen could be lots cleaner and better stocked, but on the plus side it does include such unusual items as popcorn poppers and a waffle iron.

A typical scene here consists of someone sitting on a couch strumming one of the house guitars or discussing the day's extreme hike. (You also get the feeling that a lot of beer is consumed here on the weekends, albeit in a convivial setting.) Though the feeling is very, very low-key, the management is fanatical about ecology in that same laid-back way: Everything is recycled, food scraps are composted, and short showers are requested.

There's plenty to do in the area around this hostel. Nine-thousand-foot mountains rise from the edge of town, and Bozeman's main drag is full of interesting stores and bars in which to poke around. A friendly little city, it seems safe as can be; so safe that the front door is left unlocked twenty-four hours a day. Late-night arrivals are greeted with a note on a blackboard to find their own bunk and square up in the morning.

We'd feel better if the policy weren't quite so open-door, but you shouldn't overlook the fact that guests absolutely rave about this place in a rather artistic comment book. A number of them say it's the best place they've ever stayed, and that's saying something. Only quibble? These laid-back dudes are too laid-back about grown-up issues like security. Would it hurt to lock the door? That shouldn't be an issue, but it is. Otherwise this place is very cool.

How to Get There:

By bus: Greyhound stops in Bozeman. From station walk north on Seventh to Main, then make a left and walk to Fourth. Turn right on Fourth and walk 2 blocks to Olive. Turn right on Olive.
By car: Follow I-90 into downtown Bozeman; call hostel for directions.

Backpacker's Inn

29 Dawson Avenue (P.O. Box 94), East Glacier Park, MT 59434

(406) 226-9392

Fax: (406) 226-9138

E-mail: serranos@cyberport.net

Web site: www.serranosmexican.com/backpackers-inn.php

Rates: $12 per person; $30 for private room

Credit cards: AMEX, DISC, MC, VISA

Season: May to October

Beds: 10

Private rooms: 2

Affiliation: None

Office hours: Vary; call

Extras: Restaurant

W hat's this? A hostel attached to a great Mexican restaurant?? Have we died and gone to heaven?!

Well, actually, no. This isn't heaven. It's Montana. And the hostel here actually predates the restaurant.

It's got real western heritage, too: The building was originally a lodging house built by mountaineer Tom Dawson; he constructed it to house workers staying to construct Glacier Park Lodge in what would become the national park. Later owners added log cabins. But the current owners really scored when they put in showers and the bunkhouse and added more cabins.

If you're coming, you're in luck—great food, great views of the park, and the proximity of both bus and train transit work to your advantage. Remember, though, that they only take reservations twenty-four hours in advance.

Best bet for a bite:
Pretty obvious
Gestalt:
Hot Burrito #1
Safety: *A*
Hospitality: *A*
Cleanliness: *A*
Party index:

How to Get There:

By bus: Greyhound stops in East Glacier Park. From bus stop, walk to hostel on Dawson Avenue.

By car: Contact hostel for directions.

By train: Amtrak stops in East Glacier Park. From train station, walk to hostel on Dawson Avenue.

Brownie's Hostel ✶✶✶✶

1020 Montana Highway 49 (P.O. Box 229), East Glacier Park, MT 59434
(406) 226-4426

Fax: (406) 226-4426
E-mail: browniesegp@yahoo.com
Rates: $15 per Hostelling International member
Credit cards: DISC, MC, VISA
Season: June to mid-October
Beds: 16
Affiliation: Hostelling International
Office hours: 7:30 a.m. to 9:00 p.m.
Extras: Laundry, bike rentals, fax, store, deli, coffee, pickups, kitchen, grill, Internet access

---

*H*ostellers seem to like this place, especially the novelty of having a small-town grocery store beneath them and the majestic peaks of Glacier Park out the front door. There are tons of things to do here: Drive the Going-to-the-Sun Road in the park, take boat trips on one of the 250 local lakes, hike, fish; you can't go wrong. The hostel has a camping area, too, and offers a discount at the local Whistle Stop restaurant.

Best bet for a bite:
On premises
What hostellers say:
"Fantastic area."
Hospitality: *B*
Cleanliness: *B*
Party index: 🎉

How to Get There:

By car: Take U.S. Highway 2 to Montana Route 49; turn north for ¼ mile to hostel.

By train: Amtrak stops near Glacier Park twice daily; call hostel for details and pickup.

North Fork Hostel

80 Beaver Drive, Polebridge, MT 59928

(406) 888-5241

> **E-mail:** nfhostel@nfhostel.com
> **Web site:** www.nfhostel.com
> **Rates:** $15 per person; $40–$65 for private room or cabin
> **Credit cards:** AMEX
> **Beds:** 25
> **Private rooms:** Yes
> **Affiliation:** None
> **Office hours:** 8:00 a.m. until 10:00 p.m.
> **Extras:** Bike, canoe, ski, kayak, and snowshoe rentals

---

*W*hat this hostel lacks in modern amenities, it makes up for with its pristine surroundings and back-to-the-land ethic. The place is actually part of the Square Peg Ranch, an actual ranch. Perched against Glacier National Park down a gravel highway, North Fork provides its hostellers with a truly rustic experience.

The hostel—in fact, the entire town—eschews electricity, opting instead for propane generators and woodstoves. A propane cooking range and refrigerators are available for guests—a good thing, considering you'll be hungry after your outdoor adventure days. The facilities include men's and women's bunks, couples' accommodations, a clawfoot bathtub and

Best bet for a bite:
Northern Lights Café (June–September)
Insiders' tip:
Bring a flashlight
Gestalt:
Fork in the road
Hospitality: *A*
Cleanliness: *B*
Party index: 🎉🎉

showers, common space, communal kitchen, and, as John the owner puts it, "the spiffiest outhouses on the North Fork."

The pristine natural setting allows for lots of activity—hiking, skiing, bicycling, and water sports are all encouraged by the owner. But if you just feel like hanging around this homey hostel, that's okay, too. Keep your camera on hand for when you catch glimpses of deer, moose, elk, mountain lions, and even bears through the hostel windows.

When skipping out to use the al fresco loo, you'll probably be asked to carry in some wood on your return trip to the main building. But you likely won't mind. Hostellers uniformly tell us that it's a very pleasant hostelling experience.

How to Get There:
By car: From West Glacier take Camas Creek Road to Beaver Drive. Or call hostel for directions.
By train: Amtrak stops at West Glacier (Belton); take shuttle.

West Yellowstone Hostel at the Madison Hotel
139 Yellowstone Avenue (P.O. Box 1370), West Yellowstone, MT 59758
(406) 646-7745; (800) 838-7745
Fax: (406) 646-9766
Rates: $22 per person; doubles $39
Credit cards: AMEX, DISC, MC, VISA
Season: Late May to early October
Beds: 25
Private rooms: 6
Affiliation: None
Office hours: 9:00 a.m. to 10:00 p.m.
Extras: Gift shop, grill, tour, Internet access, television

*T*his hostel occupies a motel made partly of logs. Okayyyy. You don't get a kitchen for cooking but do get to cook outdoors on a fireplace if you wish. The dorms have some nice touches, such as hand-carved headboards and chenille bedspreads, and folks seem friendly here. Just remember that the primary emphasis here isn't on hostellers but on hotel guests (hence the gift shop), and that the delights of Yellowstone aren't far away at all.

How to Get There:
By car: Call hostel for directions.

UTAH

The Lazy Lizard International Hostel

1213 South Highway 191, Moab, UT 84532
(435) 259-6057

E-mail: reservations@lazylizardhostel.com
Web site: www.lazylizardhostel.com
Rates: $9 per person; $26–$31 for private room or cabin
Credit cards: MC, VISA
Beds: 60
Private rooms: 10
Affiliation: None
Office hours: 8:00 a.m. to 8:00 p.m.
Extras: Television, hot tub, laundry, barbecue, Internet access, kitchen

You'll probably start hearing cheery college kids tell stories about the Lazy Lizard the second you get within 300 miles or so of Moab. The atmosphere here is unprecedented in its laid-backness; that's what its fans love about it. You will, too, if you're looking to make a dozen new best friends. Families and more "mature" (translation: older) travelers seeking solace may be overwhelmed here, however.

The hostel's design reflects its bargain-basement price tag. The ceilings are low, the sizable four- to eight-bedded dorm rooms are filled to the brim with beds, the kitchen can't accommodate more than a couple of people at a time, and there is a definite bathroom shortage. A bunch of log cabins offer a more upscale (and romantic) alternative, each fitted with beds, braided rug, and front porch. These are *not* to be confused with the hostel's interior private rooms, which are bare-bones and rather drab. Anyway, both non-dorm alternatives require walking outdoors to a central restroom.

Nevertheless, the hostel attracts a crowd that uses the overall space shortage to its advantage, and you're likely to find the Lazy Lizard more relaxed than restricting. Bonuses for all guests include a lavish hot tub and an outdoor patio with propane grill that's an ideal place to barbecue and mingle. Wild sunflowers add a charming touch to the grounds. The indoor television lounge is comfortable, too, the way a basement is in a fancy suburban home.

Arches National Park, one of the most fascinating natural wonders of the West, is only a few miles down the road. It is definitely worth a detour if it is not in your plans. The other major attraction in the area is mountain biking. Bikers rave about their days shredding around the area's trippy sandstone formations. The hostel fills with serious athletes who come to bike when temperatures cool down in spring and fall. Whitewater rafting is a more popular option in the summer, when the sweltering heat requires you to drink two gallons of agua daily. And Moab is a decent little town any time of year.

How to Get There:

By car: From Arches National Park, drive through the main commercial drag of Moab and at the opposite end (past all the stores) you will see a billboard for the hostel on the right side of the road. Driveway is a few hundred feet down on left (billboard will instruct you further).

The Avenues Hostel ♥

107 F Street, Salt Lake City, UT 84103

(801) 359-3855

  Fax: (801) 532-0182

  E-mail: hostel@sisna.com

  Rates: $16–$19 per person; $29–$45 for private room

  Credit cards: MC, VISA

Beds: 56
Private rooms: Yes
Affiliation: None
Office hours: 7:30 a.m. to 12:30 p.m.; 4:00 to 10:30 p.m.
Extras: Fireplace, bike rentals, parking, television, piano, laundry, shuttle, kitchen, Internet access

*S*alt Lake is just a little bit of a weird place, plain and simple. This Mormon bastion happens to be home to one of the biggest Saturday night cruising scenes we have ever witnessed. Pickup trucks full of college students and teenage boys drive up and down the main drags making catcalls at whatever female happens to be in their path. Not exactly what we expected. Lucky for you the Avenues is tucked away in a residential area, with a several-block buffer from the unfortunate downtown silliness.

Sure, there's the Mormon Tabernacle—very close by the hostel—and a bunch of chic restaurants, but a cultural mecca Salt Lake is not. The value of the area lies in its outskirts, where the world's best ski areas can be found. Utah is renowned for its dry powder, seen by many downhillers as a gift from God. Of course off-season there are unlimited hiking, biking, and rafting opportunities in the area. All of this is also only a forty-five-minute bus ride from the hostel.

Oh yes, the hostel. First, the good news: The neighborhood is ideal. When we asked about parking, one manager joked that not only could we park our car out front but we could also leave the keys in the ignition, the doors unlocked, and the car running all night, and it would still be there in the morning. After spending the night, we believe him. Rarely is a city hostel in such a safe, peaceful section of town. And the building is perfectly suited for a hostel, with the exception of a tight kitchen.

But that's where the happy feeling starts to end. This used to be a very good

> **Best bet for a bite:**
> *Supermarket a block away*
> **Insiders' tip:**
> *Alta ski resort has great snow and cheap tix*
> **What hostellers say:**
> *"Show me the moguls!"*
> **Gestalt:**
> *Snow business*
> **Safety:** *B*
> **Hospitality:** *D*
> **Cleanliness:** *D*
> **Party index:**

place, but of late it is going downhill *fast*. The common areas, once nice and commodious, are sagging—perhaps from overuse. Private rooms were once very comfortable with wide beds and firm mattresses, but wear and tear is showing and the kitchen was downright dirty when we came. This could be a nice place to wind down after a day shredding the slopes, but instead the frequent long-term guests (boarders) have made it less pleasant and more downbeat than ever before. It's rapidly becoming a sort of flophouse, and you don't need that. Avoid it until (if) things change.

How to Get There:

By airplane: Airport in Salt Lake City. Call hostel for free pickup, or take #50 bus all the way to the end and transfer to #3 bus. Get off at F Street and walk south to hostel.

By bus: Greyhound stops in Salt Lake City. Take #3 bus and get off on F Street. Walk south to hostel.

By car: Take Second Avenue east from Interstate 15 to F Street and turn left. Hostel is on left.

By train: Amtrak stops in Salt Lake City. Take #3 bus and get off on F Street. Walk south to hostel.

WYOMING

North Cache, Jackson, WY 83001

(307) 733-668; (800) 234-4507

  Web site: www.anvilmotel.com
  Rates: $25 per person
  Credit cards: MC, VISA
  Beds: 25
  Private rooms: Vary; call
  Private bathrooms: Vary; call
  Affiliation: None
  Office hours: 8:00 a.m. to 10:00 p.m.
  Extras: Laundry, television, kitchen, lockers

*P*art of the Anvil Motel, the red-roofed Bunkhouse fills up during the extreme seasons: summer, when hikers tackle the surrounding peaks, and winter, when Jackson becomes ski bum central.

A bunkhouse located in the hotel's basement, it offers very basic service: something of a kitchen, with a microwave and refrigerator; a large lounge; and lockers under your bunk for storing stuff. You also get the use of ski lockers, and believe us, hostellers use 'em. Unfortunately, showers here cost an additional six bucks per shower! Ouch. If you need more privacy than the massive bunkroom, get a cheap room at the attached Anvil.

How to Get There:
By car: Call hostel for directions.

> **Best bet for a bite:**
> *Billy's Burgers*
> **Hospitality:** *B*
> **Cleanliness:** *C*
> **Party index:**

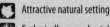 Attractive natural setting

 Ecologically aware hostel

 Superior kitchen facilities or cafe

 Offbeat or eccentric place

 Superior bathroom facilities

 Romantic private rooms

 Comfortable beds

A particularly good value

Wheelchair-accessible

Good for business travelers

Especially well-suited for families

Good for active travelers

 Visual arts at hostel or nearby

 Music at hostel or nearby

 Great hostel for skiers

 Bar or pub at hostel or nearby

Editors' choice: Among our very favorite hostels

Key to Icons

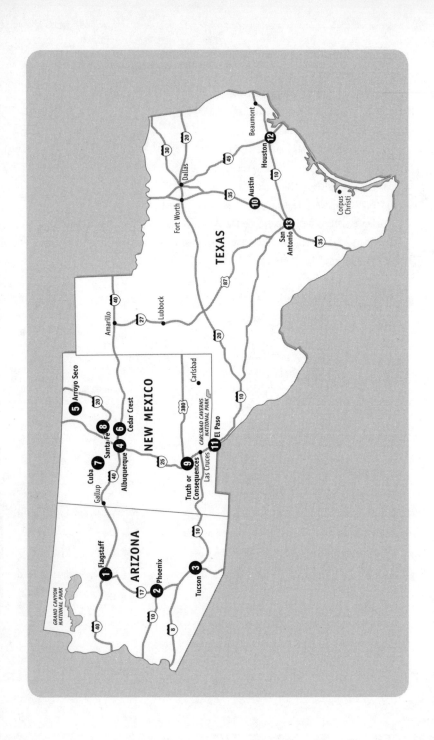

Southwest

ARIZONA

DuBeau International Hostel ✴✴✴✴

19 West Phoenix Street, Flagstaff, AZ 86001

(928) 774-6731; (800) 398-7112

Fax: (928) 774-6047

E-mail: info@dubeauhostel.com

Web site: www.grandcanyonhostel.com

Rates: $18–$20 per person; $41–$48 for private room

Credit cards: DISC, MC, VISA

Season: Early March to mid-October

Beds: 75

Private rooms: 8

Private bathrooms: 8

Affiliation: None

Office hours: 7:00 a.m. to 1:00 p.m.; 6:00 p.m. to midnight

Extras: Shuttle, grill, pool tables, television, VCR, tours, laundry, free pickups, free breakfast, coffee and tea, local phone, off-street parking

*T*he DuBeau Hostel has quite a reputation to sustain. The building is notorious in Arizona for its heyday decades ago, when it operated as a hotel under the same name—the first hotel in Flagstaff, we are told—and catered to a steady clientele of gangsters and prostitutes. In the 1970s Burt Reynolds checked into the joint while on location for a film shoot. Come hell or high water, the staff and guests at today's DuBeau are still up to the challenge of keeping their joint on the map, if only as a haven for people looking to hang out and have a good time.

The DuBeau is a magnet for the partying set. Planned and spontaneous parties regularly erupt in the multiroom common area. "Sometimes we just crank up the music and people get crazy," said one former manager who shall remain nameless (for now). Once, we dropped in at mid-afternoon in the off-season to find several guests communing to the sounds of New Age music. There seems to be a core group that hangs around the hostel day and night, holding the fort and trying to wash the hangovers out of their systems with java infusions.

The DuBeau's rooms are nice because they have only two bunks each, and each room has its own bathroom. The upkeep is about what you'd expect at such a laid-back place: suitable, but certainly not sparkling. The exception is a series of units that management has renovated a block down the way in a charming stone building with turquoise trim. Each of the spiffy southwestern-style units is graced with such luxuries as old Mexican-style tile work and authentic hardwood floors. These units are ideal for families.

Remember that summer is one high season here, when desert dwellers come to escape the parching heat (yeah, but it's a dry heat). Then winter sees another uptick, when a toned-down party atmosphere continues at the DuBeau for ski bums and their kin. Our tip? Come in spring or fall.

Best bet for a bite:
The Black Bean
Insiders' tip:
Brewery across street
What hostellers say:
"Bottoms up!"
Gestalt:
Wild West
Hospitality: *A*
Cleanliness: *B*
Party index:

How to Get There:
By airplane: Flagstaff has a small airport. Call hostel for pickup.
By bus: Call hostel for pickup.
By car: From Grand Canyon south rim: Take U.S. Highway 180 south into Flagstaff and turn right at Humphreys light. Follow to end and turn left on Santa Fe (U.S. Route 66) and then right onto Beaver. Hostel is 1 block down on left.

From the south (Phoenix, Tucson): Take Interstate 17 until it turns into South Milton Road and follow 1½ miles to Phoenix Avenue, then turn right. Hostel is on right.
By train: Amtrak stops in Flagstaff. From station walk 1 block south on Beaver. Hostel is on left.

Grand Canyon International Hostel
19½ South San Francisco, Flagstaff, AZ 86001
(928) 779-9421; (888) 442-2696 (U.S. and Canada)
  E-mail: reservations@grandcanyonhostel.com
  Web site: www.grandcanyonhostel.com

Rates: $18–$20 per person; $38–$45 for private room
Credit cards: None
Beds: 50
Private rooms: 8
Private bathrooms: Yes
Affiliation: None
Office hours: 7:00 a.m. to midnight
Extras: Shuttles, tours, free breakfast, in-room refrigerators, laundry, barbecue, television, VCR, Internet access, meals ($), kitchen

---

*T*his hostel is so much fun and so well equipped that the only noticeable flaw we found was that it was regularly booked to capacity in peak season, leaving latecomers a slim chance of snatching a bed. (There is a related hostel run by the same company, the DuBeau, around the corner.)

The Grand Canyon has two kitchens, a decent dining room, and cozy common area—and these facilities are not even the major draws to the place. People come here because they feel welcome. The staff are mostly young transitory internationals, as professional and friendly as any we've seen. Original owner Jeff Irvin had his finger on the pulse of hostelling when he opened this joint in 1995: He took what looked like an old hotel building and transformed it into a backpackers' mecca. While other hostel owners figure guests are happy just to have a bed and a television, Irvin took nothing for granted and built a base of backpacker loyalty that remains unsurpassed.

The building is decked in a nifty southwestern motif, much like the DuBeau. You're sure to be impressed by the adobe-colored walls, Native American stencils, and hardwood floors. Even the hallway lighting is set to fit the mood. Many of the walls are also peppered with murals, the mark of some quite talented work-exchange artists who have passed through the hostel. Rooms are a bit tight, but none has more than two bunks, all covered with Arizona-style bedspreads.

> **Best bet for a bite:**
> *Hip (note: it's vegetarian)*
> **Insiders' tip:**
> *Vertical relief climbing wall 1 block away*
> **What hostellers say:**
> *"Can I move in?"*
> **Gestalt:**
> *Canyon Ball*
> **Hospitality:** *A*
> **Cleanliness:** *A*
> **Party index:**

There's no lockout, no curfew, no rules prohibiting alcohol on the premises (but things never get out of hand, as far as we can tell). The hostel also offers great tours of the Canyon.

This place sets a great example for other hostels to follow. Check it out.

How to Get There:

By airplane: Flagstaff has a small airport. Call hostel for pickup.

By bus: Call hostel for pickup.

By car: From Grand Canyon south rim: Take U.S. Highway 180 into Flagstaff and turn right at Humphreys light. Follow to end and turn left on Santa Fe (U.S. Route 66) and then right onto Beaver. Left at next light onto Butler and another left at San Francisco. Hostel is 1½ blocks down on left.

From Interstate 40: Take exit 198 and turn right onto Butler Avenue. Follow for 2 miles; at fifth light turn right on San Francisco. Hostel is 1½ blocks on left.

From the south (Phoenix, Tucson): Take I-17 into Milton Road and follow 1½ miles to fifth light. Turn right on Butler and left at second light onto San Francisco. Hostel is 1½ blocks on right.

By train: Amtrak stops in Flagstaff. From station walk 1 block south on San Francisco. Hostel is on right.

Metcalf House Phoenix Hostel

1026 North Ninth Street, Phoenix, AZ 85006

(602) 254-9803

> **E-mail:** phxhostel@earthlink.net
> **Web site:** http://home.earthlink.net/~phxhostel
> **Rates:** $18 per Hostelling International member;
> **$35 for private room**
> **Credit cards:** No
> **Season:** Year-round except closed in August
> **Beds:** 14
> **Private rooms:** None
> **Affiliation:** Hostelling International
> **Office hours:** 8:00 to 10:00 a.m.; 5:00 to 10:00 p.m.
> **Extras:** Laundry, kitchen, piano

---

*H*ostelling International's entry in Arizona's capital city is surprisingly small—just fourteen beds in all, all in tight dorm rooms—and hard to spot from the outside thanks to lush vegetation covering the entryway. But don't count these as points against it: It is a lush little tree- and plant-lined surprise amidst downtown Phoenix's sea of concrete and steel. This hostel is both central and extremely welcoming, and it sports both a laundry and a homey kitchen: the salt 'n' pepper of essential hostelling. There are books, a globe, even a piano in the lounge—rumor has it that there's a musical bent to the place, in fact. You might try whipping out your double-O Martin, Gibson jumbo, or Telecaster and seeing what sorts of collaboration happen.

While in town, check out the botanical gardens in Papago Park: They showcase desert plant life in a way you've probably never seen before. There's also a good museum of Native American artifacts, as well as tons of restaurants and nightlife; pro baseball, football, and hockey; and of course the crystal-clear weather that predominates most of the year. You can even take a city bus out into the desert if you're so inclined (bring water; in summer, it gets dangerously hot out there).

How to Get There:

By airplane: From airport, take a shuttle Red line bus west to Central Bus Station, then take #10 bus east to Ninth Street and Roosevelt. Walk north; hostel is fifth house on west side of Ninth Street.

By bus: Greyhound stops in Phoenix. From Central Bus Station, take #10 bus east to Ninth Street and Roosevelt, then walk north; hostel is fifth house on west side of Ninth Street.

By car: Contact hostel for directions.

By train: Amtrak stops in Phoenix. Contact hostel for transit route.

Road Runner Hostel

346 East Twelfth Street, Tucson, AZ 85701

(520) 628-4709; (520) 940-7280

E-mail: roadrunr@dakotacom.net

Web site: www.roadrunnerhostel.com

Rates: $24 per person; $48 for private room

Credit cards: None

Beds: 18

Private/family rooms: 1

Single rooms: 1

Affiliation: None

Office hours: 7:00 a.m. to midnight

Extras: Air-conditioning, lockers, laundry, bike rentals, television, movies, free Internet access, juicer, bread machine, kitchen, pickups

This place gets raves for its staff and extras. Management has outfitted the place with a big-screen television as well as high-speed Internet so you won't have to wait like a million years to download—and, as a bonus, the service is free. There's even a juicer for juicing, since few of us bring our juicers on vacation. Movies are available for the terminally bored, but you won't be bored given the hostel's proximity to Tucson's downtown and the bustling nightlife.

Bed count in the shared accommodations is low, with just six beds per room. Private rooms are available, too, to avoid snorers and lame people who make noise very late at night or very early in the morning. Interestingly, the hostel was once the home of the deputy sheriff who nabbed the notorious bank robber John Dillinger.

Best bet for a bite:
Food Conspiracy Co-op on Fourth Avenue

Insiders' tip:
Bring carrots for juicing

What hostellers say:
"Beep beep!"

Gestalt:
Road rules

Safety: *B*

Hospitality: *A*

Cleanliness: *A*

Party index:

(We don't know if Dillinger was the guy so mean he once shot someone for snoring, but we know the urge.)

Last-minute hostellers will most likely find a bed given a day's notice but will need to book waaay ahead the first two weeks of February on account of Tucson's high season: winter. Come in summer and you'll appreciate the air-conditioning, a hostelling rarity.

Tours of the area are provided by the staff for an additional cost; they could include trips to the Arizona-Sonora Desert Museum, the town of Tombstone, the University of Arizona, or other places. Or you could hop across the border to Nogales, Mexico, and make your visit a tad more culturally interesting.

How to Get There:

By bus: Call hostel for pickup from Greyhound station.

By car: From I-10, take Broadway/Congress exit and go east at traffic light. Continue ½ mile and turn right on Fourth Avenue. At first stop sign, turn left onto Twelfth Street. Hostel is on right, at corner of Twelfth Street and Third Avenue.

By train: Call hostel for pickup from Amtrak station.

NEW MEXICO

Route 66 Hostel ✳✳✳

1012 Central Avenue Southwest, Albuquerque, NM 87102

(505) 247-1813

> **Web site:** www.rt66hostel.com
>
> **E-mail:** reservations@rt66hostel.com
>
> **Rates:** $20 per person; $25–$35 for private room
>
> **Credit cards:** None
>
> **Beds:** 30
>
> **Private rooms:** Yes
>
> **Affiliation:** None
>
> **Office hours:** 7:30 to 10:30 a.m.; 4:00 to 11:00 p.m.
>
> **Extras:** Herb garden, parking, free food, kitchen

*W*e won't lie to you: We had read some not-so-nice things about the Route 66 Hostel before we got here and were apprehensive when we arrived. To be honest, we were expecting an Alba-turkey. In fact, though, the place is all right. Not great, but all right.

An architectural anomaly, this large, welcoming hostel would look more at home on Cape Cod than in landlocked New Mexico. Though the interior leaves certain amenities to be desired, the place is perfectly located to serve as a home base while exploring the Land of Enchantment, as well as set in the backyard of some of the most happening neighborhoods in the city.

Best bet for a bite:
Lindy's diner
What hostellers say:
"Get your kicks."
Gestalt:
Number of the bunks
Hospitality: *B*
Cleanliness: *C*
Party index:

"One of the things we're best at is serving as guides to our guests," said one manager, a former aerospace engineer who ended up running the hostel for a while. He meant it literally: On top of great insights into what to do in the area—the staff is young, hip, and helpful—there is great info on day tours. Most hostellers are gone during the day, except maybe on holidays, which are celebrated in full force.

The hostel has a shabby elegance to it, manifested in contrasting ways. On the one hand, the place is a bit run-down: The subterranean men's dorm is hip if you like spelunking where you sleep; otherwise it's less than ideal. But it'll do. On the other hand, the grand second-story private rooms—capable of accommodating up to three hostellers apiece—are very good, most having their own bathrooms, and some even have private kitchen areas. Private apartments are available by the month, too.

According to hostel staffers, Albuquerque is a hidden treasure. That's debatable, but at least there is plenty to do downtown and on trendy Nob Hill nearby for a couple days. Additionally, the Pueblo Cultural Center, botanical gardens, and zoo are all easily reached, as is historic Old Town. Considering this and the easy access to all forms of transportation, this hostel is a keen, secure, New England–esque springboard for taking in New Mexico's largest city.

How to Get There:
By airplane: Airport nearby; call hostel for transit route.
By bus: Greyhound stops in town. Call hostel for transit route.

By car: Drive I-25 to Albuquerque; get off at Central Avenue going west (away from mountains).

By train: Amtrak stops in town. Call hostel for transit route.

The Abominable Snowmansion ✳✳✳✴

Taos Ski-Valley Road, Arroyo Seco, NM, (P.O. Box GG, Taos, NM 87571)
(505) 776-8298

E-mail: snowman@newmex.com
Web site: www.abominablesnowmansion.com
Rates: $18–$22 per person; $32–$54 for private room
Credit cards: MC, VISA
Beds: 38 to 80 (depending on season)
Private rooms: Yes
Affiliation: None
Office hours: 8:00 a.m. to noon; 4:00 to 10:00 p.m.
Extras: Storage, pool table, smoking lounge, camping, kitchen, Internet access, grill, laundry

---

*T*he Abominable Snowmansion has both winter and summer personalities. These personalities scarcely resemble each other because things change so drastically once the ski season starts. No matter when you arrive, though, the Snowmansion is a good bet.

First things first: Reports are mixed about downtown Taos. Some find it agreeable; some abhor its crass commercialism. We're cynical, so we side with the latter camp. But, in the end, you make the call. Arroyo Seco is where ranchers peacefully coexist with an influx of artists and craftspeople. It makes for an interesting mix. Management will point you in the direction of the area hot springs (clothing optional), which happen to be among the best we experienced in the West. Adjacent to the refreshing hot baths is an icy river perfect for swimming.

> **What hostellers say:**
> *"Great for skiers."*
> **Gestalt:**
> *Da bomb-inable*
> **Hospitality:** *A*
> **Cleanliness:** *A*
> **Party index:** 🎉🎉

The Snowmansion is arranged to offer hostellers a true New Mexican experience. The main building offers a pleasant southwestern motif, with a high-ceilinged common area and a balcony. More adventurous souls have the option of roughing it in one of the hostel tepees or bunkhouses, bare-bones shelters that you can later brag to your friends about having stayed in. The kitchen is spacious and well-equipped, a godsend in this relatively expensive corner of the universe that is the Southwest.

The hostel has a steady stream of people coming through in the summer, but things remain pretty relaxed. The activities of choice during this season seem to be hiking and hot springs–soaking. Overall Taos remains pretty active during the summer, with a melange of festivals and workshops going on. There is a lot of exploring to be done on the outskirts of downtown. Conspiracy theorists, writers, artists, and other interesting sorts run amok. A few miles outside of town is a community of Earthships (environmentally sound homes built from recycled tires) that offers tours. To find out what is really going on in the community, strike up a conversation with a local at the hot springs.

The ski crowd takes over in the winter. Taos is a first-class ski resort, and the hostel really packs in the bodies when there's snow on the mountain. All the extra bunks come out of the closets, and the place gets pretty crazy. On the upside, your breakfast is included in the price during ski season, and hostellers also have the option of going on a dinner meal plan during that time, as well.

How to Get There:

By bus: Take taxi from downtown Taos.

By car: From Taos Plaza (downtown), go north 4 miles on U.S. Highway 64/68 to traffic light, then east for 5 miles on New Mexico Highway 150 to Arroyo Seco. Hostel is on left.

Attractive natural setting	Comfortable beds	Visual arts at hostel or nearby
Ecologically aware hostel	A particularly good value	Music at hostel or nearby
Superior kitchen facilities or cafe	Wheelchair-accessible	Great hostel for skiers
Offbeat or eccentric place	Good for business travelers	Bar or pub at hostel or nearby
Superior bathroom facilities	Especially well-suited for families	Editors' choice: Among our very favorite hostels
Romantic private rooms	Good for active travelers	

Key to Icons

Sandia Mountain Hostel

12234 Highway 14N, Cedar Crest, NM 87008

(505) 281-4117

Rates: $14 per person; $35 for private room

Credit cards: None

Beds: 25

Private rooms: Yes

Affiliation: None

Office hours: 4:30 to 10:00 p.m.

Extras: Laundry, porch swing, kitchen

NOTE: Always call ahead about availability.

This out-of-the-way hostel has its pros and cons. For starters, it's appropriately set in the Sandia Mountains, famous for their arid beauty and bountiful hiking opportunities. The actual grounds of the place, a tumbling disarray of half-rebuilt cars and run-down cabins for warm-weather boarders, don't do the locale justice. On the plus side, the hostel's modern and spiffy main building—built expressly for lodging travelers—is as wheelchair-accessible as they come.

Yet it's just a bit too far from Albuquerque to conveniently get there without a car (there's no public transportation to Cedar Crest) and too close to Albuquerque along gorgeous New Mexico Highway 14 to make it a reasonable stop for cyclists or hitchhikers making the scenic trek north to Santa Fe or Taos.

Best bet for a bite:
Cedar Salad
What hostellers say:
"Nice setting."
Gestalt:
Meat is murder
Hospitality: *B*
Cleanliness: *A*
Party index:

Still, Sandia Mountain will do you right if you need a place to crash after a day of tromping, especially if you have friends to keep you company. The dorm rooms in the main building are super clean, and the kitchen facilities are expansive and accommodating, capable of seating many and backed by an enormous woodstove used to heat the building. Hostellers seem to eat communally, and "90 percent are vegetarians," according to one herbivorous tenant. There is no limit to how long you can stay, said one of the managers. "[But] if you're not nice, we tell you the limit's three days," she joked.

Sandia Mountain is welcoming enough. It's a subdued place with few draws in terms of entertainment once the sun goes down, other than a quiet game of Scrabble. The doors lock at night, but hostellers are given the combination to the door so they may come and go as they please. Showers and bathrooms, both pristine, are available for a fee to those not spending the night.

Private rooms, located in the office building and in small houses out by the auto grave-yard, are cute enough, though perhaps not worth the extra cost unless you're really big on personal space.

How to Get There:

By car: New Mexico Highway 14 (from Albuquerque: exit 175 north off Interstate 40; from Santa Fe: exit 278 south off Interstate 25). Travel north on Highway 14 to mile marker 3. Travel ½ mile more and hostel is on the east side of Highway 14. (Look for the sign with a donkey on it.)

Circle A Ranch Hostel

510 Los Pinos Road, Cuba, NM 87013
(505) 289-3350

> **Web site:** www.circlearanchhostel.com
> **Rates:** $20 per person; $50–$60 for private room
> **Credit cards:** AMEX, DISC, MC, VISA
> **Season:** May 15 to October 15
> **Beds:** 32
> **Private rooms:** 4
> **Private bathrooms:** 1
> **Affiliation:** None
> **Office hours:** Vary; call
> **Extras:** Horses, bears, lynx, library, kitchen

"*N*ot for everyone, perfect for some," reads one brochure for this idyllic hideaway. The only reason we can imagine anyone passing up a stay here is that they couldn't find this 330-acre dreamland, set in an orchard high in the Nacimiento Mountains. "People who come here tend to need to be here. Often, they don't realize how badly they needed to get away," noted one bubbly manager, whose family had owned this former hunting lodge for more than forty years at the time we visited.

It's no surprise that the hostel—sublimely arcadian, complemented by a herd of roaming horses, and a tarn for warm-weather swimming—is for many a final destination, rather than a stop along a route. The house itself is as stately as it is rustic: With a fireplace so big you could pitch your tent in it, it conjures images of an English country estate after a fox hunt. (Animal pelts are a ubiquitous means of decoration.) Upstairs four creaky, quaintly named private rooms are oh-so-charming, with (be still our hearts!) brass beds and cast-iron tubs available. Though less striking, the dorm space (a bunkroom, basically) is quite pleasant. Hostellers should be gentle with the "country plumbing," though.

Hiking trails are well-marked, and strolls to the lovely High Meadow and The Big Tree (the biggest piñon tree in North America) are recommended, as is simply lounging around the patio. The place is pretty much without rules: Don't feed the bears, a staffer told us, and swim at your own risk. Otherwise, folks are allowed to do as they please, mostly because the hostel attracts a mature crowd rather than college kids on spring break: folks looking for a bed-and-breakfast feel without a heavy price tag rather than ones looking for a beer blast beneath the stars.

Reservations are suggested, due to the place's enormous popularity. But beware of the occasional gaggle of geologists who book the place solid. They're dangerous. Really. Not.

Best bet for a bite:
BYOF (where F=food)
What hostellers say:
"One-of-a-kind experience."
Gestalt:
Havana good time
Hospitality: *A*
Cleanliness: *B*
Party index:

How to Get There:

By bus: Take Greyhound from Albuquerque to Cuba; call hostel for pickup.
By car: From Albuquerque, take I-25 to New Mexico Highway 44 north. Turn right through gate at mile marker 65, drive 5⅒ miles, always going left when road forks. Road turns to dirt before leading to the hostel.

Santa Fe International Hostel

1412 Cerrillos Road, Santa Fe, NM 87501

(505) 988-1153

E-mail: santafehostel@comcast.net

Web site: www.users.qwest.net/~epreston1/

Rates: $12–$18 per person; $45 for private room

Credit cards: None

Beds: 90

Private rooms: 4

Private bathrooms: Yes

Affiliation: None

Office hours: 7:00 a.m. to 11:00 p.m.

Extras: Piano, guitar, lockers, alarm clocks, stamps, kitchen, off-street parking, Internet access, grills

This busy downtown pit stop represents the bare-bones tradition of hostelling, both in philosophy and amenities. With enough bunks to board nearly one hundred hostellers during Santa Fe's tourist-infested summer and Christmas seasons, the hostel is sociable and convenient. Management insists that this urban refuge is committed first and foremost to hostellers, and an out-of-state picture identification is required of all guests. The backpacking variety will find the best treatment.

That's probably just as well, as these digs aren't glamorous by any stretch of the imagination. They're more of a crash pad, with a "put 'em where we can" credo in regard to sleeping space. Management will ask guests to do a chore or two while they're here as well—and it's not really optional. This suits easygoing travelers just fine, but those who are looking for a quiet place to withdraw may do better elsewhere. The sparkling industrial-strength kitchen is a huge improvement over its diminutive predecessor, though.

Despite sometimes-dingy dorm rooms with four to seven beds, the hostel is quite a swinging hangout, centered on an attractive courtyard with grills and flower gardens. Communal barbecues and informal social actions, ranging from impromptu musical jams to Trivial Pursuit marathons, are the norm. The crowd is decidedly international—helpful tourist pidgin in several languages is posted to facilitate communication—as is its live-in staff, for which management claims foreign travelers are consistently grateful. Most guests we interviewed did not give the staff such high marks, though; many commented that the folks who run the place have a habit of being aloof.

As a guide to Santa Fe and the surrounding area, this hostel is well-equipped: Maps, brochures, and recommendations line the front hall. Really, though, if you're interested in the city and its plaza, all you have to do is head outside. The hostel is that well-placed. City bus lines stop right outside the door, but with all the town's nooks and crannies to discover, it might be worth the 1½-mile walk. With dozens of outgoing backpackers on hand, it shouldn't be hard to find someone to keep you company. Just remember, if you come in winter (the place is open year-round, with long office hours—a plus): This is at 7,000 feet of elevation. It can and does snow, sometimes a lot.

How to Get There:

By airplane: Small airport in Santa Fe, or fly into Albuquerque and take shuttle. Call hostel for transit route.
By bus: Greyhound stops downtown. Call hostel for transit route.
By car: Drive I-25 to exit 278 (Cerrillos Road); or take Cerrillos Road exit from U.S. 84 (St. Francis Drive).

Riverbend Hot Springs Hostel ✳✳✳✳✳

100 Austin Street, Truth or Consequences, NM 87901
(575) 894-7625
   E-mail: riverbendsprings@gmail.com
   Web site: www.nmhotsprings.com
   Rates: $24 per person; $45–$89 for private room (discounts for AAA members and students)
   Credit cards: AMEX, DISC, MC, VISA
   Beds: 16

Private rooms: 4

Affiliation: None

Office hours: 8:00 a.m. to 10:00 p.m.

Extras: Air-conditioning, mineral baths, tepees, river deck, laundry, barbecue, Internet access

*T*his place just keeps on keeping on, one of the most distinctive hostels in North America (perhaps the world), and one of the most fun, too. The fact that it's pretty well kept-up, and incredibly friendly, only enhance the experience further.

Right from the get-go, it's an amazing concept: a hostel with a hot mineral bath right on the premises. Think about *that* the next time you're stuck shoehorned into a grimy urban hostel bed anywhere else in the world. Twice daily a giant tub on a porch overlooking the Rio Grande is filled with steaming spring water for your soaking pleasure. This is no hangout for bored retirees, nor is it a luxe spa; instead, it's a place for healing the weary mind and body. At the hostel, travelers roll out of bed at 8:00 a.m. and into the hot springs. Starting your day by relaxing has a strikingly intoxicating effect, putting an interesting spin on the morning.

"The spirit draws you here and you either obey it or you don't," said one manager. "Lots of people seem to have some kind of magical spiritual experience here. It has something to do with the energy of the place."

Okay. All we know is, an ever-changing corps of work exchangers is on hand to learn various ous arts ranging from organic gardening to alternative architecture, and they keep things moving smoothly here. The hostel is closely in tune with the area's indigenous cultures— something they don't even advertise, but it's there. They encourage people to feel their own way around by heading out to the area's ghost towns, cliff dwellings, and mountain outposts. You'll even notice an emergence pictograph on one of the buildings, too, if you look sharp enough.

Truth or Consequences has an excellent little museum where you can learn all

Best bet for a bite:
Cheap diners downtown

Insiders' tip:
Elephant Butte Lake

What hostellers say:
"Love the springs!"

Gestalt:
Truth is "Out There"

Hospitality: *B*

Cleanliness: *B*

Party index: 🎉🎉🎉🎉

about the local area, including the origins of the town's name: formerly named Hot Springs, it changed its name in 1950 to that of a popular radio show to gain publicity. The deal was, the radio show would broadcast to thousands of listeners from the town if they took the bait, thus attracting the attention of an unlimited tourist base. It worked. (Of course, this was before selling out was unfashionable.) The town still holds an annual festival in honor of Ralph Edwards, the original host of the radio show. We have no idea why.

Anyway, in the aftermath of the name change, a lot of mainstreamers—elderly folks with arthritis, rich urban types, and so forth—descended on the town en masse. The artists and counterculture types stayed on and kept coming back, and to this day "T or C" remains an oddly balanced mix of eccentrics and retirees.

Back to the hostel. Hostellers have a bunch of housing options here. Men typically stay in the mobile home dorm, painted with an Old West facade, which is crowded but cozy. Women stay in a similarly crowded dorm room in a neighboring building. The more adventurous may opt to stay in a tepee, though there are now only two, one of which is sometimes commandeered by the dreaded long-term hostellers. If you seek more privacy and comfort, the private efficiency units, complete with private kitchen and bathroom, are among the nicest we've seen. Or you can share your own trailer with another couple for a bit less. However, one of our hostel snoops reports that the trailers were a little "smelly" and the grounds were messy.

Some of the guests never left the hostel during the two days we were there, hanging out by the river the entire day. If you want to go exploring, though, there is no shortage of things to do. Staff have an entire list with all the specifics, down to how much time you should allot for each activity. Follow their advice and do not come with any expectations. You may be disappointed with the place at first; on the surface it does look a bit shabby. But if you relax, talk to people, and let the area consume your psyche, then you are sure to leave with some groovy memories.

How to Get There:

By bus: Greyhound stops in town. Call hostel to arrange free pickup.

By car: From I-25 take exit 75 onto Broadway in downtown Truth or Consequences. Follow Broadway straight for 2½ miles to Austin Street and turn right. Hostel is on left.

TEXAS

Austin International Hostel ✳✳✳✳

2200 South Lakeshore Boulevard, Austin, TX 78741

(512) 444-2294

Fax: (512) 444-2309
E-mail: hostel@hiaustin.org
Web site: www.hiaustin.org
Rates: $19 per Hostelling International member
Credit cards: AMEX, MC, VISA
Beds: 42
Private rooms: None
Affiliation: Hostelling International
Office hours: 8:00 a.m to 10:00 p.m.
Extras: Laundry, television, VCR; bike, kayak, and canoe rentals; shuttles, Internet access, kitchen, lockers, piano, live music

Robert Earl Keen Jr., Lyle Lovett, Nanci Griffith, Waylon Jennings, Willie Nelson, Steve Earle, on and on: names synonymous with the high homegrown music standards that Austin—self-proclaimed capital of live music (at least of a certain, new-country style)—demands. And Austin's little hostel so clearly lives up to these standards, by serving both as a great place to stay and an introduction to that music, that it leaves many of its fellow hostels in the United States lying in the dust.

Occupying a former covered pool that was completely renovated with tons of volunteer help, this hostel has a superb location. Not only is it a hop, skip, and jump from downtown without the frenzy, but it's also set right on Town Lake (which is actually a slow-moving section of the Colorado River), a wonderfully tranquil spot to bike along trails or watch wood ducks and University of Texas crew teams ply the water. Yes, you can rent a cycle here, too.

We're getting ahead of ourselves, though. Hostels this great start at the top, and the managers are very involved with the daily activities. Their staff get lots of points for friendliness and helpfulness, and they take their ecology seriously here, too, recycling anything they can and using eco-friendly materials, natural pesticides, and so on.

Best bet for a bite:
Ruby's or Stubbs BBQ
Insiders' tip:
Cactus Cafe for music
What hostellers say:
"Have Gibson, will travel."
Gestalt:
Lone Star
Safety: *B*
Hospitality: *A*
Cleanliness: *A*
Party index: 🎉🎉

Dorm rooms are outfitted with comfortable handmade bunks and are nicer than one would expect from a hostel. There are up to a dozen bunks per room, perhaps the only true drawback of this place—no privacy. (Its distance from downtown could also be a negative, but bus services take care of that.) Keep in mind that this hostel is in high demand and advance reservations are recommended. The hostel hosts live music just about every night of the week, featuring local up-and-comers who just might be the next big thing to come out of Austin.

Hostel staff can help you find lots to do in town, including checking out a wildflower research center or visiting the university. But let's be honest: You're here for the music, especially if you come in March (the glitzy South by Southwest music festival) or May (the more laid-back Kerrville Folk Festival in the hills). Any time of year, though, there's someone talented playing at a little hole in the wall downtown. It's always a great pleasure to discover someone terrific but unknown. Some of our favorite clubs include the Cactus Cafe, La Zona Rosa, The Broken Spoke, and Antone's, among many others; there are a million more to pick from, too.

Eats around town run the gamut from natural foods (Whole Foods Market is headquartered here) to barbecue (many great joints) to burgers and beyond, thanks to the city's huge college-student and state government employee populations. Bring a map, though, if you go exploring; Austin's traffic patterns and signage are as confusing as any we've seen in much bigger cities. You're bound to get lost. There's also lots of Americana to explore in the surrounding countryside if you've got a car: the cowboy town of Bandera, the state parks of the Hill Country coming ablaze with flowers each spring, the old Germanic buildings of Fredericksburg, and so much more.

Only quibbles we heard? Staff wake you up at 10:00 a.m.; very reasonable, we thought, but a few night-owl hostellers disagreed. Also, a few long-termers sometimes set up shop here, hogging the TV and otherwise hanging around a lot. But that's a small price to pay for staying at a hostel that actually gets the local community involved and, by so doing, teaches both hostellers and locals that there's more to this big old world than they imagined.

From the free laundry powder to hall phones that take incoming calls, every hostel manager ought to take a look at this place and get a few ideas. And the management has always been responsive to hostellers' comments and criticism. This is a great place. Still.

How to Get There:

By airplane: Airport nearby. Take #20 bus to Capitol; then take #26 or #27 to Lakeshore Boulevard.

By bus: Greyhound stops in Austin. Take #7 bus to Lakeshore Boulevard, then walk to #2200 on river side of street.

By car: Take Interstate 35 to Riverside Drive exit; go east on Riverside. Turn left at hostel sign and follow to hostel on left; if you miss sign, continue past HEB grocery store to Pleasant Valley Road; turn left, go to Lakeshore Boulevard, then turn left. Hostel is on right.

By train: Amtrak stops in Austin. Take #22 bus, then change to #26 or #27 bus to Lakeshore.

Gardner (El Paso) International Hostel

311 East Franklin Avenue, El Paso, TX 79901

(915) 532-3661

 Fax: (915) 532-0302

 Web site: www.elpasohostel.com

 Rates: $24.00–$25.50 per person; $51–$75 for private room

 Credit cards: MC, VISA

 Beds: 32

 Private rooms: Yes

 Affiliation: None

 Office hours: Twenty-four hours

 Extras: Television, laundry, storage, lockers, pool table, kitchen, Internet access

---

*T*his hostel is housed in the pseudo-historic Gardner Hotel, a seventy-five-year-old building that is marked by a conflicting blend of charm and neglect. The Gardner is El Paso's oldest continuously running hotel; it has fifty rooms, about ten of which are dedicated to the hostel. Most of the hostellers who come through are either coming from or going to Mexico, and many take advantage of the hostel's long-term storage facilities.

If you are unfamiliar with El Paso, you may be struck by the urban desolation that surrounds the Gardner's neighborhood, which is actually the city's downtown business district, if you can believe it. During the day enough people are out and about to make the case that this is really a city, but at night things slow nearly to a halt. Many people opt to run for the border in search of action, as the schmaltzy Mexican town of Juarez is only a 1-mile jog away.

At first glance the Gardner seems like it *could* be a welcome refuge from El Paso's relentless depression and the weariness of the cross-country drive: the spacious lobby has been brilliantly restored to its original grandeur with a marble staircase, gracious leather furniture (we think it's real leather, anyway), and a prominent oak front desk.

Once you get past the lobby, though, things are pretty standard and the quality of your stay is marked more by the hostellers around you than the creaky metal beds or the stench of cigarette smoke in the rooms. The hotel and hostel are mostly filled with long-term residents or even transients, and a segment of that group resides here. Staff can be rude or pushy, as you might expect. Dorm rooms have four beds, and a toilet and shower room connects two units; they're strung out along vaguely gloomy halls. Any socializing goes on in the lobby or the basement common area. The latter offers a generous amount of space in the form of a kitchen, pool table, and television room but is also rather run-down. It could be a good or even great place, but sorry; it's not.

How to Get There:
By bus: Greyhound stops in El Paso. Walk about 3 blocks north on Santa Fe (then left with the bus station behind you), still on Santa Fe Street, to Franklin, and turn right. Hostel is 5 blocks down on the left.
By car: Exit Interstate 10 at Kansas or Stanton Streets. Hostel is on Franklin (2 blocks south of I-10), between Kansas and Stanton.
By train: Amtrak stops in El Paso. From station, exit to left, then turn right on Mission. Walk down to Stanton and turn right; hostel is 1 block down.

Houston International Hostel

5302 Crawford, Houston, TX 77004

(713) 523-1009

   E-mail: resv@houstonhostel.com

   Web site: www.houstonhostel.com

   Rates: $17 per person

   Credit cards: JCB

   Beds: 31

   Private rooms: None

   Affiliation: None

   Office hours: 8:00 to 10:00 a.m.; 5:00 to 11:00 p.m.

   Extras: Laundry, lockers, television, piano, bikes, kitchen

*H*ouston, we have a problem. The first thing we spotted at this hostel, walking onto the front porch, was a sign sternly announcing NO SMOKING ALLOWED. Next to the sign was an ashtray filled with cigarette butts. That gives you the flavor of the place in a nutshell: The hostel, located in what appears to be a pretty funky area—and one that's not terribly far from downtown, either—just doesn't live up to what it might be, certainly not what a city as big and diverse as Houston deserves.

The management has the right attitude about hostelling, mind you: They'll be glad to give you an earful about why small hostels are the lifeblood of the movement. Once the owner finishes telling you how much she hates to see hostellers spread out and live in a place like it was their own, though, you turn around to find a bunch of old guys with their feet up on the couch controlling the television like there's no tomorrow.

Half the guests, in fact, seemed to be long-termers here, a practice that isn't exactly discouraged. Their stuff (they were almost all guys) was piled high in the tiny bunkrooms, and the odor of unwashed clothing was overpowering. There is a laundry here; they just obviously don't use it. Positives? The women's dorm was cleaner, though each smallish room still contained eight bunks, which was too many. The morning bathroom situation was a little tricky because sink, shower, and toilet are all contained in one room, and there's only one of each. We like the idea of separating each facility for those anxious early-morning moments, but this place needs more plumbing. Our tip? Get yourself spruced up at night to avoid the hassle.

Chores are rigidly enforced or not enforced at all, producing a hostel that wasn't really as clean as we'd expected it to be. The kitchen is pretty decent, though, as is the big front porch and a nice courtyard area off to the side. We did notice, too, that international travelers of every stripe do make their way here, making things more interesting than the American live-ins ever possibly could. The real emphasis here is on the common area, which features the television and outdated computer games as well as a number of couches and other places to meet and greet.

This hostel's location is okay: You're very close to the city's tragically hip Montrose neighborhood, where outdoor coffee shops and chic art galleries mingle with "ice houses" (garages that pull up their doors at night to reveal honky-tonkin' streetside bars) and cowboy-boot outlets. It's one of the most interesting urban neighborhoods you'll find. Just don't walk east of the hostel at all at night; it's a dangerous area, and little-trafficked to boot.

Also within walking distance are an astonishing concentration of museums: at least seven, by our count, plus a bunch of little and big parks. This is wonderful because Houston's downtown traffic often turns out to be a hot, muggy nightmare of construction signs, detours, and backups. Best just to stick around the neighborhood. Want a bike to look around? Shouldn't be a problem, because the hostel also owns a big bike shop next door.

Food is surprisingly glorious around here, too. Houston is stuffed to the gills with an incredible array of quality affordable eats, ranging from Vietnamese and barbecue to anything else you could possibly desire. This is one of America's better food towns, believe it or not, so you won't be short on choice. This is a good thing, because you'll probably want to eat out after a few minutes of hanging out among the couch potatoes.

How to Get There:
By airplane: Two large airports in Houston. Call hostel for transit route.
By bus: Greyhound stops in Houston. From Greyhound station take #8, #15, or #65 bus down South Main Street to Rice University area; walk east to Crawford.

By car: Take I-45 or I-10 to U.S. Highway 59 south exit. Head south on 59 to Fannin Road exit; go left at stop sign, left again on Oakdale, then right on Crawford. Hostel is on right.
By train: Amtrak stops in Houston. Take #2 or #4 bus to South Main Street in Rice University area, then walk east to Crawford.

San Antonio International Hostel
621 Pierce Street at East Grayson Street
San Antonio, TX 78208
(210) 223-9426
   Fax: (210) 299-1479
   Rates: $18 per person
   Credit cards: MC, VISA
   Beds: 38
   Private rooms: 3
   Affiliation: None
   Office hours: 8:00 a.m. to 10:00 p.m.
   Extras: Pool, information desk, breakfast, Internet access, kitchen

---

*T*his hostel is part of a gorgeous bed-and-breakfast inn outside a very popular city. But it's just not worth a stay, especially when you factor in its distance from the center and the general indifference-bordering-on-rudeness of the staff.

The main building, Bullis House, was built by a military "hero" who (among other things) hunted down Native Americans in Mexico and helped capture Geronimo. It's a beautiful building, but the women's dorm is located in the basement, and female hostellers aren't completely thrilled with that location—more than one gal claims to have run shrieking from a rodent! The guys' dorm is in an attached building that reminds you of a barracks. The kitchen is so-so. Most folks seem okay about the common space, which does come replete with comfy chairs for hanging out and swapping stories with fellow hostellers. There's very little to eat in the area, though; the hostel lays out a continental breakfast of muffins, cereal, and juice. Hostellers can also use the pool out back, if it's open (and clean).

On the third floor of the main building, above the bed-and-breakfast rooms, are several good private rooms. These are your best bet; they offer top-floor views, privacy, televisions, and much nicer bathrooms than the dorms. You also get the run of a completely empty common space—just a few rugs up there—but it's something.

It's too bad that the location of this hostel isn't the greatest, unless you've got a car. This is an iffy neighborhood bounded by an army base on one side and an interstate highway on the other. Consequently, there's almost nothing to do; not a grocery store (except a quickie-mart), not a good restaurant (just a few extremely unremarkable joints), not even a decent bar (except an enlisted-men's hangout). Public transit options consist of two buses—yes, you have to *change* buses to get here—that head downtown fairly regularly, but we wouldn't stand out here at night and wait for them.

If you do have wheels, you're ten minutes or less from all of downtown San Antonio's attractions. Everyone will tell you to head for the Riverwalk, so go ahead. Just don't expect to be there alone; it's very popular. You can certainly enjoy yourself lounging around at the cafes and restaurants if you like, though. Afterward tool out to the countryside for a look at the springs, state parks, and Hill Country that really make this part of Texas so unique and picturesque.

Our pick for the ultimate Texas experience? Head for Gruene (pronounced "green") Hall, 25 miles away, on the weekends for live honky-tonkin' in the state's oldest dance hall. Or if you come in February, don't miss the San Antonio Stock Show and Rodeo; it's a very interesting event, very, very close to the hostel, and one that mysteriously doesn't book the place full.

How to Get There:

By airplane: Airport nearby. Call hostel for transit route.

By bus: Greyhound stops in San Antonio. Take #11 or #15 bus. Call hostel for transit route.

By car: Take Interstate 35 to New Braunfels Road exit; go north on New Braunfels Road, then left on Grayson and left on Pierce. Hostel is on corner.

By train: Amtrak stops in San Antonio. Take #516 bus to Grayson; walk down Pierce to hostel.

West Coast

Page numbers follow hostel names

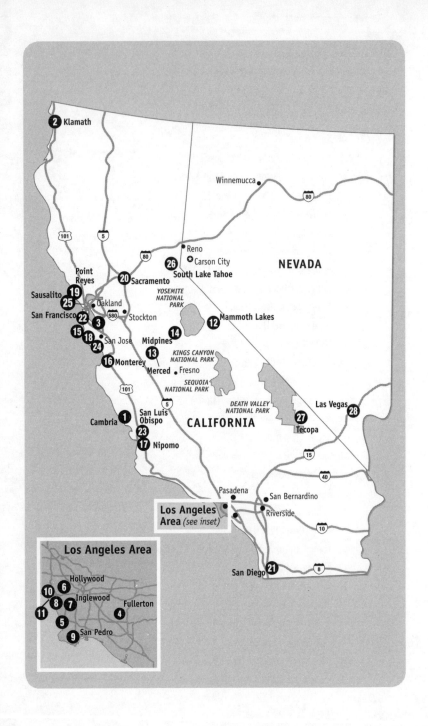

Klamath ②

Winnemucca

Reno
Carson City ✿
South Lake Tahoe

NEVADA

Point
Reyes

Sacramento ⑳ ㉖

YOSEMITE
NATIONAL
PARK

Sausalito ⑲ ㉕
San Francisco ㉒ ③
Oakland
Stockton
580

⑫ Mammoth Lakes

⑮
⑱ ㉔
San Jose

Midpines

⑭
⑬

KINGS CANYON
NATIONAL
PARK

⑯ Monterey

Merced ● Fresno

SEQUOIA
NATIONAL PARK

101

DEATH VALLEY
NATIONAL
PARK

Las Vegas

Cambria ❶ ①
San Luis
Obispo

⑤

CALIFORNIA

㉗ ㉘
Tecopa

㉓
⑰ Nipomo

15

Pasadena

Los Angeles
Area (see inset)

San Bernardino
Riverside

40

10

San Diego ㉑

8

Los Angeles Area

Hollywood

⑩ ⑥
⑧ ⑦ Inglewood
⑪

Fullerton

④

⑤
⑨ San Pedro

CALIFORNIA

Bridge Street Inn Hostel ✳✳✳✳

4314 Bridge Street, Cambria, CA 93428

(805) 927-7653

E-mail: bridgestreetinn@yahoo.com

Rates: $22 per Hostelling International member; $45–$65 for private room

Credit cards: MC, VISA

Season: Open daily from March to November; open by reservation only, December to February

Beds: 15

Private rooms: Yes

Affiliation: Hostelling International

Office hours: 8:30 to 10:30 a.m.; 5:00 to 9:00 p.m.

Extras: Kitchen

*T*his small white home contains a mini-hostel that's perhaps most notable for its lush lawn (onto which both a volleyball court and a croquet section have been laid out). It's a quiet spot with access to world-famous Hearst Castle, whale-watching, seal-watching, and the like.

The best thing about the place, inside, is the decor: lacy white frills, white-print wallpapers, and wooden chairs and furniture. This place would not be out of place at all on the Maine coast as a B&B. Yet there's a kitchen, too. It's all kept super-clean, and both ownership and staff were unfailingly friendly so far as we could tell.

As a further bonus, as if you needed one, the hostel's just a mile from cute Moonstone Beach on knockout Highway 1, and almost exactly halfway betwixt El Lay and San Fran.

Best bet for a bite:
Main Street Grill
What hostellers say:
"Cute little number."
Gestalt:
Yes we Cambria!
Hospitality: *A*
Cleanliness: *A*
Party index: 🎉

How to Get There
By car: Contact hostel for directions.

Redwood National Park Hostel ✳✳✳✳✳

14480 California Highway 101 (at Wilson Creek Road), Klamath, CA 95548
(707) 482-8265

Fax: (707) 482-4665

E-mail: info@redwoodhostel.com

Web site: www.redwoodhostel.com

Rates: $20 per Hostelling International member; $49 for private room

Credit cards: DISC, JCB, MC, VISA

Season: Open every day March to October; call ahead for open dates November to
March

Beds: 26

Private rooms: 2

Affiliation: Hostelling International

Office hours: 8:00 to 11:00 a.m.; 4:00 to 10:00 p.m.

Extras: Laundry, library, Internet access

*R*ight out the front door is a classic scene: the pounding Pacific, doing its level best to
bash a bunch of big rocks to smithereens; mist dripping from the trees; rumors of
eagles and whales and redwoods the size of a house filtering in on the wind.

You've reached Northern California.

This hostel has got more location in its little finger than most hostels can muster up in
their whole body, and an amazing place is just getting better and better every year thanks to
careful management. Tear yourself away from the views, and you'll discover a common room
stocked with games and books. Travelers seem to mix well here. Or they use the laundry—
useful after outdoors adventures—before retiring to packed bunkrooms. The lone double
room here sure is nice: a good look at the ocean out the windows, a good comfortable bed,
and art on the walls. Definitely one of the more romantic double rooms you can rent at a
hostel. (There's a single room available, as well.)

Give this hostel extra points for super educational displays around the building, too,
from a good documentation of local Native American tribes (rooms are named for them)
to a courageously honest description of the destructive local logging practices. The managers here are also expert at guiding hostellers to such outdoor activities as whale-watching
(gray whales have been known to congregate at a point just south of the hostel); redwoods-

gazing (an 8-mile hike leads to the world's biggest); and other fun Northern California stuff. If you're sticking around, hang out on the deck adorned with weatherbeaten picnic tables and chairs. Friendlier management of this hostel is striving to give guests a more positive experience by revising the previously super-strict rules, though you can expect a half-day lockout, so be prepared.

One more thing: Plan ahead for the fact that there's no nearby food except for a tiny market. It's a 2-mile walk to a little general store, the closest, but we would advise stocking up in Crescent City (if you're coming from the north) or Arcata (if you're northbound). The managers will sell you light groceries if you forget about eating until it's too late to shop.

How to Get There:

By bus: Greyhound service to Arcata (60 miles away); from Arcata Redwood Coast Transit stops at hostel twice daily by request. Call hostel for details.
By car: Drive U.S. Highway 101 to 12 miles south of Crescent City (or 7 miles north of Klamath); turn east onto Wilson Creek Road. Hostel is immediately on right.

Hidden Villa Hostel ✳✳✳✳
26870 Moody Road, Los Altos Hills, CA 94022
(650) 949-8648
  Fax: (650) 949-8608
  E-mail: hostel@hiddenvilla.org
  Web site: www.hiddenvilla.org
  Rates: $20 per Hostelling International member; $40 for private room
  Credit cards: MC, VISA
  Season: Year-round except closed June through August
  Beds: 34

Private rooms: 3
Affiliation: Hostelling International
Season: *Closed* from June through August; open the rest of the year
Office hours: 8:00 a.m. to noon; 4:00 to 9:30 p.m.
Extras: Piano, woodstove, radio, kitchen

*W*e were pretty surprised the first time we learned that the very first hostel established in the western United States is not only still standing but is also quite active. We were also downright pleased to find that Hidden Villa, tucked into one of the steep ridges that separate Silicon Valley from the blue Pacific, remains an oasis of major-league peace and quiet on the brink of one of America's fastest-growing urban areas.

The place is really a living monument to Josephine and Frank Duveneck, who lived full, generous lives here and established the first hostel west of the Hudson way back in 1937. Today the 1,600-acre Hidden Villa complex remains true to their vision. It consists of a working organic farm, a summer camp, an educational center, a bed-and-breakfast cabin, and the hostel.

As many as three or four bunkrooms at a time are dedicated to happy hostellers, depending on how many show up on a given night. These dorms are basic, but they stay cool in the afternoon heat thanks to a shady, aromatic grove of bay laurel trees. An even better deal? Booking one of the hostel's three beautiful private cabins; for just a few dollars more per night, you sleep in a romantic double bed. Those beds make up for the rather rustic bathrooms and showers, which, in true summer camp form, teem with moths and other woodsy creatures. But it's clean and friendly here.

Meet other hostellers in the spacious, but still homey, common area, which is well-kept and features such touches as a radio, woodstove, and piano. Cook in the nicely stocked kitchen. What's to eat? Well, should you come during the right time of week (weekends), there are live farm demonstrations; come during the right time of

Best bet for a bite:
Hostel farm stand
Insiders' tip:
Book the private bed-and-breakfast cabin
What hostellers say:
"Very quiet and calming."
Gestalt:
Villa and grace
Hospitality: *A*
Cleanliness: *A*
Party index:

year (late summer, early fall) and you can take full advantage of an honor-system farm stand on site. While we're on the subject of food, heed these two words of advice: Bring some. There isn't a store for quite a ways around, and you want to come well-prepared. Try to drive to a town late at night, and you might never find your way back.

These folks deserve high marks for recycling and composting practically everything in sight, too. Like many of California's Hostelling International–affiliated hostels, however, this one will lock you out during most of the daylight hours, meaning you have to get creative with your days. One option is a visit to Stanford University, which isn't very far away (you did come in a car, right?). Stanford offers a big, relaxing campus full of trails, sports, performances, and lectures—and a bunch of brainiacs, to boot.

Another possibility is a long walk or cycle. A number of hiking trails wind through the surrounding chaparral hills. (You should always wear a hat, watch for ticks, and bring plenty of water if you go; it can get surprisingly hot above treeline, especially in late summer and early autumn.) The local hills are perfect for exploring all day by bike, too, despite the lack of food and water—and, again, the ever-present heat—along the way. Oddly, though, this hostel is closed during summer when a camp takes over the place; also, if you do come, be prepared to do a chore on your way out the door. This custom is rapidly fading from U.S. hostels, and many hostellers abhor the thought of it; but at Hidden Villa, it's the *hostellers* who help keep the place clean and tuned up, and they're doing a great job so far. It seems a small price indeed to pay for so much serenity.

How to Get There:

By car: Drive on Interstate 280 to Los Altos Hills (Moody Road exit). Hostel is 2 miles west on Moody Road, on left.

By train: Caltrain stops in Palo Alto. Take bus to Foothills College, then walk 2 miles west on Moody Road.

Key to Icons

Attractive natural setting	Comfortable beds	Visual arts at hostel or nearby
Ecologically aware hostel	A particularly good value	Music at hostel or nearby
Superior kitchen facilities or cafe	Wheelchair-accessible	Great hostel for skiers
Offbeat or eccentric place	Good for business travelers	Bar or pub at hostel or nearby
Superior bathroom facilities	Especially well-suited for families	Editors' choice: Among our very favorite hostels
Romantic private rooms	Good for active travelers	

Fullerton Hostel ✸✸✸✷

1700 North Harbor Boulevard, Fullerton, CA 92635

(714) 738-3721

Fax: (714) 738-0925
E-mail: fullerton@lahostels.org
Rates: $22 per Hostelling International member
Credit cards: JCB, MC, VISA
Season: Mid-June to mid-September
Beds: 20
Private rooms: None
Affiliation: Hostelling International
Office hours: 7:30 a.m. to 11:30 p.m.
Extras: Television, VCR, fireplace, piano, table tennis, porch, storage, free laundry, parking, kitchen, Internet access, grill

*W*ho would have thought that a hostel dedicated almost entirely to serving the Disneyland-bound set could be so nice, and be so close to an Amtrak station? Yet it's true. This delightful little tile-roof house just 5 miles from Wally World (er, Disney) rests on

LOS ANGELES-AREA HOSTELS: A SUMMARY

	RATING	PROS	CONS	COST	PAGE
FULLERTON					
Fullerton Hostel	✪✪✪◗	pretty quaint	way out there	$22	p. 227
HERMOSA BEACH					
Surf City Hostel	✪✪◗	beach, bar	kitchen lacking	$27	p. 230
HOLLYWOOD					
USA Hostels Hollywood	✪✪✪	peppy		$27–$33	p. 236
Orange Drive Manor Hostel	✪◗	location	iffy	$22–$35	p. 233
Orbit Hotel and Hostel	◗	hopping	grimy	$26–$35	p. 235
Hollywood International	☻	spacious	sterile	$17–$18	p. 232
INGLEWOOD					
Los Angeles Backpackers Paradise Hostel	☻	pool	unsafe area	$16	p. 238
MARINA DEL REY					
Venice Beach Hostel	☻	loose	messy	$19	p. 240
SAN PEDRO					
Los Angeles South Bay Hostel	✪✪✪✪✪	kitchen, view	drab design	$22	p. 241
SANTA MONICA					
Santa Monica Hostel	✪✪✪✪✪	location, facilities	bunks	$28	p. 243
VENICE					
Venice Beach Cotel	✪✪	beachy	worn	$22–$26	p. 245
Venice Beach Hostel	☻		dingy	$25	p. 247

175 acres of lush green fields in Brea Dam Park. It's a perfect place to recuperate after spending the day frying your brain with capitalist cartoonery; too bad it's now only open three months out of the year (boo!).

Everything in this hostel is immaculate. The common area offers a plush white couch, gigantic television, and plenty of breathing room. The refurbished kitchen is among the better ones we've seen, and the front porch offers quiet and a bit of serenity (for L.A., at least). The dorm rooms are standard Hostelling International–type digs, with bunk beds neatly arranged. There are only three rooms, which accommodate twenty people; it's so small for a city hostel but ideal for the Hostelling International set looking for a personal atmosphere without sacrificing the rigid standards that usually come with council-run facilities. Only trouble? Scoring a bed, because there aren't many.

The major drawback to this place is also its chief selling point: location. If neither Disneyland nor Knott's Berry Farm is in your plans, you really have no reason to stay here. Fullerton is a nice enough town, for sure, but it has nothing to offer a tourist other than access to the land of make-believe. Most of the other sights in L.A. are at least an hour's drive away. (If you don't have a car and plan on taking public transportation into the city, prepare to waste half the day in transit.) One good point: a university campus in the city brings the obligatory clump of coffee shops, bookstores, and whatnot.

As for Mouseville, catching rides to Disneyland with fellow hostellers should be a cinch. And the local bus to the House of Mickey is inexpensive. The hostel does have a lockout, but you're welcome to blow off the curfew, providing you first get a special late-night key from the front desk.

How to Get There:

By airplane: Take a SuperShuttle from LAX directly to the hostel (call shuttle at 800-481-6600).

By bus: Greyhound stops in Anaheim. From station, take OCTA bus #47 north to Chapman Avenue and Harbor Boulevard intersection. Then walk north on Harbor to hostel.

By car: Take the 91 Riverside Freeway to Fullerton. Take Harbor Boulevard north of town, just past Brea Boulevard. Look for hostel entrance on right.

By train: Amtrak stops in Fullerton. From station take OCTA bus #41 north on Harbor Boulevard or walk 1½ miles to hostel.

Surf City Hostel

26 Pier Avenue, Hermosa Beach, CA 90254

(310) 798-2323; (800) 305-2901

Fax: (310) 798-0343

E-mail: info@surfcityhostel.ws

Web site: www.surfcityhostel.ws

Rates: $27 per person; $65 for private room

Credit cards: AMEX, MC, VISA

Beds: 56

Private rooms: 3

Affiliation: None

Office hours: 8:00 a.m. to 10:00 p.m.

Extras: Shuttles, free breakfast, television, free body boards, laundry, tours, rental cars, bar, kitchen, free Internet access, videos, library, parties, fax service

*S*urf City used to be one of the better-kept secrets in Los Angeles–area hostelling. Few people knew of its existence, so the word-of-mouth buzz was practically nil. All we had to go on was a flashy yellow card advertising the place with little info and a big surfer-dude graphic.

Well, that's changing. With its newfound, wild popularity has come a partying-harder ethos and a slippage in both friendliness and cleanliness. Some people still love it, but light sleepers, families, and clean freaks should steer clear. Party animals, surfers, drinkers, and really social people will probably love it.

This hostel is located right on the beach (well, it's separated from the beach by a couple of buildings, but you get the idea) in an apartment-style facility right on top of a late-opening, noisy bar. The rooms are simple, though not as bad as the ratty pits you'd find at some other beach hostels. Walls in the hallway are covered with murals painted by hostellers; trippy underwater scenes of dolphins complement surfer-man craziness. (If you've got talent, show management a sketch; they might even commission something from you.)

Some rooms have ocean views, and it costs a bit more for a private room. Yet none of the rooms have more than four beds, and all benefit from refreshing ocean breezes. The kitchen is small and the common room a bit cramped—yet it's popular nonetheless. They pile on the free services, including free body board and Internet access. As with most surf hostels, you can also always count on at least a small contingent to be crashed out watching television or snoozing in the common room in the middle of the afternoon, dreaming of perfect tubes. There's a bar downstairs (and people drink a lot here), or you can raid the free buffet at any number of local watering holes: Buy yourself a drink, then load up on cocktail wieners to your heart's delight.

Hermosa Beach is everything you wanted Los Angeles to be—cheap bars, surfers, nice people, relaxed atmosphere, music, and so on—though it's rather far from the rest of America's most sprawling metro area. This is *not* a good place to use as a base for exploring L.A., but rather a place in and of itself to chill out at for a few days (and could we use any more prepositions in a sentence??) to regain your senses—if you don't mind beer, noise, and a little dirt along the way.

> **Best bet for a bite:**
> *El Gringo*
> **Insiders' tip:**
> *Bike, in-line skate, and board rentals nearby*
> **What hostellers say:**
> *"Hang loose."*
> **Gestalt:**
> *Surf and turf*
> **Safety:** *B*
> **Hospitality:** *B*
> **Cleanliness:** *C*
> **Party index:** 🎉🎉🎉🎉

How to Get There:

By airplane: Large airport in Los Angeles. Take "C" shuttle to bus terminal, then take #439 bus to Eleventh Street and Hermosa Avenue. Walk 2 blocks north on Hermosa Avenue and turn left on Pier Avenue. Walk 1 block to the hostel.

By bus: Greyhound stops in city. From station, take #60 bus on Seventh Avenue to Long Beach Boulevard and Artesia. Transfer to #130 bus west to Pier Avenue and Monterey Avenue. Walk 4 blocks to hostel on Pier.

By car: Take Pacific Coast Highway into Hermosa Beach and turn west onto Pier Avenue. Follow Pier Avenue all the way to the ocean.

By train: Amtrak stops in Los Angeles. From Union Station, take #439 bus to Eleventh Street and Hermosa Avenue. Walk 2 blocks north on Hermosa Avenue and turn left on Pier Avenue. Walk 1 block to hostel.

Hollywood International Hostel

6820 Hollywood Boulevard, Hollywood, CA 90028

(323) 463-0797; (800) 750-6561

E-mail: info@hollywoodhostels.com

Web site: www.hollywoodhostels.com

Rates: $17–$18 per person; $40–$52 for private room

Proof of international travel required

Credit cards: None

Beds: 140

Private rooms: 5

Affiliation: None

Office hours: Twenty-four hours

Extras: Pickups, television, VCR, pool table, arcade, kitchen, laundry, free breakfast, sun deck, exercise equipment, Internet access

---

If you're looking for immediate access to the schmaltz and plastic of Hollywood Boulevard, this hostel tries to suck you in: It's just across the street from Grauman's Chinese Theatre, and within walking distance of all of Hollywood's main attractions.

But don't do it. Because if you'd like to feel safe, clean, and not have liquor rammed down your throat, we'd suggest finding somewhere else to stay in town. Fast.

Hollywood International is in desperate need of some personality, as the cheesy movie poster/stained carpet motif isn't doing it for us, and the rest of the place is even worse. The rooms at this place are spacious, but they're also unclean. Reasonably priced private rooms, complete with furniture, are as nice as any hotel room you could get at three times the price but also suffer from neglect; likewise the tile bathrooms, barely clean enough to use. Staff ranged from helpless to rude to downright threatening.

Best bet for a bite:
On the Boulevard

Insiders' tip:
Watch the stars

What hostellers say:
"Did he just spit on the floor?"

Gestalt:
Trashy Hollywood nights

Safety: F

Hospitality: F

Cleanliness: F

Party index: 🎉🎉🎉🎉

Management says this hostel is an old hotel that saw its glory in the 1930s with the likes of Humphrey Bogart on the guest list. Some of that grandeur is still evident in the antique ceiling moldings, impressive hearth, tall ceilings, and other elegant markings. Today it's given over more to, well, mass TV watching in the big common area (plush couches, a big-screen television). Commercials? Those are simply excuses to down some more tequila. Long-termers seem to camp out here, which is never a good thing.

More seriously, security is at times nonexistent. We walked around once snooping for quite awhile without anyone questioning our presence except for a creepy guy who leered at us, and we think he was curious about more than our review. The door to the street stayed wide open all the time. When we asked about lockers (none in the rooms), we were told to use one of seven in the hallway. Five were in use; two were broken. Tough luck. Lock your rucksack up during the day or leave it in storage . . . *if* you stay.

How to Get There:
By airplane: Call hostel for free pickup.
By bus: Call hostel for free pickup.
By car: Hostel is located on Hollywood Boulevard near Grauman's Chinese Theatre.
By train: Call hostel for free pickup.

Orange Drive Manor Hostel
1764 North Orange Drive, Hollywood, CA 90028
(323) 850-0350

    E-mail: info@orangedrivehostel.com
    Web site: www.orangedrivehostel.com
    Rates: $25–$35 per person; $59–$79 for private room
    Credit cards: None
    Beds: Number varies
    Private/family rooms: Yes
    Single rooms: Yes
    Affiliation: None
    Office hours: 8:00 a.m. to midnight
    Extras: Parking ($), shuttle service, Internet access, movies, event tickets, tours, phone cards

Best bet for a bite:
It's L.A.! Tacos/burritos everywhere
What hostellers say:
"Baby, I'm a star."
Gestalt:
Hollywood bowl
Safety: *D*
Hospitality: *C*
Cleanliness: *F*
Party index: 🎉🎉

The location of this quiet hostel—inside a home built in the '20s, though it now houses hostellers instead of glitterati—tries to harken back to the golden days of Hollywood. Well, the house does; the hostel doesn't. Its motto is "sleep like a king, pay like a peasant." How about we try a new one on for size: "Pay the usual rates, and take your chances."

Not quite as catchy? Well, sorry, but it's a heck of a lot more accurate.

The quiet residential street seems an anomaly to the scads of Hollywood/L.A. tourist attractions that are within a stone's throw of the property. (It's literally *right behind* the famous Grauman's Chinese Theatre, where many film premieres are hosted.) Other key sights within arm's reach include the Hollywood Walk of Fame, Hollywood Bowl, the Hollywood Sign, and Universal Studios, as well as numerous restaurants and clubs. Having said that, the main drag where all these sights are located is sketchy, so it's nice that guests can be nearby without dealing with too much slime. The hostel also arranges an L.A. tour that takes you to various celeb homes, Magic Mountain, Knott's Berry Farm, the beaches, and so on.

But that can't mask the deeper problems of this hostel. Dorms have plenty of space, yes; beds max out at four per room, and some have as few as two. Private rooms are nicely furnished with antique chairs and plants. However, the atmosphere could be livelier and cleanliness has gone way downhill. Even the staff—once an asset here—is noticeably ruder and less helpful. Buyer, beware! No king's digs here.

How to Get There:
By airplane: Free pickup service from airport with confirmed reservation.
By bus: Greyhound stops in Los Angeles. Call hostel using courtesy phone for pickup or take #60 bus (across street) to Red Line Metro and follow directions below.
By busway: Take Red Line Metro (downstairs); exit at the Highland Avenue/Hollywood exit. Walk west on Hollywood Boulevard, past Grauman's Chinese Theatre. Turn right onto Orange Drive and walk to fourth building on the right (east side of street).
By car: Take the 405 Freeway north to the 10 Freeway east. Exit at La Brea North and drive 5 miles to Hollywood Boulevard. Turn right on Orange Drive. Hostel is on the right (east) side.
By train: Amtrak stops in Los Angeles. Contact hostel for transit details.

Orbit Hotel and Hostel ⚡

7950 Melrose Avenue, West Hollywood, CA 90046

(213) 851-1129; (800) 446-7835

Web site: www.orbithotel.com

Rates: $26–$35 per person; $79–$99 for private room

Credit cards: MC, VISA

Beds: 225

Private rooms: 10

Affiliation: None

Office hours: Twenty-four hours

Extras: Television, VCR, laundry, grill, restaurant, beer, shuttle, store, arcade, weight room, Internet access, patio

The folks who brought you the famously rowdy Banana Bungalow Hostel in Hollywood are now operating in West Hollywood. Aside from the change in neighborhood, though, we can barely tell the difference; an amazing amount of partying goes on at this place, and not a whole lot of maintenance or cleaning so far as we can tell. International globetrotters come here to act like American frat boys and sorority girls, consuming mass quantities of alcohol and sleeping well into the afternoon; partake of the tours, barbecues, and myriad other activities organized by the activities director; and do it all again the next night and day. (Has anyone told these kids they're in a major city with exciting nightlife?)

The hostel sits on Melrose Avenue, just a five- to ten-minute walk from the vintage stores, coffee shops, and eateries of hip West Hollywood. It's wedged between a cheaper, cheesier shopping area and more expensive clothing shops that we think of when we think of Los Angeles. (Two blocks up Sunset is Boys Town, host to lots of gay clubs.) Despite this good position, though, hostellers seem fixated on the hostel's mod

Best bet for a bite:
Hostel cafe (if you're really staying)
Insiders' tip:
Bus service to San Diego and Tijuana
What hostellers say:
"Let's get smashed!!!!"
Gestalt:
Out of orbit
Safety: *C*
Hospitality: *C*
Cleanliness: *F*
Party index: 🎉🎉🎉🎉🎉

decor and party scene. Hanging out can happen anywhere, from the wide-screen movie room to the satellite TV room to a patio complete with disco ball. The hostel's amenities are decent— Internet access, laundry, free video rentals, for instance. Guests have access to an industrial-size kitchen and eating area. The hostel charges fair prices for shuttles to Venice Beach, Universal Studios, and LAX.

But that's where the happy mood ends. Cleanliness is not kept up; expect to feel tingles at night. Travelers also report plenty of, er, "entertaining" long-term residents at the hostel, despite a claimed four-week max stay policy. If you're intent on staying, check out the situation here *before* plunking down your cash; most of our snoops, though, advise against ever even getting as far as the front door here.

How to Get There:
By bus: Greyhound stops in in Los Angeles. Contact hostel for transit route.
By car: Contact hostel for directions.
By train: Amtrak stops in in Los Angeles. Contact hostel for transit route.

USA Hostels Hollywood
1624 Schrader Boulevard, Hollywood, CA 90028
(323) 462-3777; (800) 524-6783
  Fax: (323) 417-5152
  E-mail: hollywood@usahostels.com
  Web site: www.usahostels.com/hollywood
  Rates: $27–$33 per person; $62–$90 for private room
  Credit cards: MC, VISA
  Private rooms: Yes
  Affiliation: USA Hostels
  Office hours: Twenty-four hours
  Extras: Free pancakes, shuttle discounts, tours, TV tickets, foosball, laundry, storage, bar, comedy nights, barbecues

---

NOTE: Passport or out-of-state ID required; no guests under age sixteen.

*A*nother in the small chain of USA Hostels, this place came with big expectations. And, indeed, it was full of young people and some of the staff were friendly and helpful, which is more than we say for most of the other hostels in this city. Against the odds, it's only getting better with time. Good job!

Accommodations are adequate and clean (shocking!), though the party atmosphere can be amped up at times. The surrounding neighborhood is definitely a little bit dodgy, though, and as a result many hostellers simply end up hanging out at the hostel and drinking here. That's not really the point of coming to L.A., but okay. It's better than getting propositioned or accosted on a street corner, right? The free, U-cook-'em-and-eat-all-of-'em-you-can pancakes in the morning get a big thumbs-up, if you don't mind the wait—everybody's lining up for multiple cracks at these babies. There's also a laundry (with free powder), cheap airport transportation, free sheets, and occasional tickets to local TV program tapings. You can catch a shuttle to the same chain's San Fran or Vegas hostels for just forty-five bucks, and they do tours to Sea World and other local sights, too. Well-organized, clean, and friendly enough. Kudos, folks.

How to Get There:

By airplane: From LAX, cross over the two lanes of traffic to reach bus and van island. At "Shared Ride Vans" point, look for SuperShuttle pickup. Tell SuperShuttle driver to take you to USA Hostels Hollywood at 1624 Schrader Boulevard.

By bus: Greyhound stops in Hollywood and downtown Los Angeles. From Hollywood station, walk south on Cahuenga Boulevard, cross to south side of Hollywood Boulevard and turn right onto Hollywood Boulevard. Turn left on Schrader Boulevard; hostel is on left. From downtown, take bus to Hollywood station and follow directions above.

By car: From LAX, take Highway 105 north to Highway 110, then continue on Highway 110 east to Highway 101 north. Exit Highway 101 at Cahuenga Boulevard. Turn left onto Cahuenga, cross Hollywood Boulevard and turn right onto Selma Avenue; turn right again onto Schrader Boulevard. Hostel is on right.

> **Best bet for a bite:**
> In-N-Out Burger on Sunset
> **What hostellers say:**
> "Better than expected.
> **Gestalt:**
> Goodnight, Hollywood Boulevard"
> **Safety:** B
> **Hospitality:** B
> **Cleanliness:** B
> **Party index:**

From San Diego, take Interstate 5 north to Highway 101 north. Exit Highway 101 at Cahuenga Boulevard and follow directions above.

From Las Vegas, take Highway 15 south to Highway 10 east, then continue to Highway 101 north. Exit Highway 101 at Cahuenga Boulevard and follow directions above.

From San Francisco, take I-5 south to Highway 170 west, then continue on Highway 170 to Highway 101 south. Exit Highway 101 at Cahuenga Boulevard and follow directions above.

By train: Amtrak stops in Los Angeles. From Union Station, take red line subway going toward North Hollywood; get off at Hollywood/Vine Station. Walk west on Hollywood Boulevard and turn left onto Schrader Boulevard.

Los Angeles Backpackers Paradise Hostel

4200 West Century Boulevard, Inglewood, CA 90304

(310) 419-0999; (800) 852-0012

Fax: (310) 412-9100

E-mail: laadventurerhtl@yahoo.com

Web site: www.backpackersparadise.com

Rates: $16 per person; $45–$70 for private room

Credit cards: AMEX, DISC, MC, VISA

Beds: 220

Private rooms: Yes

Affiliation: None

Office hours: Twenty-four hours

Extras: Pool, bar, champagne, shuttles, breakfast, car rentals, pool table, arcade, laundry, Internet access

This hostel is also known as the "L.A. Adventurer," but we're not sure whether that or Backpacker's Paradise is an appropriate name for this joint. The hostel's motto ("Parties Every Night!!") tells you all you need to know about the place, and the only attraction within walking distance of this converted hotel is . . . the LAX airport.

That's right. You're smack dab in the middle of one of Los Angeles's most dodgy neighborhoods, with only airport-service-road fare for company. At least you can watch a plane take off (without you).

No, you don't want to stay here. Yes, they have a pool in the middle, complete with poolside bar. Guests sun themselves and drink fruity concoctions throughout the day. And night. Most of the folks hanging around the afternoon we dropped in looked quite tipsy. This was well before 6:00 p.m., too, when cheap beer and wine are served to all who desire them.

Such poolside pleasures are nice, but we figure they get a little tiresome by the end of the day. Surely people will want to get out and see the City of Angels? No, not so much. Dorms were packed too tight, and not clean at *all*. Staff were indifferent. Security was lax or nonexistent. Walking out the door and exploring the neighborhood on foot is very ill-advised. We didn't feel safe on these streets even in the middle of the day, not to mention at night; this is South Central L.A., the stuff of which gangsta films are made.

Maybe when the Eagles sang, "You can check out any time you like, but you can never leave," they were staying at *this* place.

Best bet for a bite:
LAX food court
Insiders' tip:
Don't walk around alone
What hostellers say:
"I'll drink to that."
Gestalt:
Tipsy turvy
Safety: *F*
Hospitality: *C*
Cleanliness: *D*
Party index:

How to Get There:
By airplane: Large airport in Los Angeles. Use free hotel-information phone to dial 56858 for free pickup.
By car: From Interstate 405 take Airport exit onto Century Boulevard. Turn right onto Century; hostel is a few blocks down on the right.

Attractive natural setting	Comfortable beds	Visual arts at hostel or nearby
Ecologically aware hostel	A particularly good value	Music at hostel or nearby
Superior kitchen facilities or cafe	Wheelchair-accessible	Great hostel for skiers
Offbeat or eccentric place	Good for business travelers	Bar or pub at hostel or nearby
Superior bathroom facilities	Especially well-suited for families	Editors' choice: Among our very favorite hostels
Romantic private rooms	Good for active travelers	

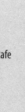

Key to Icons

Venice Beach Hostel

2915 Yale Avenue, Marina del Rey, CA 90292

(310) 306-5180; (800) 390-2632

E-mail: venicebeachhostel@yahoo.com

Rates: $19 per person; $38–$42 for private room

Credit cards: None

Beds: 35

Private rooms: 3

Affiliation: None

Office hours: 9:00 a.m. to 10:00 p.m.

Extras: Television, VCR, free breakfast, trips, parking, laundry, storage, kitchen, pool tables, lockers, Internet access, airport pickup, free Wi-Fi

Yale Avenue is a small residential street in Marina del Rey, a wanna-be suburb in downtown L.A. that borders Venice. From the outside this hostel fits right into this aesthetic. It's just a home with a fence around it and presentable landscaping. There isn't even a sign, so the hostel may be hard to find. Once inside, though, there's no mistaking that you are in a tried-and-true hostel.

That's right, this hostel isn't actually in Venice Beach (though an annex building *is*—got that?). And it is among the more lived-in places we've seen. Everything is worn to the bone, just the way some of the laid-back guests like it, apparently. Folks sit on the broken chairs puffing away, not worrying about putting their feet on the coffee table. We've heard harsh reports about bedbugs, roaches, and filth. Don't expect sympathy or help from the staff, though.

What's a typical day here? At night groups pile into clunker cars and head out for the bars. The next morning they convene in the disorderly kitchen to overcome hangovers with the help of free sandwiches

Best bet for a bite:

Twenty-four-hour supermarket nearby

Insiders' tip:

Hit the pubs on Washington

What hostellers say:

"So where's the cheapest beer?"

Gestalt:

Slack attack

Safety: D

Hospitality: *F*

Cleanliness: *F*

Party index:

and instant coffee. Some may try to shower, but with thirty-five beds and only two shower-heads, that can be a tough proposition.

Upstairs beds are crowded into the dorms in whatever direction they'll fit. There are sturdy metal bunks, wood platforms with foam covering, and traditional beds with springs. Get there early to find the type of bed that suits your fancy.

Keep in mind that the beach is a good fifteen-minute walk from this hostel—most everything is a bit of a ways, in fact—so you'll probably want a car if you opt to stay here.

How to Get There:

By airplane: Call hostel for free pickup from Los Angeles airport. Or take #3 Santa Monica Blue Bus north. Get off at Washington Boulevard and walk 3 blocks to Yale Avenue. Turn left on Yale; hostel is on right.

By bus: From Greyhound station take #33 RTD Bus on Spring Street to Venice Boulevard. Cross Venice and walk south on Lincoln to Washington Boulevard. Turn right on Washington and walk 3 blocks to Yale Avenue.

By car: Take Lincoln Boulevard from North Sepulveda Boulevard to Washington Boulevard. Go west 3 blocks on Washington; then go left on Yale. Hostel is immediately on right.

Los Angeles South Bay Hostel ✹✹✹✹

3601 South Gaffey Street #613, San Pedro, CA 90733
(310) 831-8109

Fax: (310) 831-4635
E-mail: southbay@lahostels.org
Rates: $22 per Hostelling International member; $44 for private room
Credit cards: JCB, MC, VISA
Season: Mid-June to mid-September
Beds: 52
Private rooms: 7
Affiliation: Hostelling International
Office hours: 7:30 a.m. to 11:00 p.m.
Extras: Laundry, lockers, television, VCR, barbecue, garden, Internet access, kitchen

---

*W*hat makes this summer-only hostel shine—plain and simple—is its view. Who would have thought such an astonishing sight could be seen from within the confines of Los Angeles? The hostel is in Angel's Gate Park, overlooking a panoramic view of the Pacific Ocean that extends out to Catalina Island. All that lies between you and the ocean is the Korean Friendship Bell, an inspiring example of Asian craftsmanship that lends international flair to the experience. (We once happened upon two martial arts students sparring by the bell as the sun set behind them. It was a scene right out of a Bruce Lee movie.)

San Pedro is technically within the L.A. metro area, but it's really not near any of the major tourist sights. So it's not a good base for exploring the city, but instead a great place to wind down and recover from sightseeing, traffic, or cross-country driving for a few days. Once you get past the strip malls and sprawl of downtown, you'll find yourself on a heavenly peninsula. A cruise out to Catalina is a popular option, as is exploring the local seashore on foot. There's plenty of fishing and boating to enjoy. You also have numerous seafood restaurants, whale-watching cruises, and the rest of the good stuff that comes with a quaint seaside village to try out.

The facility itself is a decommissioned army barracks, which isn't really a problem—no unexploded warheads here, so far as we know. The one thing we found fault with, though, was the huge barbed-wire fence that surrounds the place. It's there to serve as a boundary between the park and the hostel, but looks and feels a bit extreme. Otherwise this hostel is just a series of long, narrow shotgun-style structures with a bunch of dorm rooms inside. The common facilities—all grouped together in one central building—are stellar and clean, and the hostel is small enough to encourage a warm communal feel. This place also deserves an award for its travel library, complete with posters, tons of books, and flawlessly compiled information sheets.

Best bet for a bite:
Eggs 'n' pancakes at Gaffey Street Diner
Insiders' tip:
Gray whales can be seen from January to April
What hostellers say:
"Can't get enough of that view."
Gestalt:
Army surplus
Safety: *A*
Hospitality: *A*
Cleanliness: *B*
Party index:

How to Get There:

By airplane: Large airport in Los Angeles. Use free airport shuttle marked "M," "Green," or

"Special" to the Green Line Metro. Take Metro to 110 Harbor Freeway. Transfer (with Metro ticket) to #446 MTA bus south to Korean Friendship Bell.

By bus: Call hostel for transit route.

By car: Hostel is 3 miles south of Interstate 110 on Gaffey Road, in Angel's Gate Park.

By train: Take #446 MTA bus directly to hostel.

Santa Monica Hostel

1436 Second Street, Santa Monica, CA 90401

(310) 393-9913

    Fax: (310) 393-1769

    E-mail: reserve@hilosangeles.org

    Web site: www.hilosangeles.org

    Rates: $28 per Hostelling International member; $62–$65 for private room

    Credit cards: MC, VISA

    Beds: 260

    Private rooms: 10

    Affiliation: Hostelling International

    Office hours: Twenty-four hours

    Extras: Television, VCR, laundry, travel store, bike storage, barbecue grill, piano, shuttle, breakfast, Internet access, kitchen

---

*W*hat amazes us most about this beautiful hostel is that the bulk of the locals we met in Santa Monica actually know it exists. Imagine that: an urban community that takes pride in its hostel. Well, they'd better, because their city coughed up big bucks to help fund the purpose-built facility. By our estimate, and that of most everyone else we talked to, it's an investment that has paid off handsomely, bringing tons of cool young people to a great city for a taste of the L.A. life. (A fourteen-day-per-year max stay rule keeps the long-termers out.)

In some ways, the facility is more like a Hilton hotel than a hostel. After being checked in by the professional staff, you have a choice of entering the soothing courtyard—complete with working fountain—or passing through a hearthside sitting room. A few steps down the hallway is a giant dining room and commercial-quality kitchen. The pleasure of cooking in such a grandiose facility may quell your desire to blow the entire month's budget on a meal at one of the many exquisite cafes in the neighborhood. (But we still went out for eats sometimes, just to see what was out there. Answer: a lot.)

On the front side of the building is an old meeting room that has been handsomely restored for community use. It's actually part of the oldest brick building in Santa Monica, dating back to 1875 and once known as the Wrapp Saloon. Regular lectures and educational series keep some spunk in this place, with speakers running the gamut from environmentalists to massage therapists and a host of other public programs, such as barbecues, movie nights, and so forth.

As for beds, guests have the option of staying in a dorm with four, six, or eight beds; eight-bedded rooms are cheapest, of course. The bunks are somewhat narrow and mattresses could be thicker, but it's okay. Try not to roll over too much in your sleep, though.

There's so much to do just outside the hostel that you'll be hard-pressed to find time to do everything you'd like, inside or out. The Third Street Promenade, offering a huge array of outdoor cafes, bars, movie theaters, and whatnot, is just a block away—wow. A few blocks in the other direction is the city's justly famous boardwalk, where you can break the city's auto addiction and walk all the way to happening Venice Beach. Or stick around and hang out on the famous Santa Monica Pier, which pops up in Hollywood films all the time (though the giant Ferris wheel here isn't the original; that one was auctioned off on eBay in 2008 and hauled to—yikes—Oklahoma). Want to do even more? There's almost always staff on hand to point you in the right direction.

If anything, this place's guests are a little *too* serious as tourists. Everyone is busy with his or her own thing, rushing around so much that little energy is devoted here to communing with fellow travelers; it's kind of a nutshell experience of California itself, a bit self-absorbed. Stick around the courtyard long enough, though, and sooner or later some scruffy backpacker will connect with you. Soon you'll find yourself immersed in senseless pseudo-philosophical chatter 'til the early morning light. All in all, this is a nice place, and a great base from which to explore L.A.—the best hostel in the city from which to do so (there are

Best bet for a bite:
Stroll the Third Street Promenade
Insiders' tip:
Snapshots at Santa Monica Pier
What hostellers say:
"Hey, is that Hasselhoff??"
Gestalt:
California dreamin'
Safety: *B*
Hospitality: *B*
Cleanliness: *A*
Party index: 🎉🎉🎉

buses into the downtown if you need to go there). Too bad the beds are jammed together so closely; otherwise, it would be just about perfect.

How to Get There:

By airplane: Large airport in Los Angeles. Call hostel for free shuttle details.

By bus: Take #60 MTA bus west to Seventh and Spring Streets. Transfer to #33 bus and take it to Second and Broadway in Santa Monica. Walk north on Second to hostel.

By car: Drive to Second Street, 2 blocks east of beach and Santa Monica Pier.

By train: Take #33 MTA bus from Los Angeles and Arcadia Streets to Second and Broadway in Santa Monica. Walk north on Second to hostel.

Venice Beach Cotel

25 Windward Avenue, Venice, CA 90291

(310) 399-7649; (888) 718-8287

Fax: (310) 399-1930

Web site: www.venicebeachcotel.com

E-mail: reservations@venicebeachcotel.com

Rates: $22–$26 per person; $53–$70 for private room

Credit cards: MC, VISA

Private rooms: Yes

Office hours: Twenty-four hours

Extras: Internet access ($), tours, free boogie boards, paddle tennis rentals, free coffee, bar, kitchen

---

NOTE: Valid passport required.

*O*n the top floors of the St. Mark's Hotel in Venice Beach, the Cotel is about as good a location as you could ever ask for to see the "real" L.A. It's just steps from the carnival of the boardwalk and Muscle Beach, and that's why you came to Venice, right? Plus, you can get a private room here for a fraction of what you'd pay elsewhere in town.

However, the place itself leaves much to be desired . . . it's just barely borderline acceptable by our standards. Definitely not the worst place in town (there are plenty of contenders for *that* dubious title), but it's still crowded, disorganized, less clean than it should be, and—despite a party atmosphere—it can be tough to make friends here. A so-so kitchen, lots of ambient nighttime noise from the bar below, and a messy common room don't help, either. On the upside, they provide the usual beach-hostel amens: free boogie boards, free coffee, a bar where you can buy cheap beers. That bar—and the easy access to the famed boardwalk and the amazing view—are the main reasons to consider staying. If you're young and you want to "do" L.A. once, this might be one of the better choices in a city with mostly sad selections. But it's still not appropriate for families, those with high hygiene standards, or light sleepers.

How to Get There:

By airplane: From LAX, take taxi or van to hotel. Or take free airport shuttle to Parking Lot C, then Santa Monica Blue Bus #3 and ask for MTA transfer (75 cents). Get off at Lincoln and Venice Boulevard intersection, at car wash; transfer to MTA Bus #33 to Venice Beach. Get off at post office and walk 1 block west (look for flags on roof).

By bus: Greyhound stops in Los Angeles. Contact hostel for transit route.

By car: From downtown Los Angeles or Las Vegas, take Santa Monica Freeway (Highway 10) west to Lincoln Boulevard exit; turn left (south) onto Lincoln and follow to Venice Boulevard. Take Venice west to Pacific Avenue, turn right (north) then make a left on Windward Avenue. Look for flags on roof of hostel.

From San Diego, take San Diego Freeway (Highway 405) north to Venice Boulevard exit; go west to Pacific Avenue, turn right, and then turn left on Windward Avenue.

From San Francisco, take I-5 south, then San Diego Freeway (Highway 405) south to Venice Boulevard exit; go west to Pacific Avenue, turn right, and then turn left on Windward Avenue.

By train: Amtrak stops in Los Angeles. Contact hostel for transit route.

Venice Beach Hostel on Pacific

1515 Pacific Avenue, Venice, CA 90291

(310) 452-3052

E-mail: vbh@caprica.com

Web site: www.caprica.com/venice-beach-hostel

Rates: $25 per person; $64 for private room

Credit cards: None

Beds: 65

Private rooms: 5

Affiliation: None

Office hours: Twenty-four hours

Extras: Free Sunday meal, movies, television, VCR, laundry, piano, pool table, free breakfast, Internet access, kitchen, library

*T*here have been a bunch of hostels named Venice Beach Hostel or something like that in L.A. We're not sure how this came about, but as is typically the case with such hostel controversies, the disagreement is rife: Accusations and counteraccusations fly about whose hostel is legitimate and whose is not. We're not going to get into that; we'll just advise you to mind the addresses so you know which one you're at.

Mark Wurm's Venice Beach Hostel—located in the heart of Venice—is a dive with character. Worn mattresses, dim lighting, and cracked ceilings are contrasted with bright hallway murals, exotic plant life, and an owner who is the cream of the eccentric crop.

Wurm gives free accommodations to street performers "if they do what I think is good stuff out there." The man loves Venice and all it represents. "This is P. T. Barnum at large," he said. "It is a total freak show, and you want it to exist in the most humane and pleasurable way possible."

Best bet for a bite:
Pizza on Ocean Front Walk
Insiders' tip:
Go on a weekend
What hostellers say:
"Will perform for food."
Gestalt:
Barnum & Bailey
Safety: *C*
Hospitality: *F*
Cleanliness: *D*
Party index: 🎉🎉🎉🎉

On the guest list when we popped in were a human robot and a sand sculptor. The hostel's common areas reflect this Renaissance attitude. Guests can go "day-tripping" through the upstairs hallway's Grand Canyon theme, walking through the corridor into a sunset. Most of the dorms have a theme to them as well. The "Saloon" is surrounded by a boozing couples mural, and the "Maine" room is, you guessed it, chock-full o' nature. The highly utilized kitchen and comfy common area allow for a chill, pleasant social scene.

Once you get over this fun, though, the place has a somewhat seedy feel. Despite the murals, the dorm rooms have that dreary subsidized housing aura about them. We suggest looking at them before committing yourself to stay the night.

How to Get There:
By airplane: Large airport in Los Angeles. From airport, take shuttle (call hostel for details; hostellers get $2 discount).
By bus: Greyhound stops in Los Angeles. From station, take #33 RTD bus to Venice post office. Look for hostel sign on Pacific Avenue.
By car: Hostel is at the corner of Pacific and Windward Avenues (downtown, by the beach).
By train: Amtrak stops in Los Angeles. From station, take #33 RTD bus to Venice post office. Look for hostel sign on Pacific Avenue.

Davison Street Guest House Hostel
19 Davison Street, Mammoth Lakes, CA 93546
(760) 924-2188

 Web site: www.mammoth-guest.com
 Rates: $25–$35 per person; $53–$93 for private room
 Credit cards: None
 Beds: 28
 Private rooms: Yes
 Affiliation: None
 Office hours: Vary; call
 Extras: Barbecue, television, VCR, fireplace, deck, kitchen

---

*D*avison Guest House is a well-equipped ski chalet located at the base of the Mammoth Mountain ski resort. There's a good kitchen and some lovely bunk beds and private rooms, and the place seems very clean. This is a ski town, where development goes head-to-head with wilderness. It's a fine enough place for skiers when snow is on the ground, though others may get restless.

Nonskiers might consider a visit in the warmer months, however. A network of hot springs in the area offers unsurpassed soaking opportunities in the great wide open; crafty locals have set about digging and paving baths in remote locations. You'll have to look hard, but it's worth it. The forest that surrounds Mammoth Lakes also offers excellent hiking. Stop at the local ranger station for trail guides.

We happened upon the area in late August and had the whole hostel to ourselves. Not unusual, the manager told us: Turns out, summer is the slow season. So the secret is not yet out about the beauty of this community to the east of Yosemite in the warm season. Definitely worth a stop before, or after, a visit to the national park.

> **Best bet for a bite:**
> *Supermarkets downtown*
> **Insiders' tip:**
> *Hot springs nearby*
> **What hostellers say:**
> *"Anybody come here in the summer?"*
> **Gestalt:**
> *Mammoth fun*
> **Hospitality:** *A*
> **Cleanliness:** *A*
> **Party index:**

How to Get There:

By car: From Highway 395, take Highway 203 west 3 miles to the town of Mammoth Lakes. Go up Main Street through two traffic lights, past Minaret Road, and then ¾ mile toward the fishing lakes (Main Street becomes Lake Mary Road) and turn right at Davison, which is the first right turn after the turnoff to the Canyon Lodge ski area. The hostel is at 19 Davison—it is the first building on your left after you have turned right onto Davison.

 Attractive natural setting

 Ecologically aware hostel

 Superior kitchen facilities or cafe

 Offbeat or eccentric place

Superior bathroom facilities

Romantic private rooms

 Comfortable beds

 A particularly good value

 Wheelchair-accessible

 Good for business travelers

 Especially well-suited for families

 Good for active travelers

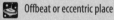 Visual arts at hostel or nearby

Music at hostel or nearby

 Great hostel for skiers

 Bar or pub at hostel or nearby

 Editors' choice: Among our very favorite hostels

Key to Icons

Merced Home Hostel

P.O. Box 3755 (call for street address), Merced, CA 95344

(209) 725-0407

E-mail: merced-hostel@juno.com

Rates: $16 per Hostelling International member

Credit cards: None

Beds: 6

Private rooms: 1

Affiliation: Hostelling International

Office hours: 7:00 to 9:00 a.m.; 5:00 to 10:00 p.m.

Extras: Kitchen, storage, ice cream, breakfast

*E*verybody seems to like this little hostel, tucked into a home not far from Yosemite National Park. The owners are friendly enough, offering free pickups from the local bus depot or train station and complimentary ice cream. There's a nightly scripted talk on the park, and they'll also school you on local tour outfitters and other outdoorsy-type options.

The hostel itself consists of just a couple bunkrooms and a private room: You're basically staying in a wing of the owners' home outside town. They've set up a kitchen and lay out a small breakfast in the mornings, too.

Best bet for a bite:
Fish tacos at El Asadero

What hostellers say:
"Tiny but adequate."

Gestalt:
Oh Merced

Hospitality: *B*

Cleanliness: *A*

Party index:

For fun, the owners recommend the town's farmers' market—that's Thursday nights, spring through fall—or the nearby Castle Aircraft Museum. There's a Courthouse Museum, park, and zoo, too. We'd recommend hanging at the local lake over all that, though if you've got wheels you're probably heading up to the big trees at Yosemite. (Even if you don't have a car, you can take a bus to the park from here for about $20 round-trip; the bus ticket includes park admission.) The hostel's owners will rent you tents and sleeping bags if you're going camping.

How to Get There:

By bus: Contact hostel for transit route.
By car: Contact hostel for directions.
By train: Contact hostel for transit route.

The Yosemite Bug ✹✹✹✹

6979 Highway 140 (P.O. Box 81), Midpines, CA 95345
(209) 966-6666

Fax: (209) 966–6667
E-mail: bughost@yosemitebug.com
Web site: www.yosemitebug.com
Rates: $20 per Hostelling International member; $40 for private room
Beds: 55
Private rooms: 5
Affiliation: Hostelling International
Office hours: 7:00 a.m. to 11:00 p.m.
Extras: Cafe, laundry, grill, table tennis, pool table, shuttles, hammock, fireplace, Internet access, lockers, kitchen, spa

---

*T*hough not as picture-perfect as it used to be, the Yosemite Bug remains a good pick for hostellers who have long searched for an affordable bed near the gates of California's awe-inspiring Yosemite National Park. A few bunks with good access would have been fine, but this place goes far beyond that. A bungalow community surrounded by forest, the hostel provides a relaxing retreat after a day on the trail.

The quaint bungalows are set on a hill, and each is equipped with five spacious bunk beds and a bathroom. The private cabins are great for couples who want a view. Most guests pass their time by the fireplace in the rustic main lodge down below. There's even a health spa. The Cafe at the Bug serves American and Mediterranean dishes, desserts, and beer on tap. The large front porch, equipped with a pool table, is also a popular hangout—and if enough interest and enthusiasm is there, management will sometimes build an evening bonfire at the base of the hostel's amphitheater.

Best bet for a bite:
In-house cafe
Insiders' tip:
Buy supplies in Mariposa
Gestalt:
Love Bug
Hospitality: *A*
Cleanliness: *A*
Party index: 🎉🎉🎉

The national park is only a thirty-minute drive from the Bug, and rides there are easy to get. Otherwise there is a shuttle bus. Get out early, as most of Yosemite's stunning hikes require a full day. Within walking distance from the hostel is a local swimming hole, and strenuous mountain bike trails are also in the immediate area. Rentals can be arranged through the hostel. During winter, hard-core snowboarders come to take on some of the state's toughest terrain, which is accessible only by hiking. Snowshoeing is also a popular Yosemite winter pastime.

The owners are enthusiastic and ambitious, and it reflects in the work they've done to the place.

How to Get There:

By bus: Greyhound stops in Merced. From Merced station take VIA bus to hostel.

By car: From San Francisco, take Bay Bridge to Interstate 580 east, then take California Highway 132 east to California Highway 99 south to Merced; take California Highway 140 east 2 miles past Midpines. Sign is on left.

From Yosemite, take State Highway 140 east from the El Portal gate and go 20 miles. Hostel is on right, 2 miles after Merced River Wild and Scenic Area.

By train: Amtrak stops in Merced. From station take VIA bus (included with some Amtrak tickets) directly to hostel. Call hostel for schedule.

Point Montara Lighthouse Hostel ✴✴✴✴✦

16th Street at California Highway 1 (P.O. Box 737), Montara, CA 94037
(650) 728-7177

Fax: (650) 728-7058
E-mail: himontara@norcalhostels.org
Rates: $22 per Hostelling International member; $59 for private room
Credit cards: MC, VISA
Beds: 45

Private rooms: 2
Affiliation: Hostelling International
Office hours: 7:30 to 10:00 a.m.; 4:30 to 10:00 p.m.
Extras: Hot tub, laundry, bike rack, souvenir shop, kitchen, Internet access

*W*hen it comes to setting, we're giving Point Montara the top prize among all U.S. hostels. A state park, the hostel comes complete with its own lighthouse, secluded pocket beach, hot tub, views of the Pacific, and glimpses of harbor seals, great blue herons, and migrating gray whales. For hostellers coming from the ultra-urban experience of nearby San Francisco, a night or two in this fabulous place is a much-needed tonic and many enthuse that it's nearly life-changing. We agree.

Bikers and bus riders are given top priority for beds on the spread, which consists of a main building and several cottages. The main house holds fairly crowded dorms, but most come with their own bathroom. Another building contains private rooms with shared bathrooms, and the fog-signal house includes two more private rooms (one of which is coveted by many couples seeking a bed-and-breakfast style experience and view for a fraction of the cost).

Amazingly, the main building boasts two well-equipped kitchens: There are four (count them) refrigerators and scads of counter space. Sometimes one of the kitchens is reserved for groups, but there's always ample space for everyone to cook. There's a laundry here, too; just don't plan on doing it between 9:30 a.m. and 4:30 p.m. Like many Northern California hostels, this one locks you out all day and asks you to do chores before you leave.

Lots of school groups visit during the fall, but otherwise most folks make it here to unwind from the wearying drone of city life. What to do if you're a Type A personality and just can't turn off? Well, Half Moon Bay's got some shops. Agricultural festivals are a big deal during the fall; the coast's soil and climate produce perfect pumpkins. Surfing is an even bigger deal, and you can

Best bet for a bite:
Caffe Lucca
Insiders' tip:
Pumpkin harvest in the fall
What hostellers say:
"I have to leave?"
Gestalt:
Excellent Point
Hospitality: *A*
Cleanliness: *A*
Party index: 🎉

shred some stick at Mavericks Beach a little way down famed Highway 1. Or watch some-body else do it from the comfort of your own blanket.

Then, at night, after a hard day of cycling, whale-watching, or doing nothing at all, you can reserve a private hour in the hot tub for just $5 a person. Now that's what we call hostelling perfection.

How to Get There:
By bus: Bus service from San Francisco MUNI and BART systems. Contact hostel for details.
By car: Take California Highway 1 for 25 miles south of San Francisco (or just north of Moss Beach). Turn toward lighthouse on unmarked road.
By train: Bus service from San Francisco; contact hostel for details.

Monterey Carpenters Hall Hostel
778 Hawthorne Street, Monterey, CA 93940
(831) 649-0375
> **Fax:** (831) 649-0375
> **E-mail:** info@montereyhostel.org
> **Web site:** www.montereyhostel.org
> **Rates:** $22.50 per Hostelling International member; $59 for private room
> **Credit cards:** MC, VISA
> **Beds:** 32
> **Private rooms:** 2
> **Affiliation:** Hostelling International
> **Office hours:** 8:00 to 10:30 a.m.; 5:00 to 10:00 p.m.
> **Extras:** Laundry, lockers, parking, Internet access, kitchen, breakfast

*T*his West Coast hostel is in a great coastal town. The Monterey Peninsula was noticeably void of budget digs; hostellers are mighty happy to have this place as an option to crash. Expect it to be often booked full on weekends or in summer, but if you can get in, do so—staff here are considered especially friendly by our snoops, and they help make this an ideal starter course on the smorgasbord of world travelers who pass through hostels.

It is a great place, clean and quiet and well-situated. The free pancakes are a boon.

However, one past quibble: The early curfew has left us scrambling to get back. Luckily it has been changed. We also liked the free parking, movies, and cut-rate aquarium tickets.

The facility is close to tourist attractions like Fisherman's Wharf and the Monterey Bay Aquarium, but if you have transportation, we'd suggest you hoof it to Point Lobos State Reserve—a beautiful point of land jutting into Monterey Bay, rampant with deer, seals, and other unique flora and fauna. You might also want to coast down the highway toward Carmel—an exclusively exclusive town where buildings have no numbers. Come during February and you may get to see PGA favorites swing into action in a golf tournament at the gorgeous Pebble Beach golf course here.

However, the course itself is incredibly expensive to play—they don't really take very well to the ripped-jeans set, either. So don't count on squeezing in a round while you're here.

Best bet for a bite:
Red's Donuts on Alvarado
Insiders' tip:
KPIG radio station
What hostellers say:
"Let's play 18! Or not."
Gestalt:
Full Monterey
Hospitality: *A*
Cleanliness: *A*
Party index:

How to Get There:
By bus: Take #1 bus from Monterey Transit Center to Irving Street; bus runs until 10:30 p.m. Monday to Saturday, to 7:50 p.m. Sunday.
By car: From Highway 101 take Route 156 west to Monterey Peninsula, continue 5 miles to Highway 1. Go through Seaside and take Del Monte Avenue–Pacific Street exit; continue 2 miles and bear right through tunnel to Lighthouse Avenue. Continue 6 stop lights to Irving Street and turn left; hostel is 1 block up, on corner of Hawthorne and Irving.

Bill's Farm Hostel
10404 Cielo Lane, Nipomo, CA 93444
(805) 929-3647
  E-mail: bdenneen@slonet.org
  Web site: www.kcbx.net/~bdenneen/

Rates: $18 per person (free with work exchange)
Credit cards: None
Beds: 6
Private rooms: 2
Affiliation: None
Office hours: 8:00 a.m. to 9:00 p.m.
Extras: Television, piano, horses, bikes, darts, fireplace, weights, dinner

NOTE: Strictly no smoking.

*B*ill Denneen's hippie farm hostel is for travelers who want to get their hands dirty. Don't come here for a simple bed and kitchen to retreat to after a day of sightseeing. No, at Bill's you work with the earth and tend to the animals, experiencing life on a small organic farm firsthand.

Denneen's over eighty but never stops, moving from feeding the horses to tending the garden to milking the goats without skipping a beat. The man loves his farm. "I don't like L.A.," he told us once. "When I come back from there, I like to spend some time shoveling (word that means manure) to get the place out of my system." And you'll get the most out of your stay if you shovel it right beside him. Work exchange is favored over greenbacks here.

Time spent with the eccentric Denneen is, well, educational. He is proud of his reputation as an "environmental extremist" in the town of Nipomo. He even advertises it on his brochure, and his hostel Web page counsels you to "become a tree hugger." Signs spouting messages about boycotting oil and legalizing medical marijuana pepper his lawn. He wears shirts advocating vehicle-free Nipomo Dunes in a town where off-roading is basically a form of religion. And he's leading an unpopular push to gain federal protection for a large chunk of local seaside property. "Real estate developers hate me," he says, laughing.

The inside of his hostel is not the cleanest we've ever seen, but it's about at the level of what you'd expect from the type

Best bet for a bite:
Liquid lunch at Santa Maria Brewing
What hostellers say:
"Autocratic, idiosyncratic, unsympathetic."
Gestalt:
Weird beards
Hospitality: *C*
Cleanliness: *C*
Party index:

of place that attracts dudes in fuzzy goatees and felt hats. "People feel intimidated if you keep your house *too* clean," Denneen says by way of explanation. (Note to Bill: We're *not* in that category, man. Keep it clean! It's all good!) Guests are encouraged to participate in the communal evening meal, which is helpfully billed as "the only chance you'll have of Bill sitting still long enough to chat." Um, just wondering, is that a plus?

Explorers can check out the Nipomo Dunes or one of the several stunning beaches. Denneen has more information than you'll care to carry, and he arranges tons of events such as coastal hikes and bird-watches (check the Web site for updates) so he can impart his unique local knowledge all that much more thoroughly. Experienced riders are also welcome to saddle up a horse, and there are plenty of bikes for guests to borrow, too. Nice place. Not spic-and-span, and there's a huge leftward tilt to everything, but otherwise it's okay by us.

How to Get There:
By car: Take Teft Street exit off U.S. Highway 101 and head west (right turn from Highway 101 southbound). Drive a few blocks to Orchard Street, then turn left. Turn right at Primavera Lane, then take immediate left on Cielo. Hostel is on the right.

Pigeon Point Lighthouse Hostel
210 Pigeon Point Road, Pescadero, CA 94060
(650) 879-0633
  Fax: (650) 879-9120
  E-mail: pplhostel@norcalhostels.org
  Rates: $20 per Hostelling International member; $55 for private room
  Credit cards: MC, VISA
  Beds: 41
  Private rooms: 4
  Affiliation: Hostelling International
  Office hours: 7:30 to 11:00 a.m.; 3:30 to 11:00 p.m.
  Extras: Hot tub, kitchen, cafe, games, television

A jutting, lonely slab of rock on a windswept and remote stretch of coastline, Pigeon Point is named for the Boston ship *Carrier Pigeon* that wrecked off its jagged rocks in

1853. Now globe-trotters can gaze out on the vast expanse of water from the comfort of a cute little hostel that replaces the former living quarters of lighthouse keepers.

Like at its sister hostel, Point Montara just up the coast, hostellers are housed dormitory-style in four buildings. Remarkably, three out of the four buildings come replete with their own common areas and kitchens. The surrounding grounds consist of a small state park where day-trippers mostly gawk at the lighthouse; its amazing original Fresnel lens is still displayed inside, but a newer electric light does the job today.

Lockout and chores are strictly enforced, so it's a good idea to have an activity planned. What to do all day? This area of the coast is rife with parks; you can visit the only mainland breeding colony of elephant seals at Año Nuevo, south of the hostel on California Highway 1, or stroll through groves of redwoods 6 miles east in Butano State Park.

Whatever you do, you would be seriously remiss if you didn't cap off your day soaking in the gorgeously situated outdoor hot tub, and you can reserve it for private use.

Pigeon Point finds itself on a sparsely populated stretch of road, so there aren't many choices for eats. The hostel sells a variety of quick fixes in the way of soups and snacks, but if you really want to nosh in style, check out Duarte's in the tiny nearby town of Pescadero; the cream of artichoke soup—made from artichokes harvested in the area—is widely renowned.

We frequently heard this complaint, though: Some staff members aren't especially friendly. Professional, yes. Also, though there's supposedly a no-pets policy, we did note a couple of critters roaming the premises, which probably belong to a manager. Lastly, the walls are a bit thin.

Anyhow, this is one gorgeous hostel and a terrific place to score a private room if you can.

How to Get There:
By car: Drive California Highway 1 to 20 miles south of Half Moon Bay (or 27 miles north of Santa Cruz). Turn toward water and lighthouse at Pigeon Point Road.

Point Reyes Hostel

Box 247, Point Reyes Station, CA 94956

(415) 663-8811

Fax: (415) 663-8811

E-mail: prhostel@norcalhostels.org

Rates: $20 per Hostelling International member

Credit cards: MC, VISA

Beds: 45

Private rooms: None

Affiliation: Hostelling International

Office hours: 7:30 to 10:00 a.m.; 4:30 to 9:30 p.m.

Extras: Grill, kitchen

I t's hard to imagine a road being more full of sinewy twists, transmission-bustin' inclines, and breathtaking views than the one leading to the hostel at Point Reyes National Seashore. You really have to want to get there, but—once you've arrived—you might want to stay for a few days just to recover from the journey.

Tucked into a hillside within the Point Reyes National Seashore, this hostel is ideal for peace seekers, cyclists, and nature-lovers because hostellers here have access to one of the state's largest and best beaches. A forest fire a few years back nearly did it in, but the hostel survived and maintains a small, friendly facility. In a verrrry small space (this is the only complaint we have), it can house almost fifty hostellers at once when fully booked; reservations are a must, as are groceries purchased in advance. And don't expect a lot of breathing room. Everyone is welcome to take advantage of the patio, grill, and awesome views, so that tight packing might not bother you much so long as the weather's good.

Conserving natural resources is really the focus of this hostel, one of Hostelling

Best bet for a bite:
Back in civilization
Insiders' tip:
Got to check out Limantour Beach
What hostellers say:
"Awesome, dude."
Gestalt:
Silent night
Hospitality: *A*
Cleanliness: *A*
Party index:

International's few facilities to be designated as a Sustainable Living Center. They don't recycle just cans and bottles here. They have also developed a totally organic system to clean mopwater right on site, and a composting area exists to nurture the organic gardens. Wow!

Before you start making plans, though, keep in mind that this hostel is closed tighter than a drum between 11:00 a.m. and 3:30 p.m. The nearest bus stop is an 8-mile walk, so either plan to stick out your thumb or start hoofing it.

How to Get There:

By car: From San Francisco, drive north on U.S. Highway 101 to California Highway 1; go toward Olema and Point Reyes Station. Turn left onto Bear Valley Road, then take second left onto Limantour Road. After 5½ miles, turn left at crossroad. Hostel is on left.

Sacramento International Hostel

925 H Street, Sacramento, CA 95814

(916) 443-1691; (800) 909-4776 (U.S. only)

  Fax: (916) 443-4763

  E-mail: hisac@norcalhostels.org

  Rates: $22 per Hostelling International member

  Credit cards: MC, VISA

  Beds: 67

  Private rooms: 3

  Affiliation: Hostelling International

  Office hours: 7:30 a.m. to 10:30 p.m.

  Extras: Travel library, television, VCR, movie rentals, piano, barbecue/patio, bike storage, laundry, Internet access ($), kitchen

---

*H*ostelling International outdid itself with this one. A landmark Victorian home that dates to 1885 and stands practically in the shadow of California's capitol building, the Sacramento hostel is one of the organization's ten best in the West.

This was a big effort: More than $1 million in city funds, plus another chunk of Hostelling International's change, went into the renovations. It paid off in spades; there are frescoed ceilings, hand-carved fireplaces, elegant staircases, and immaculate upkeep. What else do you want? You're getting spoiled, no question about it—you'll feel like you're at a four-star hotel until the shock wears off—though breakfast doesn't come with it. Oh well. This is still great hostelling, and it's in a safe part of the city, as a bonus. It's not cheap, not at all, but for once a hostel delivers more than expected.

The facilities include a sociable basement dorm—it's next to the television room and an amazing travel library, so it's not nearly so bad as it sounds—plus some really nice private rooms with views of downtown Sacramento. Bathrooms are spacious and plentiful. The kitchen is a joy: big, well stocked, and a happy place to make a meal. Then you get

Best bet for a bite:
Midtown's chock-full
Insiders' tip:
Thursday night market
What hostellers say:
"Excellent value."
Gestalt:
Pot of gold
Safety: *A*
Hospitality: *A*
Cleanliness: *A*
Party index:

to eat in one of two first-class dining rooms and relax afterward in a parlor with scrapbooks, a piano, and other features. For travelers with special needs, there is a well-located—and roomy—first-floor private room called the River City Suite. It comes with its own bathroom, and the hostel's kitchen is also designed to easily accommodate wheelchairs.

What to do around town? Seek out Sacramento's interesting Midtown neighborhood: an alphabet-street mixture of funky shops, homes, and clubs that stretches for block after leafy block. It's a surprisingly fun place to check out for a day, making frequent stops for juice or ice cream if you're hoofing it around during Sacramento's stifling summer.

Closer to the hostel, try beers at a microbrewery or food at a street stall, check out Old Sacramento, a touristy, but still fun, little area nearby—a large railroad museum, a Kings basketball game, or whatever.

How to Get There:

By airplane: Medium-size airport outside city. Take shuttle to hostel.

By bus: Greyhound stops in Sacramento. From station walk 4 blocks north on Eighth Street to H Street; turn right and continue 2 blocks to hostel. Or take cab.

By car: Take Interstate 80 to I-5 north, then take J Street exit to Eighth Street. Turn right onto H Street and follow to corner of Eighth. Park on street (meters) or at hostel ($5 per day).

By train: Amtrak stops in Sacramento. From station, walk 4 blocks east to Tenth Street, turn left, and walk 1 block to hostel on H Street.

SAN DIEGO HOSTELS: A SUMMARY

	RATING	PROS	CONS	COST	PAGE
Point Loma Hostel	✹✹✹✹✹	common space	full dorms	$17	p. 265
Metropolitan Hostel	✹✹✹✹✹	skylights, location		$19	p. 264
Banana Bungalow	✹	on the beach	boozy	$20–$25	p. 262

Banana Bungalow Youth Hostel ✹

707 Reed Avenue, Mission Beach (San Diego), CA 92109

(858) 273-3060

Web site: www.bananabungalowsandiego.com

Rates: $20–$25 per person; $65–$105 for private room

Credit cards: AMEX, MC, VISA

Beds: 65

Private rooms: Yes

Affiliation: None

Office hours: Twenty-four hours

Extras: Barbecue, free breakfast, tours, kitchen, parking

NOTE: International passport required to stay.

Make no mistake about it: This beach institution (yes, it's right on the beach) is a magnet for burnouts, party animals, surfer dudes, and the like. The San Diego Banana Bungalow—one of the last Bungalows left standing—tries to create a fun atmosphere but ends up as a virtual free-for-all, with scarcely a rule to consider and no regard whatsoever for basic hygiene or cleanliness. It is one of the most sociable hostels we've come across in America, but our snoops consider it one of the grimiest. Consider the other hostels in town first. And second.

For true beach bums, though, no location can beat this one. The hostel is right on oceanfront property, closer to the inviting blue swells of the Pacific than any other hostel in Southern California. The back patio is a good place from which to watch the whole beach scene; sucking down beers is the preferred activity while doing so.

Too bad the rest of the facility is seriously lacking, closer to indoor camping than hostelling. Beds are crammed every which way, the kitchen can be a disaster area, and the common areas need work—as they have, for ages. Expect noise and merriment at night; light sleepers won't be happy. None of this seems to bother the hard-core partiers a bit, and anybody looking for a party will find it here and make loads of new buds. The rest of us will move along.

Best bet for a bite:
Kojak's
Insiders' tip:
Build up your alcohol tolerance
What hostellers say:
"Dude, let's get some brewskies."
Gestalt:
Banana daiquiri
Safety: *C*
Hospitality: *C*
Cleanliness: *F*
Party index:

How to Get There:

By airplane: Airport in San Diego. Take bus #2 to Broadway downtown. Transfer to bus #34 and get off at Mission Boulevard and Reed Avenue. Walk ½ block along Reed to hostel.

By bus: Greyhound stops in San Diego. From station take #34 bus to Mission Boulevard and Reed Avenue. Walk ½ block on Reed to hostel.

By car: From I-5, go west on Garrett Avenue. Turn south on Mission Boulevard and right on Reed Avenue. Drive ½ block on Reed to hostel and hunt for parking.

By train: Amtrak stops in San Diego. From station take #34 bus to Mission Boulevard and Reed Avenue. Walk ½ block on Reed to hostel.

Attractive natural setting	Comfortable beds	Visual arts at hostel or nearby
Ecologically aware hostel	A particularly good value	Music at hostel or nearby
Superior kitchen facilities or cafe	Wheelchair-accessible	Great hostel for skiers
Offbeat or eccentric place	Good for business travelers	Bar or pub at hostel or nearby
Superior bathroom facilities	Especially well-suited for families	Editors' choice: Among our very favorite hostels
Romantic private rooms	Good for active travelers	

Key to Icons

Metropolitan Hostel

521 Market Street, San Diego, CA 92101

(619) 525-1531

Fax: (619) 338-0129

E-mail: downtown@sandiegohostels.org

Rates: $19 per Hostelling International member; $47 for private room

Credit cards: MC, VISA

Beds: 74

Private rooms: 24

Affiliation: Hostelling International

Office hours: Twenty-four hours

Extras: Laundry, television, VCR, lockers, bike rental, Internet access, free parking, pool table

*H*ostelling International had big plans for this joint in San Diego, and it has become one of its star properties nationwide. A lot of bucks were poured into this lavish Mediterranean facility.

The accommodations here seem basic at first glance but are neat, clean, and reliable: better than 95 percent of the other places in this book just on those basic counts. Dorms come in combinations of four, six, eight, or ten beds per room. Smaller dorms share bathrooms, while larger dorms have their own bathroom facilities. Private rooms are equipped with a desk and a lamp. The kitchen gets a special nod for its size, setup, cleanliness, and convenience.

The hostel is right in the heart of the historic Gas Lamp district, an area filled with charming shops and restaurants. The place could not be more central, with public transportation to all outlying attractions practically at the hostel's doorstep. The big advantage here is that Americans are not barred from the premises.

Best bet for a bite:

Croce's Top Hat

What hostellers say:

"Outstanding!"

Gestalt:

Get Met

Safety: *A*

Hospitality: *B*

Cleanliness: *A*

Party index:

How to Get There:

By airplane: Large airport in San Diego. From airport, take #992 (The Flyer) bus to Fifth Street and Broadway. Walk south 4 blocks on Fifth to Market. Hostel is at corner of Fifth and Market.

By bus: Greyhound stops in San Diego. From station, walk east on Broadway to Fifth Street, then south 4 blocks on Fifth to Market. Hostel is at corner of Fifth and Market.

By car: From I-5, exit at Front Street and turn left at Market. Hostel is at corner of Fifth and Market.

By train: Amtrak stops in San Diego. From station, take Bayside Trolley to Convention Center. Walk north 3 blocks to hostel on corner of Fifth and Market.

Point Loma Hostel ✳✳✳✳✺

3790 Udall Street, San Diego, CA 92107-2414

(619) 223-4778

> **Fax:** (619) 223-1883
>
> **E-mail:** pointloma@sandiegohostels.org
>
> **Rates:** $17 per Hostelling International member; $42 for private room
>
> **Credit cards:** MC, VISA
>
> **Beds:** 52
>
> **Private rooms:** 8
>
> **Affiliation:** Hostelling International
>
> **Office hours:** 8:00 a.m. to 10:00 p.m.
>
> **Extras:** Laundry, table tennis, television, VCR, DVD player, boogie board rental, bike rental, barbecue, Internet access, kitchen, storage

---

"People use our hostel like they use a home," said one manager of this big red house in a residential San Diego neighborhood. "They come here because they don't like the atmosphere of the beach hostels, but they want to be near the beach." Sounds about right. The Point Loma offers more of a family-type atmosphere than do the city's other hostels. Think of it as "San Diego Lite," and *don't* come if you want to party.

The airport and downtown are both about a half-hour bus ride away, and the beach is a bit of a hike. Staffers speak of restaurants in the immediate area, but all we found was a strip mall and a few random joints. You need to get in a car—something most of the visitors to the Point Loma possess—or bus to find any nightlife. That's okay, however, because the hostel is actually hopping most evenings (in a sedate way)—between table tennis tournaments and video screenings, there should be enough going on to keep you occupied. There is a tremendous amount of common space in the building divvied up as outdoor courtyard, lounge area, and humongous kitchen and dining room. The hostel caters to a few long-termers, mostly folks who are just arriving in San Diego and looking for an apartment, but it seems to work out okay. There is a two-week max for stays, and it is not just apartment hunters who take advantage of it. Many travelers do, too, because once they get settled they feel comfortable here.

The sleeping arrangements are not quite as inviting as the common space. The hostel is actually an old house of worship—we're not sure what faith—that has been carved into several rooms. This works to your advantage in terms of a spacious downstairs. The spacing in the upstairs sleeping quarters is a bit awkward, though, with beds fitted tightly into narrow rooms. The private rooms, most with a bunk and a double, are small but thoughtfully furnished.

No need to worry about a lockout here; guests may come and go as they please, and most do. At any time of day you're likely to find a few stragglers hanging around reading a newspaper or studying a map. Staff are pleasantly friendly and helpful. The typical guest seems to be a few years older and a bit more mature than at most hostels; we're not talking the golden-age set, just a higher ratio of thirtysomethings finding themselves as they cycle the Bikecentennial trail (easily accessible from the hostel) or make their soul-searching journey in some other fashion.

How to Get There:
By airplane: Leave airport to North Harbor Drive. Take #922/923 bus on airport side of street. Get off bus at Voltaire and Poinsettia. Follow Poinsettia, turn right onto Udall Street. Hostel is red building on right. *NOTE:* Bus runs only Monday through Friday.

By bus: Take #35 bus westbound to Ocean Beach and get off at Voltaire and Poinsettia. Walk 1 block back along Voltaire to Worden and turn left to Udall.

By car: Take I-5 to Sea World Drive exit and go west. Bear right onto Sunset Cliffs Boulevard, then turn left onto Voltaire. Turn right a few blocks down on Worden and go up 1 block to Udall.

By train: Call hostel for transit route.

SAN FRANCISCO HOSTELS: A SUMMARY					
	RATING	PROS	CONS	COST	PAGE
San Francisco City Center Hostel	★★★★★	bathrooms	location	$23	p. 280
USA Hostels San Francisco	★★★★☆	fun	popular	$25–$36	p. 281
Fisherman's Wharf Hostel	★★★★☆	view, parking	stiffness	$28	p. 272
Adelaide Hostel	★★★	fun	busy	$23–$26	p. 268
Pacific Tradewinds Guest House	★★★	friendly	tight	$26–$28	p. 278
Downtown San Francisco Hostel	★★☆	central	iffy	$25	p. 269
Green Tortoise Guesthouse	★★☆	fun	worn	$28–$33	p. 276
Globetrotter's Inn	★★	active	poor neighborhood	$20	p. 275
Globe Hostel	👎		partying residents	$20–$22	p. 273
European Guest House	👎	laundry	unsafe area	$17–$20	p. 270

Adelaide Hostel ✹✹✹

5 Isadora Duncan Lane, San Francisco, CA 94102

(877) 359-1915

Web site: www.adelaidehostel.com

E-mail: info@adelaidehostel.com

Rates: $23–$26 per person; $60 for private room

Credit cards: AMEX, DISC, JTB, MC, VISA

Beds: Number varies

Private rooms: Yes

Affiliation: None

Office hours: Twenty-four hours

Extras: Laundry with free soap, Internet access, free Wi-Fi, storage, free breakfast, parking ($), television, kitchen, dinner ($)

NOTE: Passport and ID required for check-in.

*W*e've long been shocked by the poor stock of hostels in San Fran, which is one of America's greatest cities and ought to possess some of its very finest accommodations, at all levels. Yet the hostels here generally suck (see elsewhere in this section for a few notable exceptions, though).

So we were glad to see this place open near Union Square, a popular shopping and sightseeing hub downtown, in an old house with "character." It's not a bad place at all. They've got the right attitude, mostly—keeping it pretty clean so far—offering dorms with four, six, or ten beds apiece, plus some decent private rooms. There's also a big kitchen with two (count 'em) stoves; a good-size lounge/dining room with satellite TV; free Wi-Fi throughout; and huge free breakfasts that were very popular with hostellers we spoke with. (They also cook and serve good dinners for a small fee.) It draws a fun, young, international crowd and that is a big plus over other places that just draw, say, Americans or families. One caveat: The hostel maintains relationships with some annexes and neighboring hotels, so you might book a room in the main building

Best bet for a bite:
Cook it yourself
What hostellers say:
"Thanks for opening."
Gestalt:
San Fun
Safety: *B*
Hospitality: *C*
Cleanliness: *B*
Party index: 🎉🎉🎉

and end up shunted off to another building (without a kitchen in it). We hate that. So ask before you arrive, to ensure you'll be in the main building.

All in all, a much-needed addition to the local hostelling scene.

How to Get There:

By airplane: Large airport outside San Francisco. From airport take 7B or 7F bus, shuttle, or BART into city; call hostel for transit route.

By bus: Greyhound stops downtown. Call hostel for transit route.

By car: Call hostel for directions.

By train: Caltrain and BART stop downtown. Amtrak stops in Emeryville; take shuttle bus into San Francisco. Call hostel for transit route.

Downtown San Francisco Hostel

312 Mason Street, San Francisco, CA 94102
(415) 788-5604; (800) 909-4776 (U.S. only)
   E-mail: dtinfo@sfhostels.com
   Rates: $25 per Hostelling International member; $69 for single room
   Credit cards: JCB, MC, VISA
   Beds: 192
   Private rooms: 38
   Affiliation: Hostelling International
   Office hours: Twenty-four hours
   Extras: Television, nightly movies, local tours, Internet access, lockers, kitchenette

---

For all the advantages of the downtown San Francisco Hostel, you have to scratch your head about a couple things here: first, the location. Set in the former Hotel Virginia, it's smack on the borderline between one mighty run-down neighborhood (the Tenderloin) and one super-glitzy one (Union Square). The result is a complete dearth of budget eats or parking or entertainment—unless you count the numerous peep shows—in the immediate vicinity. Head out for Nordstrom, turn the wrong way, and you could be in trouble. No, you don't really want to be walking down any dark alleys in this neck of San Francisco. They also took far too long to outfit this place with a decent kitchen and laundry.

On the plus side, the staff is mostly helpful—a few glaring exceptions here, too—despite the high traffic (people without reservations line up outside the door to try to snag beds at check-in time) and general strangeness of the neighborhood. The facilities do include an Internet connection. But it's not really enough to overcome the crowded bunkrooms. Traffic noise is a problem, too. On the upside, the private rooms are essentially hotel-quality: pretty good. Would we stay here again? Sure, though there are definitely better deals—and hostel experiences—in the city. Check the two other HI-run hostels for space first. This place is just okay, not great.

How to Get There:

By airplane: From airport take shuttle or use 7B or 7F bus to bus terminal; then take #38 bus to Geary and Mason. Walk down Mason Street ½ block. Hostel is on left.

By bus: Greyhound stops in San Francisco. Take #2 bus to Sutter and Mason, then walk 3 blocks south to hostel.

By car: Drive on U.S. Highway 101 (Van Ness Avenue) to Geary or Post; turn east, drive to Mason Street and park.

By train: Caltrain and BART stop in San Francisco. Take #2 bus to Sutter and Mason, then walk 3 blocks south to hostel. Or take #38 bus to Geary and Mason and walk to hostel. Amtrak stops in Emeryville; take shuttle to San Francisco.

European Guest House

761 Minna Street, San Francisco, CA 94103
(415) 861-6634

Rates: $17–$20 per person; $30–$50 for private room
Credit cards: DISC, MC, VISA
Beds: 60
Private rooms: Yes
Affiliation: None

Office hours: 6:00 a.m. to 2:00 a.m.

Extras: Laundry, TV, VCR, kitchen, Internet access ($), roof deck

W e're not sure if this hostel lives up to the expectations a tired traveler would have about a place called the European Guest House. Resembling a residential hotel, the place is sort of dark and gloomy, and the many plants that management has spread around the hostel don't do much to change that impression. There are several floors of hallways and a common room/eating area that reminded us of a hospital cafeteria. Half the rooms here are quad rooms, half are doubles, but the hostel gets very crowded at times, with excess numbers bunking down wherever they can, even on the floor.

Judging from the amount of food lying around and in lockers, you might guess this place has its share of long-term residents. You'd be right: Half (all?) the guests here seemed to be either transient, homeless, or otherwise in transition. The only other "tourists" we met here were trying desperately to book new rooms for the following day! A TV/VCR mounted on the wall (and left running twenty-four hours a day) doesn't seem to work as a social mixer, but that's not surprising; many guests were simply passed out cold. Staff leave something to be desired, too—these folks seem to enjoy keeping secrets about the place, and we don't think they're pretty.

The location of this hostel is also grim: The south of Market area *can* be fun, but it can also be sketchy. The narrow alleyway that is Minna Street makes people nervous even during the height of the day; needless to say, be very careful at night if you choose to stay at this hostel.

Best bet for a bite:
Burritos in the Mission
What hostellers say:
"Horrible neighborhood."
Gestalt:
Euro-trash
Safety: *F*
Hospitality: *D*
Cleanliness: *F*
Party index:

All things considered, we'd definitely place this at or near the bottom of the San Fran options. There are some great hostels and neighborhoods to stay at in this city, so take a pass on this one.

How to Get There:

By airplane: Large airport outside San Francisco. From airport, take 7B or 7F bus, shuttle, or BART into city; call hostel for transit route.

By bus: Greyhound stops downtown. Call hostel for transit route.

By car: Call hostel for directions.

By train: Caltrain and BART stop downtown. Amtrak stops in Emeryville; take shuttle bus into San Francisco. Call hostel for transit route.

Fisherman's Wharf Hostel ✳✳✳✴

Building 240, Fort Mason, San Francisco, CA 94123

(415) 771-7277

> **Fax:** (415) 771-1468
>
> **E-mail:** fwinfo@sfhostels.com
>
> **Rates:** $28 per Hostelling International member; $75 for single room
>
> **Credit cards:** JCB, MC, VISA
>
> **Beds:** 144
>
> **Private rooms:** None
>
> **Affiliation:** Hostelling International
>
> **Office hours:** Twenty-four hours
>
> **Extras:** Pool table, stamps, laundry, lockers, cafe, movies, info kiosk, tours, Internet access, kitchen, free parking

---

*N*ow this is a hostel worth knowing about and one worthy of such a great city. Occupying the former infirmary building of Fort Mason, the hostel perches on a cliff overlooking the Golden Gate Bridge, the Marin Headlands, Alcatraz, and even the Bay Bridge. What an unbelievably fantastic piece of real estate; the views alone would be worth millions to developers. Yet a bunk here costs you less than one at Hostelling International's downtown hostel.

Unlike many HI-affiliated hostels, this one locks you out for only two hours. But no matter: There's lots to do both in the neighborhood and inside the hostel itself. Besides a common room with a fireplace, the place has a good kitchen with big tables and lots of counter and stove space. A small cafe serves coffee and simple breakfasts as well. At night you can avail yourself of the pool table. There's even a stamp machine, if letter writing is your thing. A number of clubs and good restaurants are nearby on Lombard, Chestnut, and Union Streets, not to mention the usual tourist attractions and views at Fisherman's Wharf. The free parking is a big bonus if you've brought a car (just lock up at night, to be safe).

The most common complaints we heard from hostellers here were that some members of the staff are cool, that it's a bit boring here (which is true), and that it's a little far from the main sights—also true, with the exception of the Golden Gate Bridge, which is so close you can practically eat off it (not recommended).

Taken as a whole, this joint is clean, well-managed, a little rigid: much better for a group of soccer moms and their team than serious Euro-hostellers or spring-breakers. But if you're in a pinch and need a clean bed that's no more than a cab ride from most of San Fran, it'll work.

Best bet for a bite:
Taste of the Himalayas (Tibetan!)
Insiders' tip:
Stroll across that big orange bridge
What hostellers say:
"What a view!"
Gestalt:
San Francisco treat
Safety: *B*
Hospitality: *B*
Cleanliness: *B*
Party index:

How to Get There:

By airplane: Large airport forty-five minutes from hostel. Take 7B or 7F bus to city bus terminal or BART to downtown, then take #42 bus to Bay and Van Ness, walk 1 block west to Fort Mason gates, enter fort, and follow signs. Or take shuttle to hostel.

By bus: Greyhound stops downtown. Take #42 bus to Bay and Van Ness, then walk 1 block west to Fort Mason gates. Enter fort and follow signs.

By car: Take U.S. Highway 101 (Van Ness Avenue) to Lombard Street, then turn onto Franklin and drive through Fort Mason gates toward water to the end.

By train: CalTrain and BART stop downtown. Take #42 bus to Bay and Van Ness, then walk 1 block west to Fort Mason gates. Enter fort and follow signs.

Amtrak stops in Emeryville; take shuttle bus into San Francisco, then take #42 bus to Bay and Van Ness. Walk 1 block west to Fort Mason gates. Enter fort and follow signs.

Globe Hostel ◯

10 Hallam Place, San Francisco, CA 94103

(415) 431-0540

 Rates: $20–$22 per person; $50 for private room

 Credit cards: None

Beds: 150
Private rooms: Yes
Affiliation: None
Office hours: Twenty-four hours
Extras: Laundry, fax, cafe, television, sundeck, bar, pool table, storage, free tea and coffee

---

*W*e have to admit that we used to like this chill, social hostel and its fun staff. While the neighborhood was okay, you could hang around the place all day and night and have plenty to do without ever going anywhere. Check out the aquarium, drink beer on the sun roof and admire the view, play pool with some of the other international guests. For sure, it was a place for partiers; even during a quick stop in, we've often been invited to parties here.

Trouble is, some of the guests stay on. And on. And on. Some people have been here, like, ten years!! Folks, that is not a hostel. It's something else. And it's no longer clean or friendly or safe enough to get our recommendation, though Eastern Europeans wishing to see a beer-blast version of the U.S.A. would probably still love it.

The hostel sits in the SoMa (South of Market) district, where there are plenty of coffeehouses, computer geeks, and retro clothing around if you know where to find them. There are also plenty of galleries and clubs, and there are remnants of a gay-biker heyday, such as leather shops, as well. (This hostel itself used to be a gay bathhouse, and the owner has decorated it with lots of photography and articles related to its former days. Um, okay.)

Best bet for a bite:
Trader Joe's on Ninth Street
Insiders' tip:
Clubs and coffee in SoMa
What hostellers say:
"Party hard, hipsters!"
Gestalt:
Gin blossoms
Safety: *D*
Hospitality: *F*
Cleanliness: *D*
Party index: 🎉🎉🎉🎉🎉

Each dorm room holds about five people and has its own private bath. Guests can't usually use the "staff" kitchen, so they have to either settle for something microwaved or hit the Mexican place down the street. On the refrigerator, there's a listing of all the free meals given away in San Francisco (what does this say about the hostel?); we say, open up the kitchen to the rest of us, and hungry guests will keep their mitts off the staff grub.

All in all, if you like to party and don't care about nutrition or hygiene, hey, check it out. But it's not for us.

How to Get There:

By airplane: Take airport shuttle, city bus 7B, or BART. Then take #12 bus to corner of Folsom and Harrison or #41 bus to corner of Harrison and Eighth and turn left at Folsom. If you take BART, get off at Civic Center Station and walk west on Seventh or Eighth Streets.
By bus: Greyhound stops nearby. Take cab at night.
By car: Call hostel for directions.
By train: Amtrak stops nearby. Take cab at night or call hostel for bus route.

Globetrotter's Inn

225 Ellis Street, San Francisco, CA 94102
(415) 346-5786

Fax: (415) 346-5786
E-mail: info@globetrottersinn.com
Web site: www.globetrottersinn.com
Rates: $20 per person; $58 for private room
Credit cards: MC, VISA
Beds: 30
Private rooms: 7
Affiliation: None
Office hours: 8:00 a.m. to midnight
Extras: Laundry, television, kitchen, free Internet access, free breakfast

---

The Globetrotter's Inn used to be one of the worst hostels in town, but by default (others are fading away) it is inching up the ladder ever so slightly. Not a great choice, though: For starters, it's smack in the heart of the Tenderloin, San Francisco's worst neighborhood. You don't want to fool around here at night, trust us. At least this street gets twenty-four-hour traffic, being right downtown, but it's no place to wander; use a cab.

Rooms crowd along two narrow halls, and your roomie will probably be somebody

Best bet for a bite:
Union Square diners
What hostellers say:
"Any other hostels in town?"
Gestalt:
Global warning
Safety: C
Hospitality: C
Cleanliness: D
Party index: 🎉🎉🎉🎉

who's living here for several months while he/she tries to find a job (or simply avoids reality). The kitchen is tiny, bathrooms are serviceable but not plentiful, and the neighborhood is just plain lousy. One staffer actually referred us to another, "cleaner" hostel elsewhere in the city. You definitely can do better and should try. On the upside, the crowd is usually young and international, so it's not as morose—or as dirty—as some of the other total dives in town. That's hardly a glowing recommendation. We're just saying.

How to Get There:

By airplane: Large airport outside city. Take airport shuttle, BART, or the 292 Samtrans bus ($2). Take bus to corner of Mission and Fifth Street. Cross Mission and walk up Fifth Street past Market to Ellis Street. Turn left, walk 1 block to Mason Street. Hostel is at corner of Mason above Red's Corner bar.

By bus: Greyhound stops nearby. Take cab at night, or call hostel for bus route.

By car: Call hostel for directions.

By train: Caltrain stops nearby. Amtrak stops in Emeryville. Take shuttle to San Francisco, then call hostel for bus route (or take a cab at night).

Green Tortoise Guesthouse

494 Broadway, San Francisco, CA 94133

(415) 834-1000; (800) 867-8647

  Fax: (415) 956-4900

  E-mail: hostel@greentortoise.com

  Web site: www.greentortoise.com

  Rates: $28–$33 per person; $65–$78 for private room

  Credit cards: None

  Beds: 130

  Private rooms: 10

  Affiliation: None

  Office hours: Twenty-four hours

  Extras: Television, parties, sauna, locker storage, free breakfast, free dinner (sometimes), laundry, pool table, kitchen, Internet access, foosball

*T*his is it: headquarters for the justly famous Green Tortoise bus network and mini-hotel dynasty.

This hostel, located on the edge of San Francisco's Italian North Beach neighborhood, originally developed as a place for the bus-trippers to hang out for a while in the city by the bay; eventually, though, the hostel business became more important than the travel service.

First things first: This is definitely not a place for the shy. Front desk personnel sport various pierced body parts. Party types congregate in a big former ballroom, smoking butts or sipping brews. Management is generally friendly, giving the place a laid-back feel. At times, though, it begins to resemble chaos, especially on a weekend night, and you might not like that if you've come seeking peace and quiet in San Fran.

The dorm rooms here are adequate; that's all—though a few coats of paint and improved aeration have helped. There's a small sauna, a few bathrooms, and a postage-stamp-size kitchen, if that gives you some idea of the place. This is a crash pad, basically, though much more fun and social than many others we've seen. A free continental breakfast, occasional beer parties, and free dinner three times per week all help lube up the social interaction.

Much better, especially if you're traveling as a pair, is the small number of private rooms. These rooms offer more breathing space, fewer hostellers per bathroom, and decent kitchen facilities—at very affordable prices. (We did hear complaints about Green Tortoise's propensity to charge a few bucks for each of various extras.) Also, they supposedly do not check in any guests with local ID, trying to crack down on the "long-termer's disease" that plagues so many other hostels in town.

The neighborhood is very happening, so almost anything can happen. Nude dance clubs mingle with open-air coffeehouses, Korean restaurants, and more. It's pretty well lit and safe, but just be aware at night—this *is* a city, after all. Our picks? City Lights Books (next to Jack Kerouac Alley, don't you know) is practically across the street. There's the Italian district of Nob Hill, with its own various charms, down Columbus Avenue. Good health food, Asian, and hamburger joints rise up from the hills around the hostel, too; while overpriced, they offer welcome relief from the usual fast-food junk.

Best bet for a bite:
Taqueria next door
Insiders' tip:
Italian coffeehouses in the nabe
What hostellers say:
"Bottoms up."
Gestalt:
Ballroom blitz
Safety: *C*
Hospitality: *B*
Cleanliness: *C*
Party index: 🎉🎉🎉🎉🎉

This is not a bad place, not at all. It's not pristinely clean or serenely quiet, either. But if you're seeking fun and fun only, it's a pretty good pick.

How to Get There:
By airplane: From airport take shuttle, city bus, or BART (call hostel for route).
By bus: Greyhound stops on Mission. Take #12 or #42 bus to Pacific; walk to Broadway. Or take #15 bus.
By car: Call hostel for directions.
By train: Call hostel for directions.

Pacific Tradewinds Guest House
680 Sacramento Street, San Francisco, CA 94111
(415) 433-7970; (888) SF-HOSTEL
   Fax: (415) 433-7970
   E-mail: info@pactradewinds.com
   Web site: www.pactradewinds.com
   Rates: $26–$28 per person
   Credit cards: AMEX, MC, VISA
   Beds: 28
   Private rooms: None
   Affiliation: None
   Office hours: 8:00 a.m. to midnight
   Extras: Laundry, fax machine, kitchen, free Internet access

---

*T*o get to this tiny, popular hostel, you're forced to run an upstairs gauntlet past two floors of a Chinese restaurant. If there's anything hostellers complain about here, it's the size of the place: Just two bathrooms serve the entire twenty-eight-bed facility, which is rough at times, and dorm rooms obviously get a bit cramped. There are no doors, by the way; the bunks are literally out in the hallways, and even the four-bedded, partitioned-off sections feel like they are part of a thirty-bed room. Joyful revelers also tend to stay up late, foiling attempts at early sleep. It really depends on who's booked in: losers, sex partners, and drifters will ruin your sleep. Cool people will befriend you. Quiet travelers will soothe you. You can't control any of it, because of the proximity of everything. Beds really aren't that comfortable, either.

The common area is also small, but very well-utilized by a generally happy and convivial crowd; games and binders full of travel info line the walls, and a long dining room table encourages conversation. Tradewinds does seem to attract an unusual proportion of friendly, curious travelers from all over the globe, so that's probably the biggest draw. Also, you're relatively close to some cool sights (China-

Best bet for a bite:
Henry's Hunan downstairs
Insiders' tip:
Don't leave valuables in your car
What hostellers say:
"Good atmosphere, though tiny."
Gestalt:
Trade-off
Safety: *C*
Hospitality: *B*
Cleanliness: *C*
Party index:

town, Lombard Street, Nob Hill, and so forth)—staff can helpfully direct you. The place is like a short course in international relations, and for that it's worth a look. The kitchen and free Internet access are also gaining positive reviews. But that's about it, for services; you're mostly on your own, which is fine in a city like San Fran with so much to do. Just don't plan to spend hours hanging out alone in this hostel enjoying your personal space; it ain't gonna happen, because there *is* no space.

A warning: Don't leave your car in this neighborhood overnight (we tried; bad idea), and don't walk around alone late, late at night, either. Cabs exist for a reason.

How to Get There:
By airplane: Take airport shuttle, 7B or 7F bus, or BART to city. Call hostel for transit route.
By bus: Greyhound stops in city. From station walk up First Street through Market onto Battery; continue north to Sacramento, then turn left; walk 3 blocks to hostel.
By car: Call hostel for directions.
By train: Amtrak stops in Emeryville; take shuttle to San Francisco's Ferry Building. Walk across Embarcadero to Justin Herman Park. Sacramento Street begins to left of tall building; walk 6 blocks to hostel.

San Francisco City Center Hostel

685 Ellis Street, San Francisco, CA 94109

(415) 474-5721

Fax: (415) 776-0755

E-mail: ccinfo@sfhostels.com

Rates: $23 per Hostelling International member; $82 for private room

Credit cards: MC, VISA

Beds: 185

Private rooms: 8

Affiliation: Hostelling International

Office hours: Twenty-four hours

Extras: Internet access, television, lockers, kitchen, tours

A much-needed addition to San Fran's hostel scene, this is yet another renovated older hotel in the beating heart of the city by the bay—only 5 blocks from the other downtown HI hostel, but much better. Keep in mind that the Tenderloin 'hood is sketchy, especially in the section near this hostel; don't walk alone in this area at night.

Otherwise, it's great. You'll be very comfortable in the place, a former hotel that's been retrofitted with dorms topping out at no more than four beds apiece. The hostel's building is elegantly decorated and a specimen of the fine architecture San Francisco is known for. Staff works the front desk 24/7/365, mostly friendly and helpful, and all rooms contain their own bathrooms. Guests seem to enjoy socializing with each other in the beautiful lobby; the music sets a nice mood to compare travel tales.

The kitchen rocks, too. It's huge, clean, and well-utilized without being crowded. There is an elegant reading room and a dining room converted from a classy old bar.

Best bet for a bite:
Double Rainbow ice cream parlors

Insiders' tip:
Beware of parking laws

What hostellers say:
"Great digs!"

Gestalt:
Nice-a-roni

Safety: *B*

Hospitality: *B*

Cleanliness: *A*

Party index: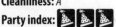

No laundry, though—serious bummer there—and no free breakfast. Whaa? Anyway, this place stands out in a city full of dumpy hostels; compared to them, it's practically a hotel. If only the neighborhood were safer—or at least better-policed.

Anyway, best bunk in the city? Yes, yes. You've found it here.

How to Get There:

By airplane: Take airport shuttle, 7B or 7F bus, or BART to city. Call hostel for transit route.
By bus: Contact hostel for transit details.
By car: Contact hostel for directions.
By train: Amtrak stops in Emeryville. From station, take shuttle to Ferry Building in San Francisco. Walk to Embarcadero BART station and take BART subway train to Civic Center. Continue to Ellis Street.

USA Hostels San Francisco

749 Taylor Street, San Francisco, CA 94108
(415) 440-5600; (877) 483-2950
Fax: (415) 651-8802
E-mail: sanfrancisco@usahostels.com
Web site: www.usahostels.com/sf
Rates: $25–$36 per person; $56–$76 for private room
Credit cards: MC, VISA
Private rooms: Yes
Affiliation: USA Hostels
Office hours: 6:00 a.m. to 6:00 p.m.
Extras: Storage, Internet access ($), laundry, television, patios, tours ($), meals, free breakfast, foosball

---

NOTE: Foreign passport or out-of-state ID required.

*T*his newish hostel, in a three-story townhouse with nice architectural touches of trim and lighting, scores big in hostel-plenty (yet quality-poor) San Fran. It's fun, clean enough, and not saddled with the stiffness that afflicts many "official" hostels.

Big and airy dorm rooms, kitted out with four to six beds each, are clean and comfortable, with marble-tiled bathrooms. Staff claim to change the mattresses often to maintain a high sleepability factor; we'll see. And the private rooms (in an annex around the corner, on Sutter Street) are nearly hotel-quality, with such goodies as a dresser, regulation TV, big queen bed or two bunks, private bathroom, and maybe an antique mirror.

Shared amenities are plentiful, too—high-speed Internet access; free linens, coffee, and incoming phone calls; a laundry room with free powder; a patio backyard with picnic tables for socializing; free Xbox games, rockin' foosball matches, DVDs playing on the huge theater-like TV; you get the idea. Not to mention the pancakes and waffles each morning . . . again, FREE. (Are you sensing a theme?) Obviously a lot of thought has gone into this place. Wanna cook? Do it in the cool lime-green kitchen. The annex has its own kitchen, as well as an Internet cafe, too.

And the kicker is that the location is not all that bad: The place is a couple blocks from Union Square and cable cars, bookshops, department stores, Chinatown, and so on. You can book cheap walking tours of San Francisco or shuttle rides to L.A. right at the front desk. Meals are served, pub crawls and parties conducted, and there's neither a curfew nor a lockout to crush your daytime or nightlife plans. In short, it's close to perfect and it's fast becoming a favorite.

How to Get There:
By airplane: From Oakland Airport, take the AirBART shuttle to the Coliseum/Oakland Airport BART station. Take a train in the direction of Daly City, Millbrae, or San Francisco Airport. Exit at Powell Street Station.

From San Francisco International Airport, go to the BART station found on Level 3 of the International Terminal and take a train in the direction of Dublin or Pittsburg. Exit at Powell Street Station. When you exit the train at the Powell Street station, take the escalator marked "Hallidie Plaza," and once you pass through the turnstiles turn right in the direction of Hallidie Plaza (do not enter shopping mall), exit station and to your right will be another escalator to Powell Street. Turn left at the top of the escalator and walk up Powell Street, following the cable cars. Turn left onto Sutter, and then turn right onto Taylor. The hostel is on the left (749 Taylor Street). If you're checking into the annex on Sutter Street, don't turn right onto Taylor. The annex will be on the left side of Sutter Street (#717).

By bus: Greyhound stops in San Francisco. From bus station, walk southwest on Mission Street to First Street; turn right and cross Market Street. Turn left on Market and continue southwest, bearing right onto Sutter Street at See's Candy store. Continue along Sutter to Taylor Street and turn right; hostel is on left. (For annex building, do not turn onto Taylor; annex is on Sutter Street at #717.)

By car: From I-5, take Highway 505 south or Highway 580 West, then merge onto 80 Freeway West. Take Fremont Street exit, turning left onto Fremont. Fremont becomes Front Street; turn left onto Pine Street, then left again onto Mason Street and right on Sutter Street. Finally, turn right onto Taylor Street. Park in street or at nearby lots (about $15 daily).

By train: Amtrak stops in Emeryville. Take shuttle to Shopping Center stop in San Francisco. Walk up Powell Street, following cable cars. Turn left onto Sutter Street, then right onto Taylor. Hostel is on left. (For annex building, stay on Sutter; hostel is on left at #717.)

Hostel Obispo ✳✳✳✳

1617 Santa Rosa Street, San Luis Obispo, CA 93401
(805) 544-4678

> **E-mail:** reservations@hostelobispo.com
> **Rates:** $20 per Hostelling International member; $45 for single room
> **Credit cards:** None
> **Beds:** 22
> **Private/family rooms:** 4
> **Affiliation:** Hostelling International
> **Office hours:** 8:00 to 10:00 a.m.; 4:30 to 10:00 p.m.
> **Extras:** Laundry, bicycle rentals, grill, store, piano, fireplace, garden, breakfast

---

This sunny California joint, located right in downtown San Luis Obispo, scores big with us and our hostelling buddies.

We really like the laid-back atmosphere, which manifests itself in a number of forms;

discounts for hostellers who cycle into town; a patio-and-barbecue setup; and even pancakes and (sometimes) free bagels in the mornin'. The owner/manager is often on duty, and she's doing a great job.

Events like guided hikes, bikes, and tours act as social lube while introducing the unfamiliar to the one-and-only Southern California. You're not far from gorgeous coastal views along famous Highway 1, either, if you've got two or four wheels. (If you've got eighteen, keep on truckin'.) The lounge here features a piano and fireplace. Nice. Only negative? An all-day (okay, 6½–hour) lockout.

The city of San Luis Obispo itself—"Slo-town" to locals—is rather sleepy and not exactly right on the water, but it's a fine college city to chill out in for a couple of days and catch a ride west to the beach. There's a historic Spanish mission, a creek, tons o' coffee shops, bars, and galleries . . . you know the deal. Great weather, too.

How to Get There:

By bus: Greyhound stops in San Luis Obispo. Call hostel for transit route.
By car: Call hostel for directions.
By train: Amtrak stops in San Luis Obispo. Call hostel for transit route.

Carmelita Cottages Hostel ✴✴✴✦

321 Main Street (P.O. Box 1241), Santa Cruz, CA 95061
(831) 423-8304
  Fax: (831) 429-8541
  E-mail: info@hi-santacruz.org
  Web site: www.hi-santacruz.org
  Rates: $25 per Hostelling International member; $55–$65 for private room
  Credit cards: None
  Beds: 27
  Private rooms: 2

Affiliation: Hostelling International
Office hours: 8:00 to 11:00 a.m.; 5:00 to 10:00 p.m.
Extras: Bikes, bike shed, fireplace, barbecue, lockers, kitchen, laundry

*S*anta Cruz evokes images of surfers, hippies, and other counterculture types who've come here to chill out, lay back, and hang loose. The kind of town where the local university mascot is a banana slug. What a surprise, then, when we arrived at the Carmelita Cottages Hostel to find an ironclad 11:00 p.m. curfew and an all-day (well, six-hour) lockout imposed, among other rules.

At least there's a good reason why. The curfew is maintained because the hostel is located within a city park, and residents of the neighborhood worried about late-night revelry. Curfew aside, the Carmelita Cottages consist of three historic buildings—former sea captains' cottages, actually—that are being scrupulously restored and maintained by an army of volunteers. Even better, they're located on some darned nice grounds that include an herb garden and some fantastic big trees.

Inside the main cottage are an office, kitchen, dorms, a common room, the only guaranteed private room, and a nice big tub for soaking. The other cottages are smaller, though one has a mini-kitchen and piano for late-night socializing. (A curfew, after all, doesn't mean you have to go to bed.) These smaller dorms are just the right places to hang out and meet other travelers from distant lands.

Smoking is allowed on a porch, where smoke wafts directly into the poorly heated and ventilated private room; it could be better situated. The kitchen, however, is just like your grandmother's. True to the overwhelming community spirit in the town of Santa Cruz, there's always some free food such as pizza, pastries, or fruit being donated by a local store or restaurant.

Best of all the renowned Santa Cruz beach—a surfing mecca, plus the home of an amusement park in summertime—is just a block or so away. A lovely university

Best bet for a bite:
Free food box
Insiders' tip:
Farmers' market each Wednesday
What hostellers say:
"Curfew schmurfew."
Gestalt:
Cruz control
Safety: *A*
Hospitality: *C*
Cleanliness: *B*
Party index: 🎉🎉

campus is farther afield but also worth a look, as are a park full of redwoods and a Frisbee-golf course. (You're in California now, baby.) There's an on-site cyclery where you can borrow retrofitted bikes for cruisin' around town. The staff here is nuts about ecology, by the way, so much so that when hostellers queue up for first dibs on beds, the cyclists, hikers, and bus passengers get first pick.

A few years back when the restorations were beginning, Santa Cruz operated two hostels: an original hostel located closer to downtown and the Cottages, which were used as supplemental accommodations. Judging from comments in the hostel guest book, some of the convivial magic of the first hostel has disappeared with the strict rules of the new one. These rules and attitude somewhat dampen the experience of staying here, to be truthful.

How to Get There:

By bus: From station walk down Front Street toward beach. Cross Pacific Avenue, take footpath up hill, go left on Main Street. Hostel is on right.
By car: Drive California Highway 1 to Santa Cruz; call hostel for more specific directions.

Marin Headlands Hostel
941 Rosenstock Road, Sausalito, CA 94965
(415) 331-2777
> **Fax:** (415) 331-3568
> **E-mail:** marinhdl@norcalhostels.org
> **Rates:** $20 per Hostelling International member; $60 for private room
> **Credit cards:** JCB, MC, VISA
> **Beds:** 100
> **Private rooms:** 6
> **Affiliation:** Hostelling International
> **Office hours:** 7:30 a.m. to 11:00 p.m.
> **Extras:** Laundry, bike storage, Internet access, kitchen

H ere you are at the northern threshold to one of the most-visited cities in the world, and you sight a graceful elk galloping up the side of a steep hill. You're so anxious to see San Francisco for the first time that you scramble up another hill, turn a corner, and run smack into a glorious view of the Golden Gate Bridge. Right then and there you decide to savor the scent of eucalyptus and the Kodachrome glow of a sunset over the Pacific awhile longer. It's at that moment you see the sign pointing to a hostel.

Nestled among a grove of cypress trees and protected by high steep bluffs, the Marin Headlands Hostel is a stone's throw away from the densely populated peninsula that's home to San Francisco. It's actually situated on a former military base, and with a little walking, you can view what looks like an old missile cordoned off by barbed wire.

Best bet for a bite:
Munchies candy shop in town
What hostellers say:
"Not bad."
Gestalt:
Clean and serene
Hospitality: *A*
Cleanliness: *B*
Party index: 🎉🎉🎉

Accommodations are split between two buildings on spacious grounds. The commanding officer's home—decorated with period furniture and containing good-size couple's rooms, its own kitchen, and human-scale bathrooms—is the nicer of the two.

In the main building, dorm rooms are reasonably sized. The kitchen is efficient and well stocked; pictures painted on the cabinets show you which cooking implements are stored where. (Better stock up on groceries well beforehand, however: There aren't any stores for miles.) Though we liked the kitchen and the recreation room (more on that in a moment), the main building's bathrooms were a different story; showers have no privacy, no changing rooms, or any real place to hang up clothing. Beds, as well, were far from comfy.

Kids (and adults who refuse to grow up) love the big recreation room in the basement. It has a pool table, foosball, and table tennis; ask at the front desk for equipment. You can also munch on some Almond Joys from a vending machine while doing laundry, but that's for nighttime. Hiking the local hills is the best use of your daylight hours, particularly because you'll be locked out all day long anyway. Luckily the hostel sponsors hikes through the Headlands as part of a new outdoors program for groups of at least ten. The justly famous hikes of Muir Woods and Mount Tamalpais are also nearby.

There's only a little not to like here, and it's the rules. Being locked out all day isn't fun, and neither is the closing of the kitchen at night. It's really little inconvenience, though, to put up with for such low-priced digs in such a beautiful place.

How to Get There:

By airplane: From San Francisco Airport take 7B or 7F bus to city. Then take #76 bus (Saturday and Sunday only) to hostel area.

By bus: From San Francisco take #76 bus (Saturday and Sunday only) to hostel area. Weekdays, take Golden Gate Transit bus to Sausalito and walk 4 miles or take cab to hostel.

By car: Call hostel for directions.

By train: Contact hostel for transit route.

Doug's Mellow Mountain Retreat

3787 Forest, South Lake Tahoe, CA 89449

(P.O. Box 2764, State Line, NV 89449)

(530) 544-8065

> **Rates:** $25–$40 per person
> **Credit cards:** None
> **Beds:** 17
> **Private rooms:** None
> **Affiliation:** None
> **Office hours:** Twenty-four hours
> **Extras:** Television, barbecue, bike rentals, fireplace, shuttles, studio apartment

---

*E*xpect to hear the word "dude" spoken often here. There is a significant emphasis on partying in that "mellow" manner stereotypical of Northern California. Rasta designs are painted throughout the hostel, there is a mini-bar on the generous front patio, and a giant poster of beer flowing from a bottle to a glass covers the side-entrance door. All prepare you for the attitude of Doug Hall (he prefers to use just his first name) and his retreat.

Relatively speaking, it is clean and comfortable. Doug offers a small house in a wooded area only 1 mile from the renowned Tahoe casinos. Pine trees surround the place, giving a sense of privacy on the front porch (which is party central), and the pleasant neighborhood feels like it could be a thousand miles away from the gaudy gambling strip. The house is small, though, and if partying with your fellow guests—ganja included—doesn't interest you, the cheap hotels down the road are a better option. Doug makes no apologies about having guests sleep on the couch in the spacious lounge or jammed in a stairway crevice. "All my mattresses are full-sized," he boasted instead. For a few dollars extra, up to three people can stay in the rear studio with its own kitchen and bathroom. It's more spacious than most private rooms and refreshingly clean.

Doug's location can't be beat. The Tahoe area is full of tourist attractions. In the winter it's a skier's dream, with a number of challenging resorts to choose from; just be ready to shell out $50 for a ticket. In warmer months the Tahoe Lake Lapper ferry boat runs around the entire lake, making twenty stops in less than three hours. There are also a number of state parks around the lake from which to choose. Where else can you hit the jackpot, then be on a challenging wilderness hike only minutes afterward?

Doug's is not a bad choice with which to be stuck, but only if you've got an attitude that matches the milieu. After all, Doug is a guy who jokes about being shocked when a guest asked him if it was okay to drink. Doug's reply to the guest: "It's not okay if you don't."

Best bet for a bite:
Casino buffets
Insiders' tip:
Hiking info at the South Lake Tahoe visitor's center
What hostellers say:
"Doug is an asp."
Gestalt:
Area code 420
Best bet for a bite:
Big Daddy's burgers (to decompress)
Hospitality: *D*
Cleanliness: *C*
Party index:

How to Get There:

By bus: Stops near hostel. Follow car directions or call for free pickup.

By car: From east, take U.S. Highway 50 through casinos in Nevada portion of town and continue 1 mile to Wildwood intersection (at streetlight). Turn left and drive 3 blocks to Forest; turn left again. Hostel is #3787 on left. From west, take U.S. Highway 50 into South Lake Tahoe and look for Ski Run Boulevard. Continue past Ski Run to next light and turn right on Wildwood. Drive 3 blocks and turn left on Forest. Hostel is #3787 on left.

Ranch House Inn Hostel ✸✸✸✸

2001 Old Spanish Trail Highway (P.O. Box 14), Tecopa, CA 92389

(760) 852-4580

Web site: www.ranchhouseinn.com

Email: reservations@ranchhouseinn.com

Rates: $22–$25 per person; $75 for private room

Credit cards: MC, VISA

Beds: 10

Private rooms: 1

Affiliation: None

Office hours: 4:00 to 8:00 p.m.

Extras: Kitchen, lockers, decks, bikes, television, VCR, volleyball, telescope, movies

These no-frills digs on the eastern border of Death Valley are a pretty good option, for a couple reasons: One, it's only two hours of beautiful driving away from Vegas (four hours from L.A.). And, two, it's open year-round. Finally, they've added a kitchen, some tipis, and a more upscale section that improve upon what used to be basically a collection of trailers.

The old section still consists of several mobile homes with small bedrooms and tiny common areas. That part of the facility is nothing to write home about, but it is getting better—front and back decks, the small kitchen, and so forth. And the surrounding area is so fascinating that you will get over the plainness of the hostel quickly. Then there's the new section, known as China Ranch, which is about a five-minute drive down into the canyon: It has some sweet B&B rooms and tipis (which are expensive, because the owners assume a bunch of people will be staying in there).

Tecopa itself is a dot of a town, with only about 130 residents and one hot

Best bet for a bite:
Pastels

Insiders' tip:
Ghost town of Rhyolite

What hostellers say:
"Getting better all the time."

Gestalt:
Just deserts

Safety: A

Hospitality: A

Cleanliness: B

Party index: 🎉

springs (labeled as a "resort"). The springs are indoors, rather than outdoors, but we were pleased to learn that bathing in them is inexpensive. The town itself, while otherwise featureless, is near any number of amazing desert sights not on any tourist's map. If you've got a solid car, wander through ghost towns, up and down the hills of the basin and range, and across the dunes of the Valley; you'll begin to feel like you're in some kind of futuristic movie.

The hostel is also right outside the gates of Death Valley National Monument, one of America's weirdest (and hottest) parklands. Sagebrush blows across the road, and sand periodically whips up in a fury. On the grounds is a watchtower from which you can stargaze at night, and a few miles down the road is the China Ranch date farm, an intriguing desert oasis where palm trees and lush green growth sprouts in an area where there is nothing but sand and stone for miles.

One caution: Bring supplies with you when you come here. The only thing nearby is a local greasy spoon in Shoshone, which leaves a lot to be desired. Take note that gas is also ridiculously expensive in the area—the station can charge what it wants, so it does.

Okay, one more caution: If you come in summer, dress super-cool (and check the coolant and radiator hoses in Vegas before setting out). The mercury here in the desert can touch 120!

How to Get There:

By car: From Los Angeles, take I-10 about 40 miles east to I-15; switch to I-15 and continue 135 miles north to Baker; exit at Baker and take Highway 127 north 50 miles to Old Spanish Trail Highway (use the Tecopa turnoff). Head east on Old Spanish Trail Highway 5 miles to hostel.

From Las Vegas, drive I-15 south to Highway 160 about 35 miles toward Pahrump; turn left (west) onto Tecopa Road at the junction, and continue west about 32 more miles to hostel (Tecopa Road changes name to Old Spanish Trail Highway at Nevada state line).

Attractive natural setting	Comfortable beds	Visual arts at hostel or nearby
Ecologically aware hostel	A particularly good value	Music at hostel or nearby
Superior kitchen facilities or cafe	Wheelchair-accessible	Great hostel for skiers
Offbeat or eccentric place	Good for business travelers	Bar or pub at hostel or nearby
Superior bathroom facilities	Especially well-suited for families	Editors' choice: Among our very favorite hostels
Romantic private rooms	Good for active travelers	

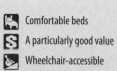

Key to Icons

NEVADA

Sin City Hostel ✹✹

1208 South Las Vegas Boulevard, Las Vegas, NV 89114

(702) 868-0222

    Web site: www.sincityhostel.com

    E-mail: party@sincityhostel.com

    Rates: $18 per person; $36 for private room

    Credit cards: AMEX, DISC, MC, VISA

    Beds: 58

    Private rooms: Yes

    Affiliation: USA Hostels

    Office hours: 6:00 a.m. to 2:00 a.m. (April to mid-October); 7:00 a.m. to 11:00 p.m. (rest of the year)

    Extras: Laundry, television, DVD player and VCR, tours, barbecue, kitchen, Jacuzzi, movies, breakfast, parking, pool table, business center

---

NOTE: Passport, student ID, hostel card, or proof of international travel required

*G*uests don't come to Sin City Hostel looking for first-class digs or a major bargain: Those can be found at a million other places in town. And with some advance planning you can get a sparkling hotel room right on the Strip for about the same price it costs to stay at this hostel, providing your visit will be midweek. People come here to hang out, meet others, and partake in shenanigans. Don't mistake our meaning. That means: A PARTY. Got it? Despite all the action up and down the Strip, Vegas can be a difficult place to meet fellow adventurers. Senior citizens, families, and cheesy couples clog the place. So it's nice for hostellers to have a respite where they can pair up with like- minded souls in the world capital of tackiness.

The hostel's physical condition is only so-so, a mixed bag of cleanliness and upkeep. But there are some pluses. A business center on site offers printing, scanning, CD burning, and even local use of a fax machine—useful for those looking for fast work in the casinos, maybe? Other good stuff includes half a basketball court, a pool table, a TV room with DVD player and VCR; a grill, gazebo, and Jacuzzi; and a laundry with free powder. The hostel kitchen is adequate. Dorms consist mostly of four-bedded rooms, incredibly bare-bones. Private rooms add a lamp and a few other basic furnishings. The real story here, though, is the social docket. They jazz the place up with weekly barbecues, parties inside Hummer stretch limos cruising the Strip, and the like.

Note that this is definitely not the safest part of Las Vegas, one of America's most crime-ridden cities. You need to take a bus to reach the Strip, and it can take a bit of time to get there. Shady characters abound in the neighborhood, so watch yourself at night—or simply don't go out walking. It's the typical mix of weird-meets-scary Vegas by night. Just met a foxy hosteller or hostellette? There's an all-hours, get-married-fast chapel right across the street. (Rumor has it that it's the one where Britney Spears got quick-hitched.) How's that for one-stop shopping?

Best bet for a bite:
All-U-can-eat casino buffets
Insiders' tip:
Wedding chapel across street
What hostellers say:
"Know when to fold 'em."
Gestalt:
Snake eyes
Safety: *C*
Hospitality: *B*
Cleanliness: *C*
Party index:

How to Get There:

By airplane: Airport in Las Vegas. Take #108 bus from airport all the way to its end (Oakey Boulevard). Walk north on Las Vegas Boulevard to the hostel.
By bus: Greyhound stops in Las Vegas. Take cab to hostel.
By car: Hostel is on the Boulevard past the Strip and in the downtown business district.
By train: Amtrak stops in Las Vegas. Take cab to hostel.

Northwest

Page numbers follow hostel names

OREGON

Ashland Hostel

150 North Main Street, Ashland, OR 97520

(541) 482-9217

Web site: www.theashlandhostel.com
E-mail: ashostel@earthlink.net
Rates: $28 per person; $40–$84 for private room
Credit cards: None
Beds: 50
Private rooms: 4
Affiliation: None
Office hours: 8:00 a.m. to noon; 5:00 p.m. to midnight
Extras: Piano, lockers, laundry, bike storage, woodstove, Internet access, tea and coffee, kitchen, movies

*A*shland is so well-known for the eight-month-long Oregon Shakespeare Festival that this hostel's brochure features a big grinning line drawing of the bard. This hostel, located 3 blocks from downtown, gets busiest around April. Hostellers hang out on a big porch or try out the piano. The hostel has two family rooms with a queen-size bed, two sets of bunks, and a shared bathroom.

Recent improvements to the hostel have impressed visitors; a fully equipped kitchen, great common space, and brightly painted murals on bedroom walls have transformed this place. The hostel is extremely clean but manages to keep it together while avoiding that institutional feel common of bigger hostels. You feel like you're visiting a friend's home—okay, a

Best bet for a bite:
Morning Glory cafe
Insiders' tip:
Park and skating rink nearby
What hostellers say:
"To be or not to be . . ."
Gestalt:
Bard beyond belief
Safety: *A*
Hospitality: *B*
Cleanliness: *A*
Party index: 🎉🎉

friend with a lot of rules. But still. The renowned Pacific Crest Trail, a long hiking trail, is just 10 miles away, as are ski resorts, horseback riding, and the scenic and wild Rogue River.

How to Get There:

By car: Drive I-5 south to exit 19; follow signs to Oregon Shakespeare Festival. Travel 2½ miles to Bush Street. Hostel is on right.

From I-5 north, take exit 14. Cross overpass and go left on Ashland Street. Turn right onto Siskiyou Boulevard and follow through downtown. Pass plaza and stoplight and hostel is on the right.

PORTLAND-AREA HOSTELS: A SUMMARY					
	RATING	**PROS**	**CONS**	**COST**	**PAGE**
Northwest Portland International Hostel	★★★★★	location, staff	books up	$20–$25	p. 297
McMenamins Edgefield Hostel	★★★★	swank, suds	expensive	$40	p. 302
Hawthorne Portland Hostel	★★★	location	popular	$17	p. 299

Northwest Portland International Hostel

425 NW 18th Street, Portland, OR 97209

(503) 241-2783; (888) 777-0067

  E-mail: info@nwportlandhostel.com

  Web site: www.nwportlandhostel.com

  Rates: $20–$25 per Hostelling International member; $42–$74 for private room

  Credit cards: MC, VISA

  Beds: 74

  Private rooms: 20

  Affiliation: Hostelling International

  Office hours: 8:00 a.m. to midnight

  Extras: Espresso/juice bar, laundry, trips, breakfast, Internet access, kitchen, free Wi-Fi

*T*his just in: The best hostel in Oregon's best city has moved (slightly) and expanded (big-time), adding much-needed beds to Portland's busy hostel scene with the acquisition of three historic buildings around the corner from the hostel's original home. It has a much different feel from the other HI hostel in town, which is in the super-hip/hippie Hawthorne area; this one's in the trendy northwest part of town.

Best bet for a bite:
Ken's Artisan Bakery
Insiders' tip:
Rogues Ale brewpub on Flanders rocks
What hostellers say:
"Great place."
Gestalt:
Oregon transplants
Safety: *A*
Hospitality: *A*
Cleanliness: *A*
Party index: 🎉 🎉 🎉

The hostel is housed in three restored historic buildings. Dorm rooms contain two to four beds apiece, and the hostel has an espresso bar. (This is Oregon; gotta have a cuppa Joe somewhere in the mix.) But the biggest change is the addition of twenty private rooms, making this much more a destination for couples and families than it was before. Friendly international staff and the laundry, free Wi-Fi, and kitchen/dining area supply additional appeal. It's all kept immaculately clean, and there's tons of stuff to do in the immediate area as well.

Planned activities include van trips to Mount St. Helens, the Columbia River Gorge and Mount Hood, the famously beautiful Oregon coast, hot springs, and more. Closer to home, distractions include lots of parks and gardens (this is the Rose City, after all), cafes, bars, natural foods stores, the famous Powell's bookstore right downtown, and everything else that makes Portland one of America's great small cities.

How to Get There:

By airplane: Large airport in Portland. From terminal take Red Line MAX train to PGE Park and walk 6 blocks north on Eighteenth Avenue.
By bus: Greyhound stops in Portland. From terminal take #17 bus to Nineteenth and Glisan; walk 1 block to hostel. Or take #17 bus for free to 15th Street and walk three blocks to hostel.
By car: Drive I-5 to I-405 connector road; take Northwest Everett Street exit, and continue west following signs onto Glisan Street. Continue 4 blocks to hostel on left.
By train: Amtrak stops in Portland. From station take #17 bus to Nineteenth and Glisan; walk 1 block to hostel.

Hawthorne Portland Hostel ✸✸✸✸

3031 Hawthorne Boulevard Southeast, Portland, OR 97124

(503) 236-3380

E-mail: hip@portlandhostel.org

Web site: www.portlandhostel.org

Rates: $17 per Hostelling International member; $40 for single room;
$36–$46 for private room

Credit cards: AMEX, DISC, MC, VISA

Beds: 34

Private rooms: 2

Affiliation: Hostelling International

Office hours: 8:00 a.m. to 10:00 p.m.

Extras: Laundry, travel shop, Internet access

Portland's original hostel is located in the funky Hawthorne district, and it feels like it, with its colorful decor and a slightly hippo crowd. The hostel is an old Victorian with an ecoroof, large porch, and herb garden typical of the Northwest. The inside of the place fits in well with the rest of the nabe—lots of vintage furniture, funky World Planet–type chic rugs, bright walls, and fun art.

Yes, some of the bunks in the basement are too close together, and cleanliness and bathroom space can definitely become a bit of a problem—it's a house, after all, packed with Phish fans (kidding). But the private rooms are pleasantly decorated, and one has a good view of Hawthorne Street—note that traffic noise can be a problem there. Likewise, the hostel has lots of activities. If you're looking for a social atmosphere, this is great, but for families or clean freaks we'd probably recommend the Northwest Portland International (see page 297) first.

Best bet for a bite:
Fred Meyer, Grand Central, Bridgeport Ale House, People's Food Co-op . . .

Insiders' tip:
Beer and a brew at the Bagdad Theater & Pub

What hostellers say:
"Have you picked any lavender today?"

Gestalt:
Hip, hip, hooray

Safety: A

Hospitality: A

Cleanliness: B

Party index: 🎉🎉🎉

Among the other highlights here are a good travel shop where you can buy backpacks at cost. These folks also maintain a decent backyard patio, and take great pains to dispense information (on the walls) and recycle everything they possibly can (downstairs).

As for the neighborhood, suffice to say that this is the place to be, according to Portlanders in the know. Dozens of hipster coffee shops, restaurants, clubs, and stores line both sides of Hawthorne as far as the eye can see; downtown is a ten-minute drive or bus ride away; Reed College is a short stroll; and so are blocks and blocks of residential areas just off the main strip.

How to Get There:

By airplane: Large airport in city. From airport take #12 bus, then change to #14 bus to Thirtieth and Hawthorne. Walk east less than 1 block; hostel is on north side of Hawthorne.

By bus: Greyhound stops in Portland. From station take #14 bus to Thirtieth and Hawthorne. See directions above.

By car: From I-5 south, take exit 300B. Turn left at fork on exit ramp and follow signs for Belmont Street. Take Belmont to Thirtieth Avenue and turn right. Follow Thirtieth to Hawthorne Boulevard, turn left to hostel on left.

From I-5 north, take left-lane exit 299B, stay left, and take exit 1A. Turn right onto Front Avenue and another right onto Hawthorne Bridge. Cross bridge up Hawthorne Boulevard. Hostel is on left.

By train: Amtrak stops in Portland. From station take #14 bus to Thirtieth and Hawthorne. See directions above.

Key to Icons

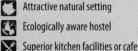 Attractive natural setting

 Ecologically aware hostel

Superior kitchen facilities or cafe

Offbeat or eccentric place

Superior bathroom facilities

Romantic private rooms

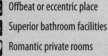 Comfortable beds

A particularly good value

Wheelchair-accessible

Good for business travelers

Especially well-suited for families

Good for active travelers

 Visual arts at hostel or nearby

 Music at hostel or nearby

 Great hostel for skiers

 Bar or pub at hostel or nearby

 Editors' choice: Among our very favorite hostels

Seaside International Hostel

930 North Holladay Drive, Seaside, OR 97138

(503) 738-7911; (888) 994-0001

Fax: (503) 717-0163

Web site: www.seasidehostel.net

E-mail: seaside@teleport.com

Rates: $20–$23 per person; $41–$53 for private room

Credit cards: DISC, JCB, MC, VISA

Beds: 56

Private rooms: 7

Affiliation: None

Office hours: 8:00 a.m. to 9:00 p.m.

Extras: Espresso bar, cafe, earplugs, VCR, hikes, canoes, kayaks, tours, kitchen, laundry, ironing board, Internet access, lockers

This former law office was converted by a former owner into a friendly hostel with common spaces on a riverside deck (with barbecue grills), a front porch, and inside at tables. An espresso bar dispenses the official Oregon state drink and baked goods from Portland, a boon to the budget traveler who has forgotten to shop beforehand. The kitchen is exemplary, as well, with free food and plenty of counter space. Bunkrooms are decent, and the comfy private rooms with televisions in the section that used to be a fading motel are good for couples. The hostel gets points, as well, for an eco ethic throughout, from recycled papers to energy-saving measures to support of salmon restoration programs.

Seaside is frankly a bit of a tourist trap: a few too many T shirt shops, beachside motels, and fast-food joints nudging the Pacific for our taste. But don't despair (if you've got wheels). The surrounding area takes in some of Oregon's most beautiful and historic coastline—near where Lewis

Best bet for a bite:
The Stand on Avenue U (great Mexican)
Insiders' tip:
Hiking Tillamook Head
What hostellers say:
"Great coastline."
Gestalt:
Whole latte fun
Hospitality: *A*
Cleanliness: *A*
Party index:

and Clark reached the Pacific and then camped out for a winter—so you can comfortably opt for either history or natural history. Try climbing the nearby Astoria column for a million-dollar view of the coast (if you're not afraid of heights); hanging out on the beach promenade; driving down to Cannon Beach and beyond to Tillamook; or—this is best—having the staff guide you to lots of local walks and hikes on the headlands and beaches.

How to Get There:

By car: Drive U.S. Highway 101 to Seaside; exit at Tenth or Twelfth Avenue, then turn onto Holladay. Hostel is on Holladay.

By bus: Oregon Coach Way runs once-daily service to and from Portland's Union Station (the train station). Contact hostel for transit details.

McMenamins Edgefield Hostel

2126 Southwest Halsey Street, Troutdale, OR 97060

(503) 669-8610; (800) 669-8610

> **E-mail:** edge@mcmenamin.com
> **Web site:** www.mcmenamin.com
> **Rates:** $40 per person; $50 single room; $80–$145 for private room
> **Credit cards:** AMEX, DISC, MC, VISA
> **Beds:** 24
> **Private rooms:** Yes
> **Affiliation:** None
> **Office hours:** Twenty-four hours
> **Extras:** ATM, restaurant, pubs, gardens, bathrobes

*W*hen we heard about a hostel attached to a microbrewery—one where they're rumored to give you free bathrobes for the length of your stay—we thought maybe we'd died and gone to heaven.

We're getting ahead of ourselves, though, because you pay through the nose for that privilege.

The Edgefield complex is, as the great Bob Young once put it, a "beer theme park." This is a place to celebrate the art of the pour, and the grounds include no less than four places to buy a beer separated by gardens, walking trails, and restored old buildings. Only in Oregon. But hostel rooms, too?

It's true, and what's more, lucky hostellers who find this place get to partake of swanky bathrooms, those spacious grounds, an ATM in the house, and all the trappings of wealth and taste that helped make the building's restoration possible in the first place.

Best bet for a bite:
Siam Sushi
Insiders' tip:
Great views and salmon runs at Multnomah Falls
What hostellers say:
"Another round."
Gestalt:
The house that beer built
Hospitality: *C*
Cleanliness: *A*
Party index:

The story goes like this: A one-time county poor farm was restored by the McMenamins brothers into a brewery and, eventually, the complex of inns, pubs, and grounds here today. Somewhere along the line, one of the brothers who had stayed in hostels in Europe decided he'd like to add some rooms to the inn. Voilá: big clean bunkrooms, astonishingly upscale bathrooms, great third-floor views. Surprisingly, there are even lots of environmentally friendly touches about the place: Toilets are low-flow, the toilet paper is unbleached and recycled, and so on.

Disappointingly, however, there is no kitchen for hostellers to use. The staff also seems uniformly chilly when queried about the hostel. You get the sense that hostellers aren't taken as seriously as high-paying guests at the inn. And when you're paying forty—yes, *forty*—bucks for a bed in a bunkroom (which must make this one of the most expensive bunkroom nights in the world), they'd better be nice.

Oh, well. This is still livin' pretty high on the hog, hostel-wise.

How to Get There:
By airplane: Airport in Portland. Call hostel for transit route.
By car: Call hostel for directions.

WASHINGTON

Columbia River Gorge Hostel ✳✳✳

Cedar Street at Humboldt (P.O. Box 155), Bingen, WA 98605

(509) 493-3363

Web site: www.bingenschool.com

Rates: $19 per person; $49 for double room

Credit cards: MC, VISA

Beds: 70

Private/family rooms: 5

Office hours: 8:00 a.m. to 1:00 p.m., 6:00 to 9:00 p.m. (Tuesday to Saturday); call hostel for Sunday and Monday hours

Affiliation: None

Extras: Laundry, kitchen, gymnasium, basketball court, climbing wall, weight bench

---

*T*he hostel complex consists of two buildings on an entire city block, with a sports field in the adjacent lot. It was an elementary school for a while, becoming a schoolhouse-themed hostel when a windsurfing nut bought the place in 1988. Chalkboards remain intact, and old lockers still line the hallway. But otherwise it's a big improvement on its parochial origins.

There are two huge eighteen-bed dorms, one twelve-bedded dorm, and five private rooms—three with two queen beds each, and two with a third bed as well. It's well-done.

The only problem is that windsurfers sometimes come for the season and practically live here, sucking a bit of life from what could be a good hostel ambience. Then again, this is far off most travelers' radar anyway. And it's pretty well-run from what we can see.

Bingen's just a tiny speck of a town—think Mexican places and taquerias for food—but you might find bargains at the local health food deli. There isn't much else

> **Best bet for a bite:**
> *Pizzas at Solstice Cafe*
> **What hostellers say:**
> *"It's rippin' out there, dude!"*
> **Gestalt:**
> *Wind tunnel*
> **Hospitality:** *B*
> **Cleanliness:** *C*
> **Party index:**

to do around here besides windsurf, though, and you're many miles from other attractions of interest. Our advice? Learn to windsurf, or keep on truckin'.

How to Get There:

By bus: Greyhound stops across river from Bingen. From station, cross Hood River bridge into Washington, continue 1 mile east to Bingen, turn left on Cedar Street, and walk 1 block off Highway 14 to hostel.

By car: Call hostel for directions.

By train: Amtrak stops in Bingen. From station, walk 2 blocks north and 5 blocks east to hostel.

Birch Bay Hostel ✳✳✳

7467 Gemini Street, Blaine, WA 98230

(360) 371-2180

   Web site: www.birchbayhostel.org

   E-mal: hostelmanager@birchbayhostel.org

   Rates: $20 per person, private rooms $45–$69

   Credit cards: MC, VISA

   Season: May through September; October through April, groups only

   Beds: 45

   Private rooms: 4

   Affiliation: None

   Office hours: 5:00 to 10:00 p.m.

   Extras: Laundry, sauna, lockers, kitchen, free weekend pancakes

---

*I*f it's peace of mind you're looking for, this place is as quiet as they come. Set way out in some fields in a county park off the beaten track, Birch Bay Hostel doesn't get many visitors thanks to the proximity of Vancouver, British Columbia. It's not a bad place, though not spectacular either. Its best asset is its location just a few miles from Canada and the Tsawassen ferry that leads to British Columbia's dazzling Gulf Islands.

     The hostel used to be part of a military base, but that fizzled out; all that's left to see are mostly empty barracks, a radio tower pointed toward the former Soviet Union, and the

State of Washington's legislative archives. In other words, not a whole lot of excitement. At least they serve free pancakes on the weekend.

This place has improved since we first started visiting. You'll surely have plenty of room: Fewer guests means an excellent chance at a private room to yourself and time to cook in the kitchen, and there are grassy fields to romp around in, as well. There's a terrific bathrooms-to-rooms ratio. A nearby state park offers up clam flats for digging. Birds are often twittering around.

The local roads are great for biking, too; unfortunately, the hostel doesn't rent two-wheelers, so you need to bring your own. Don't forget the food, either; it's a good distance to the nearest restaurant or store.

How to Get There:

By airplane: Call hostel for directions.

By bus: Call for ride to hostel. Advance notice of two hours preferred.

By car: From the north, take I-5 to exit 270 (Birch Bay–Linden Road). Go west 3½ miles to Blaine Road; turn left and drive 1 mile to Alderson Road. Go ½ mile to county park.

From the south, take I-5 to exit 266. Follow Grandview west 6 miles to Blaine Road; turn right and drive 2 miles to Alderson Road. Go ½ mile to county park.

Grays Harbor Hostel ✺✺✺

6 Ginny Lane, Elma, WA 98541

(360) 482-3119

E-mail: ghhostel@techline.com

Web site: www.ghhostel.com

Rates: $18 per person; $35 for private room

Credit cards: None

Beds: 14

Private rooms: 1

Affiliation: None

Office hours: 7:00 to 9:30 a.m.; 5:00 to 9:00 p.m.

Extras: Library, boat rental, inner-tube rental, bike shop, hot tub, Frisbee golf course, kitchen

*H*ostellers pretty much like this hostel, which is set on the southern part of the Olympic Peninsula. Hosts Jay and Linda Klemp receive good marks for their hospitality and their willingness to go the extra mile for their guests. The couple—who have been very active in the hostelling movement for years—maintain a hostel that includes a hot tub, bike repair shop, library, and other extras. They do lock the building all day, however, because they work regular jobs.

That might be okay because most of the reasons you're coming here (such as whale-watching at the beach or hiking in Olympic National Park) will take some driving to reach. The immediate area around the hostel offers little, if anything, to do. The exceptions are if you're fascinated by the goings-on inside the Washington state capitol building in Olympia or want to drive around the streets of Kurt Cobain's hometown of Aberdeen. Luckily the Klemps are expert guides to the region.

The 9:30 a.m. checkout/lockout is a bit of a drag, though. Amuse yourself with the new (eighteen-hole!) Frisbee golf course on the premises: seriously fun.

Best bet for a bite:
Rusty Tractor
Insiders' tip:
Frisbee golf!
What hostellers say:
"Friendly."
Gestalt:
Safe Harbor
Hospitality: *A*
Cleanliness: *A*
Party index: 🎉🎉

How to Get There:

By bus: Greyhound stops in Olympia; take #40 bus to Elma (one hour). Call hostel for directions.

By car: Take Washington Highway 8 to Elma; turn right on Fairgrounds Road, then right on Ginny Lane.

By train: Amtrak stops in Olympia; take Greyhound #40 bus to Elma (one hour). Call hostel for directions.

Rainforest Hostel

169312 Highway 101, Forks, WA 98331

(360) 374-2270

Web site: www.rainforesthostel.com

Rates: $9 per person; $20–$21 for private room

Credit cards: None

Beds: 14 winter; 26 summer

Private rooms: 3

Affiliation: None

Office hours: 8:00 to 10:00 a.m.; 5:00 to 10:00 p.m.

Extras: Fireplace, some food items, camping

*T*his hostel, set 23 miles outside the town of Forks, receives mixed reviews from our hostel snoops. Some applaud the management, who carefully curate an extensive file of hostel comments from wanderers and sell basic food items at minimal cost (20 cents for an egg, for example) to compensate for the hostel's remote location. We also like the friendly guests and laid-back atmosphere. This place does cater to the free spirit; truly hard-core (read: cheap) travelers will be right at home, as this is one of the cheapest hostels in the entire U.S. of A. The owner even offers a half-price deal (five bucks a night!) to those arriving by bike or public transportation who want to pitch a tent and get access to the hostel's showers and kitchen.

Best bet for a bite:
Gathering Grounds coffeehouse

Insiders' tip:
Check out Ruby Beach

What hostellers say:
"Great hostel file."

Gestalt:
Rainforest crunch

Hospitality: C

Cleanliness: C

Party index:

But some feel the owner can be both dictatorial (there's a six-hour daytime lockout, and required chores such as weeding gardens or washing windows) and insensitive. We also heard complaints about mustiness and odor in the dorms.

One thing's for sure, though: If you want to see migrating birds, whales, or fish, this is definitely the place to come. A marine sanctuary 4½ miles from the hostel is one option; gorgeous Ruby Beach is another; and the grand green peaks of Olympic National Park, of course, are yet another. The fishing is reputed to be excellent in the area's rivers, as well, if you're a hook, line, and sinker sort of person.

How to Get There:

By bus: Bus stops nearby. Call hostel for details.

By car: Take U.S. Route 101 to a point 23 miles south of Forks or 84 miles north of Aberdeen. At Milepost 169/170, look for hostel signs and turn into driveway.

Doe Bay Resort Hostel ✻✻✻

107 Doe Bay Road, Olga (Orcas Island), WA 98279

(360) 376-2291

E-mail: office@doebay.com

Web site: www.doebay.com

Rates: $35–$50 per person; $75–$100 for private room

Credit cards: None

Season: Open daily spring through fall; call for winter opening dates

Beds: 12

Private rooms: 2

Private bathrooms: 1

Affiliation: None

Office hours: 7:00 to 9:00 a.m.; 5:00 to 10:00 p.m.

Extras: Mineral baths, Jacuzzi, sauna, massages, pets allowed, cafe

---

*D*oe Bay isn't first and foremost a hostel; set on a cove on lovely Orcas Island, it's chiefly a resort where folks come to stay in a cabin for a week or so, soak in the mineral baths, kayak the clear offshore waters, and walk in a natural paradise. It's also a hippie haven.

The resort's little twelve-bed hostel (eight beds in a bunkroom, plus a couple queen-bedded private rooms) gets rave reviews from some of our hostelling correspondents. They love the landscape, the option of paying a few extra bucks for a sauna or mineral bath, the work-exchange residencies, and the quiet groove of it all, which

Best bet for a bite:
Cafe on the premises

What hostellers say:
"Far out, man! And relaxing."

Gestalt:
Doe, a dear

Hospitality: *B*

Cleanliness: *B*

Party index: 🍕🍕🍕

harkens back to the back-to-the-land 1960s. A few hostellers feel the place is getting worn, though, and that the hot tubs are perhaps not as spectacular as they had expected. But new owners (Joe and Maureen Brotherton bought it in 2003) seem committed to freshening the place up and improving the house cafe.

There's also a campground here, a rarity in the San Juan Islands, that deserves a look if other accommodations around the islands are filling up fast.

How to Get There:
By car/ferry: Take ferry from Anacortes to Orcas Island; from landing, follow signs into Olga, then continue along Point Lawrence Road 3 miles. Doe Bay complex is on right.

Thor Town Hostel ✸
316 North Race Street, Port Angeles, WA 98362
(360) 452-0931
> **E-mail:** thortown@olypen.com
> **Web site:** www.thortown.com
> **Rates:** $13.60 per person; $30 for private room
> **Credit cards:** No
> **Beds:** 10
> **Private/family rooms:** 4
> **Affiliation:** None
> **Office hours:** 5:00 to 9:00 p.m.
> **Extras:** Internet access, bike rentals, laundry, kitchen, food for sale

---

*T*his hostel, in well-positioned Port Angeles near the ferry to Canada, would seem like a serviceable choice as a place to stay on the Olympic Peninsula.

Well, it's not. In fact, it appears to be rapidly declining, according to our latest investigations. A small, plain house, the hostel is a short walk from the ferry to British Columbia as well as the entire rest of the small downtown district. It used to be a sparkling place, but no more; seems like whoever's in charge is content to let the hostellers self-police cleanliness and order . . . and that isn't really working out. The kitchen is now just okay, and the bunkroom is bare-bones rather than comfy.

Add to this the fact that you're in someone's house—the family might grumble a bit if you linger during the day—and we can't see any reason to stay here instead of beautiful British Columbia.

How to Get There:

By bus: Contact hostel for transit route.
By car: Drive U.S. Highway 101 to Port Angeles and the golden arches; turn right on Race Street and continue to hostel.
By train: Contact hostel for transit route.

Olympic Hostel ✹✹✹✹

272 Battery Way, Port Townsend, WA 98368
(360) 385-0655

 E-mail: olympichostel@olympus.net
 Rates: $17 per Hostelling International member; $45 for private room
 Credit cards: MC, VISA
 Beds: 32
 Private rooms: 6
 Affiliation: Hostelling International
 Office hours: 7:30 to 9:30 a.m.; 5:00 to 10:00 p.m.
 Extras: Laundry, piano, kitchen

You'd be forgiven if you do a double take, making your way up the winding driveway that leads to Fort Worden State Park and, eventually, the hostel there. Those barracks look, well, awfully familiar. And they are. They were featured in the film *An Officer and a Gentleman*.

Management has put together an interesting hostel. It has a well-organized kitchen setup, a strong emphasis on recycling and environmental programs, beautiful grounds, and very helpful advice on local activities, concerts, and ferry schedules. The hostel consists of two dorms, plus a few private rooms. Hostellers get the run of the state park, and the hostel sells

Best bet for a bite:

Any of the Thai places

Insiders' tip:

Elevated Ice Cream Co. in town is excellent

What hostellers say:

"Haven't I seen this place before?"

Gestalt:

Sax 'n' violins

Hospitality: *B*

Cleanliness: *B*

Party index:

some unusual but useful items—such as earplugs and condoms—in the bathroom.

Once you're set up with a bed, there's lots to do in the town itself, which oozes arts festival during the summer. Classical music is a particular favorite of the locals, and it's not uncommon to hear tuba-tooting or piano-playing protégés tuning up in a nearby building. Sometimes they, or their parents, even stay at the hostel. A fine local arts organization called Centrum brings many of these events practically to the hostel's front door.

On the downside, hostellers have complained that management sometimes messes up reservations, especially during the busy summer months, or that the staff occasionally could be friendlier. Others noted with disappointment that just three toilets serve the entire place. (There's a fourth, portable toilet for the desperate, though that hardly seems an appropriate solution.)

Nevertheless, this is still a pretty spectacular vantage point from which to chill out and enjoy Washington's unique coastal scenery.

How to Get There:

By car: Drive Washington Highway 20 into Port Townsend; turn left on Kearney at stoplight after visitors center, turn right on Blaine, then left on Cherry. Drive through state park gate. Follow signs uphill through park to hostel.

Key to Icons

 Attractive natural setting

 Ecologically aware hostel

 Superior kitchen facilities or cafe

 Offbeat or eccentric place

 Superior bathroom facilities

 Romantic private rooms

Comfortable beds

A particularly good value

Wheelchair-accessible

Good for business travelers

Especially well-suited for families

Good for active travelers

 Visual arts at hostel or nearby

 Music at hostel or nearby

 Great hostel for skiers

 Bar or pub at hostel or nearby

 Editors' choice: Among our very favorite hostels

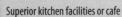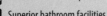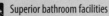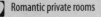

SEATTLE-AREA HOSTELS: A SUMMARY					
	RATING	**PROS**	**CONS**	**COST**	**PAGE**
Green Tortoise Hostel	✴✴✴✴	central, fun		$25–$36	p. 313
The Ranch Hostel	✴✴✴✴	island	too remote location	$17–$25	p. 315

Green Tortoise Hostel ✴✴✴✴

105B Pike Street, Seattle, WA 98101

(206) 340-1222

E-mail: info@greentortoise.net

Web site: www.greentortoise.net

Rates: $25–$36 per person; $40–$56 for private room

Credit cards: MC, VISA

Beds: 175

Private rooms: 16

Single rooms: Yes

Affiliation: None

Office hours: Twenty-four hours

Extras: Free breakfast, storage, alarm clocks, laundry, tours, television, VCR, free pick-ups, Internet access, free Wi-Fi, free dinners (three times weekly), live music

It's funny how things work out. In 2007, to our shock, the "official" Seattle International Hostel on Union Street near Pike Place Market suddenly closed its doors. You know the story: Landlord raises rent; nonprofit can't pay; expensive condos arrive; THE END. That's a shame, because the Seattle hostel was one of the best in North America, hands-down: always friendly, always clean, with great security measures, and oh-so-close to the best urban market in the United States.

Well, our loss has been the Green Tortoise's gain, because a place that used to be just so-so has seized the day, moved to a bigger and better building than the one it had before, and seriously upgraded their place . . . just in time to catch a huge wave of desperate travelers hunting budget beds in pricey downtown Seattle. For a hippie hotel, this place now almost sparkles, a rapid comeback from the so-so condition we found the former Seattle Tortoise to be in when it first opened.

The owners found this brick building in the heart of downtown, a historic former hotel that once housed itinerant miners and loggers. Hooray for history. The value of this location—just steps from the Pike Place Market—seems to appreciate every year. It's nice to see hostels take advantage of gentrification. At least it won't be yuppies taking *all* the hostels over.

The renovation was as classy as it gets. Funky rugs were salvaged from an old opera house, scores of super-firm surplus hotel mattresses were acquired for the undertaking. Floors and walls were cleaned and waxed. The clique of slightly odd, weed-puffing guests that seemed to dominate the former Tortoise has apparently all moved along (or been rounded up by the authorities). Whichever it was, cleanliness and friendliness have become the rule rather than the exception here now, and activities have been ramped up, too. Look out for free dinners three nights a week, weekly live music open-mic nights (yes!), and free breakfasts that are all very well-attended—since they're free—featuring items including brownies (no, not *that* kind), U-make-your-own waffles, fruit, eggs, and toast. It's one big happy feed, for sure. You sleep in one of thirty dorm rooms, or else in one of sixteen semiprivate rooms (semiprivate in the sense that bathrooms are shared, but the bedroom's your own).

What to do? In a location this central, that's a snap: The Needle and the market, of course. A tour to the grave sites of Jimi Hendrix and Bruce Lee is a big hit: Hostellers are encouraged to bring along paper and pencil and make rubbings of the gravestones as souvenirs. Yes, it's legal.

Sure, this crowd is more laid-back than the one that frequented the "official" hostel. (You can even work a week to pay for your bed.) Fewer people with planned itineraries and prepaid plane tickets arrive here (though that's changing); it's got that easy-come, easy-go attitude its umbrella organization is famous for—the Tortoise, after all, *did* start in San Francisco. But it has nicely segued into a modern era when hostellers expect more comforts and cleanliness (and space). Kudos, turtles!

How to Get There:

By airplane: Large airport in Seattle. From Seattle Airport, take #174 or #194 bus to Westlake Center stop. Hostel is at corner of First and Pike Streets.

By bus: Greyhound stops in Seattle. From terminal call hostel for pickup.

By car: Call hostel for directions.

By ferry: From dock call hostel for pickup.

By train: Amtrak stops in Seattle. From station call hostel for pickup.

The Ranch Hostel

12119 Southwest Cove Road, Vashon Island, WA 98070

(206) 463-2592

Fax: (206) 463-6157

E-mail: ayhranchhostel@yahoo.com

Rates: $17–$25 per Hostelling International member; $55–$75 for private room

Credit cards: MC, VISA

Season: Open May to September

Beds: 70

Private rooms: 3

Affiliation: Hostelling International

Office hours: 9:00 a.m. to 10:00 p.m.

Extras: Bike rentals, free pancakes, kitchen, Internet access

NOTE: Only private rooms (no hostel beds) and no free breakfast November through April.

*H*owdy there, buckaroos! Thar's a real nice place away yonder from Seattle you might have heard about called Vashon Island! I hear tell that they all have some mighty nice digs set up on some real pretty land. Yup. They got all kinds of lodgin' to choose from. (Funny that the only "official" Seattle hostel isn't even in Seattle, though! Well, hell!) Still, thar's some gen-u-wine Indian tepees here, some covered Conestoga wagons, a bunkhouse, and even a barn. You kin rustle up some grub in th' cookhouse or cook over the campfire by the light of the moon, if'n th' ground's not too dry. You kin saddle up one of them bikes for about eight bucks and pay just a dollar for the helmet.

Sounds perfect, don't it? Well, thar's just one thang. It might seem just a bit picky, but you see, thar's some folks who feel they don't take too kindly to you jess' havin' a good time here . . . a-fussin' about chores not bein' done and whatnot, complainin' about how hostellers is just plain uncaring. What's that, you say? You've heard the place is thinkin' about loosenin' up a bit? Well, Hallelujah! And we gots to say this: This island is just bee-you-tee-ful—the real Washington if yer askin' us. Jes' don't use this as a base to see Seattle. Nope. That there city is just too difficult to get to, and back, 'specially if you want to enjoy some nightlife.

Here's how you get there if'n you got one of them newfangled automobiles, though. You take the ferry from the Fauntleroy landing in West Seattle. You then follow the road for about, oh, 5 miles until you see the sign for the hostel. Take a right onto Southwest Cove Road and go for about 2 miles. Then you'll see them tepees, and you'll know that you're there. If'n you're goin' by your own foot power, take the foot ferry (Monday through Saturday) from Pier 50 in Seattle, then a bus to the Thriftway store on Vashon. You kin try t' ring up th' hostel from thar for a free pickup, podner.

See y'all at the ranch. Yee-haw!!

How to Get There:

By bus: Take #118, #119, or #54 city bus from Seattle to Fauntleroy dock. Take passenger ferry to Vashon Island. Catch bus to Thriftway grocery, then call hostel for free pickup.

By car: Take I-5 to exit 163A (west Seattle). Follow signs to Fauntleroy dock; take ferry to Vashon Island. Follow 160 Avenue to Vashon Highway; make right in town at sign for Cove Road. Hostel is on left, just after 121 Avenue.

By ferry: Take passenger ferry to Vashon Island. Catch bus to Thriftway grocery, then call hostel for free pickup.

Alaska & Hawaii

Page numbers follow hostel names

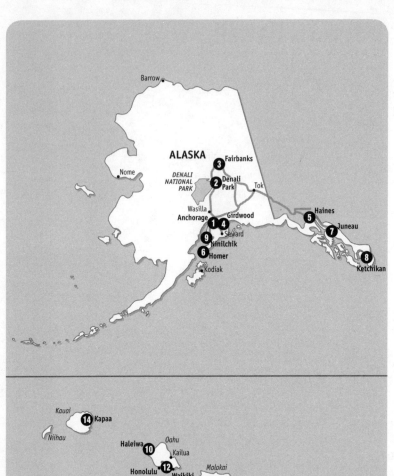

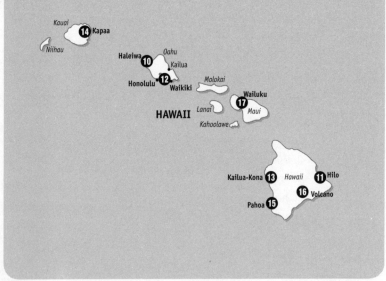

ALASKA

Anchorage Backpackers Inn Hostel

327 Eagle Street, Anchorage, AK 99501

(907) 277-2770

E-mail: info@alaskabackpackers.com

Web site: www.alaskabackpackers.com

Beds: 90

Private rooms: Yes

Affiliation: Hostelling International

Office hours: Twenty-four hours

Rates: $22–$25 per Hostelling International member; $50–$60 for private room

Credit cards: MC, VISA

Extras: Kitchen, television, laundry, lockers, grill, game room, Internet access, free coffee, bikes

*T*his newest Anchorage hostel—inside a squat blue building that looks like it could be a fish-processing plant, but isn't—fills a sorely needed gap by providing budget Alaska beds and Hostelling International–level quality control. Lots of exposed wood reminds you where you are (in the wild), but modern amenities and bright colors also predominate.

Entry is via key cards, just like in a hotel. Dorm rooms max out at just four simple beds, which is a welcome switch from the usual HI-run warehouses. Each room has a different theme, reflected in original art on the floors, and there's both a hostel kitchen and a common TV room. They've got a few Internet terminals, too.

> **Best bet for a bite:**
> *Moose's Tooth (pizza)*
> **Gestalt:**
> *Sporting wood*
> **Hospitality:** *B*
> **Safety:** *B*
> **Cleanliness:** *B*
> **Party index:**

How to Get There:

By car: Contact hostel for directions.

By bus: Bus station around corner. Contact hostel for directions.

By train: From Alaska Railroad Depot, walk along First Avenue to Eagle Street and turn right; continue to hostel.

Anchorage International Hostel

700 H Street, Anchorage, AK 99501

(907) 276-3635

Fax: (907) 276-7772

Web site: www.anchorageinternationalhostel.org

Rates: $25 per person; $65 for private room

Credit cards: MC, VISA

Season: Mid-May to mid-September

Beds: 95

Private rooms: 5

Affiliation: None

Office hours: 8:00 a.m. to noon; 1:00 p.m. to 1:00 a.m.

Extras: Storage, laundry, lockers (bring your own lock), Internet access

This monster of a facility (ninety-five beds) is the first place most hostellers come when they get into town. Located right near the bus station and convenient to all downtown locations, it's a natural draw.

Unfortunately, its tendency to draw some rather oddball characters (and we don't mean that in a good way; more like in a desperate, transient way) has seriously dragged it down as an experience, and we can't recommend it. Management seems to be slacking off. People wander in and out and around, and who's to say whether they're hostellers? Bring soap and watch your stuff.

If you do stay, you can walk to most of Anchorage's urban attractions, including the opera, the museum, and the giant Alaska Experience Theater, not to mention a handful of classy microbreweries. While there is much to do in town, some hostellers may want to use the hostel as a jumping-off point for other excursions. The five-day maximum stay limits your ability to use the place as a base, but there are still

Best bet for a bite:
Glacier Brewhouse (G Street and Fifth)

What hostellers say:
"Feels like I'm anchored here in Anchorage."

Gestalt:
Loser's circle

Safety: *C*

Hospitality: *C*

Cleanliness: *D*

Party index:

any number of day-trip opportunities: The stunning waters of Turnagain Arm, the majestic beauty of Portage Glacier, or the sheer magnificence of Kenai Peninsula are all just a short scoot from downtown.

This place doesn't cut it, and that's too bad. But at least there are other hostels in town and in the state to pick from.

How to Get There:

By airplane: Airport in Anchorage. Take shuttle.

By bus: Hostel is a short walk from station. Call hostel for details.

By car: Follow Highway 1 into downtown Anchorage. At Fifth Street or Sixth Street, turn east and continue approximately 13 blocks to H street. Turn down H Street, hostel is located at southwest corner of Seventh and H Streets, across from Arco Tower. Must park on street or in pay lot.

By train: Hostel is a short walk from station. Call hostel for details.

Spenard Hostel International ✺✺✺✺

2845 West Forty-second Avenue, Anchorage, AK 99517

(907) 248-5036

   E-mail: stay@alaskahostel.org

   Web site: www.alaskahostel.org

   Rates: $21–$22 per person; $60–$64 for private arrangements

   Credit cards: AMEX, DISC, MC, VISA

   Beds: 40

   Private rooms: None

   Affiliation: None

   Office hours: 9:00 a.m. to 1:00 p.m. and 7:00 to 11:00 p.m. (summer); 7:00 to 11:00 p.m. only (winter)

   Extras: Laundry, computer rentals, Internet access, barbecue, lockers, volleyball, bicycle rentals, three kitchens, television, games, grill, player piano

---

*O*ur scouts report that Bill Madsen's Spenard hostel serves up a "warmer, homier" feel than Anchorage's downtown hostels, with only one small drawback: It's *not* downtown. Otherwise, it's pretty good! A bus will get you to the bars and bistros of central Anchorage in a jiffy, however, and the hostel is just 2 miles from the airport, which is very convenient if you're popping in and out of Alaska. At the very least it serves as a suitable spillover for folks turned away from the downtown joint during high season.

The hostel stuffs about forty beds inside a fourplex apartment building with separate facilities for men and women. Couples and family rooms are available when there's room, too. Dorms are mostly in four-bedded rooms, and management seems ambitious and enthusiastic. Visitors can rent computers to check e-mail and cook in one of three (!) kitchens. There's also talk about a possible hot tub someday, and other ways to create cohesion among guests. Booze, cigs, drugs, and even shoes (inside the hostel) are verboten, though.

How to Get There:

By airplane: Airport in Anchorage. Walk 2 miles to hostel (call for directions) or take shuttle or bus to downtown transit center, then catch #7 bus to first stop past Gwennies Restaurant (about 3 miles out of town). Walk west on Turnagain Boulevard, then left onto Forty-second Place; hostel is on right.

By bus: Bus stops downtown. From transit center take #7 bus to first stop past Gwennies Restaurant (about 3 miles out of town). Walk west on Turnagain Boulevard, then left onto Forty-second Place. Hostel is on right.

By car: From downtown take H Street to Ninth Street, turn right on L Street, left to Northern Lights, left to Wisconsin, left to Forty-second Place and look for green building on left, #2845.

Denali Mountain Morning Hostel ✳✳✳✳
Mile 224.1 Parks Highway (P.O. Box 208), Denali Park, AK 99755
(907) 683-7503
 Fax: (907) 683-7503
 E-mail: stay@hostelalaska.com

Web site: www.hostelalaska.com
Rates: $25 per person; $75–$95 for private room
Credit cards: AE, DISC, MC, VISA
Season: Mid-May to mid-September
Beds: 25
Private rooms: Yes
Affiliation: None
Office hours: 5:30 to 10:00 p.m.
Extras: Laundry, parking, shuttles, television, breakfast, outdoor gear rentals and sales, kitchen, small store, Internet access, travel library

*T*his place really gets it right. Secure your reservations early for this bustling hostel on the border of a park that easily ranks among North America's most stunning. The hostel is fairly standard, with all the amenities you'd expect in the place, but its setting, Alaska feel, and upkeep push it to the front of the line.

The hostel consists of a series of log-and-wood cabins, clean and newish, plus private cabins that are perfect for couples or families. (One is called "The Octagon" and it's an especial favorite of visitors.)

The price may strike you as a bit high, but you're not going to find anything in this area with four walls that even comes close in terms of value. Remember where you are. As they say in the real estate biz: It's all location, location, location, and it doesn't come any better than this pristine, wild spot. Plus, you get access to a kitchen, stove, outdoor-gear rental service, and handy, cheap ($3 at last check) shuttles to Denali Park. There's a small shop on site purveying organic foods, and an Internet terminal in the common lounge for sending wondrous e-mails back home to your jealous friends; nice. Hosts Ben and Becky even light campfires at night.

Best bet for a bite:
Grizzlies (where you=the bitee)
Insiders' tip:
Bring a flashlight!
Gestalt:
Queen of Denali
Hospitality: *A*
Cleanliness: *B*
Party index:

All in all, it's just a splendid place to experience Alaska's many natural wonders.

How to Get There:

By bus: Free shuttle from bus stop. Call hostel for details.

By car: From Anchorage, follow Parks Highway to a point 14 miles north of Cantwell Village. Just after the sign for Carlo Creek Lodge and Campground on left, cross a small bridge and immediately turn left onto a dirt road and follow it to the hostel. Stop at the first cabin to check in.

From Fairbanks, follow Parks Highway to a point 13 miles south of National Park entrance (to Milepost 224.5). At McKinley Creekside restaurant (A-frame) just before Carlo Creek bridge, turn right onto dirt road and follow it to hostel.

By train: Call hostel for shuttle from train station ($3).

Billie's Backpacker Hostel ✹✹✹✦

2895 Mack Avenue, Fairbanks, AK 99709

(907) 479-2034

> **Fax:** (907) 457-2034
> **E-mail:** info@alaskahostel.com
> **Web site:** www.alaskahostel.com
> **Rates:** $35 per person
> **Credit cards:** Yes
> **Beds:** 20
> **Private/family rooms:** None
> **Affiliation:** None
> **Office hours:** Be reasonable
> **Extras:** Television, laundry, bikes, camping, free Internet access, meals ($), volleyball, stamp store, deck, grill, hammocks, kitchen, pug dogs

---

*T*his place started in July 1991 with just a toolshed and four beds, but Billie Cook's former cottage has swelled into an actual hostel of several wings: each wing with a kitchen and a private bathroom. And you know what? This grown-up hostel is now an excellent choice when in Fairbanks.

All the dorms here contain four or fewer beds, and there are several hanging-out lounge areas as well. Lots of nice extras have gradually been added, such as hammocks, a computer terminal with Internet access, stamps for sale at the reception, bikes, and a much-appreciated laundry. And Kublai and Frankie, the house pug dogs, are always happy to see you.

You've got proximity to the University of Alaska and its campus, museum, and nearby pubs. So the position is pretty good right off the bat, and the hostel's staff can direct you to various hipster coffee shops, bookstores, and what-have-you in the surrounding area. This place also shuttles guests to sights such as Denali National Park, Anchorage, and many others for a fee. All in all, a surprisingly good choice.

How to Get There:
By bus: Call hostel for transit route.
By car: Call hostel for directions.

Alyeska Home Hostel
2222 Alta Drive, (P.O. Box 953), Girdwood, AK 99587
(907) 783-2222

> **Web site:** www.alyeskahostel.com
> **E-mail:** stay@alyeskahostel.com
> **Rates:** $20 per person; $40–$50 for private room
> **Credit cards:** None
> **Beds:** 12
> **Private rooms:** 2
> **Affiliation:** None
> **Office hours:** 5:00 p.m. to midnight
> **Extras:** Storage, parking, sauna

---

nother spot-on Alaska hostel? You betcha! This nice wood-heated cabin only half a mile from the Alyeska downhill ski resort is in Girdwood, a forty-five-minute drive from Anchorage and a good diversion if you wanna get outside the city. The owners boast a location surrounded by views of towering mountain peaks with virgin snow, glaciers, and a swift-running river. Mind you, there's no shower, just cold running water. You can take pleasure, though, in the fact that there is a sauna.

Best bet for a bite:
Chair 5
What hostellers say:
"Homey as can be."
Gestalt:
Lofty
Hospitality: *A*
Cleanliness: *A*
Party index:

This friendly and clean hostel sleeps only a dozen or so, and it does fill quickly in the winter as hard-core skiers brave the Alaska cold for pristine runs. Be *sure* to call ahead during the cold months. Things around the cabin are more relaxed in the off-season (which is summer), and you might have the whole place to yourself at that time. All in all, it's a nice refuge in close proximity to the city of Anchorage.

But remember: Its charms are simple. Don't expect luxury and you'll love it.

How to Get There:

By car: From Anchorage drive south to Girdwood. Turn left onto Alyeska Highway. Travel 2 ⁵⁄₁₀ miles and turn right onto Timberline Drive. Go ²⁄₁₀ mile and turn right onto Alpina. The hostel is ⁵⁄₁₀ mile on the right.

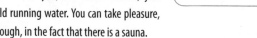

Bear Creek Cabins and Hostel ✺✺✺

Small Tracks Road (P.O. Box 908), Haines, AK 99827

(907) 766-2259

E-mail: bearcreekcabin@yahoo.com

Web site: www.bearcreekcabinsalaska.com

Rates: $18 per person; $48 for private cabin

Credit cards: None

Season: April 1 to December 1

Beds: 32

Private rooms: Yes

Affiliation: None

Office hours: 7:00 a.m. to 8:00 p.m.

Extras: Store, shuttle to ferry, camping, kitchen

*Y*es, there's a big kitschy sculpted bear right in the center of this motor-court-like cottage compound. Yes, the most impressive gathering of bald eagles to be found anywhere on the continent takes place every fall not far from here. Sound great? It is.

Just one problem: This hostel is waaaaay out there, a six-hour ferry ride from Juneau or a very long trek by auto. Veterans of the journey say it's no matter, though; the trip is worth it because the Alaska Chilkat Bald Eagle Preserve is, at times, home to as many as 4,000 eagles at once.

Best bet for a bite:
Chilkat Bakery

Insiders' tip:
Summertime salmon feasts in town

What hostellers say:
"This is natural history at its finest."

Gestalt:
Bold eagle

Hospitality: *A*

Cleanliness: *B*

Party index: 🎉🎉

You'll find the hostel to be a pretty lax place, rather what you'd expect from the name: It's a clean bunkhouse in the woods. Easy come, easy go. Hostellers stay in small units with a few beds and nothing else. Showers and toilets are out in another unit and the kitchen in another. The place draws a crowd in the summer, we're told, so do call ahead. Hiking Mount Riley or Mount Ripinski is another possible activity choice, and if you enjoy fishing, bring a rod: They're always biting around here.

How to Get There:

By car: Take Beach Road from the ferry terminal until you hit Main Street. Follow Main to Third Avenue, then take Third south to Mud Bay Road. Go left on Small Tracks Road; hostel is about 1 mile away.

Homer Hostel ✴❄

304 West Pioneer Avenue, Homer, AK 99603

(907) 235-1463

E-mail: homerhostel@homerhostel.com

Web site: www.homerhostel.com

Rates: $25 per person; $65 for private room

Credit cards: Yes

Private rooms: Yes

Affiliation: None

Office hours: 9:00 a.m. to 9:00 p.m.

Extras: Kitchen, bicycle rentals

---

*I*n a rambling blue house in the middle of Homer, this hostel's close to everything. You can experience the beach, coffee shops, a museum, the library and its Internet access, and other aspects of town life by foot—or on one of the bikes the hostel rents. (Also use those to pedal out to the end of the spit poking into Kachemack Bay.)

Accommodations consist of three five- and six-bedded dorms, one of which is coed, plus two private rooms good for couples or families. There's a kitchen for preparing simple meals, a lounge with a view, a tiny library, and a porch, all maintained by nice people. That's about it. It could be close to heaven . . . except that the upkeep is just not good enough, by a long shot. So we really can't recommend this place, although the view *is* spectacular. Homer? No. More like a pop fly.

For fun, if you are coming anyway, hang out in town or schedule a day or overnight trip to Grewingk Glacier Lake: It's filled with icebergs calving off the huge

> **Best bet for a bite:**
> *Smoky Bay Natural Foods*
> **What hostellers say:**
> *"D'oh!!"*
> **Gestalt:**
> *Broken Homer*
> **Hospitality:** *A*
> **Cleanliness:** *F*
> **Party index:** 🎉

Grewingk Glacier. Need to send e-mail? You can't do that at the hostel, but you *can* do it (for free) at the local library just a few blocks away. Whew.

How to Get There:
By car: Contact hostel for directions.

Mossy's Alaska Seaside Farm Hostel

40904 Seaside Farm Road, Homer, AK 99603
(907) 235-7850

E-mail: seaside@alaska.net
Rates: $20 per person; $50 for private room
Credit cards: MC, VISA
Season: May 1 to September 30
Beds: 14
Private rooms: Yes
Affiliation: None
Office hours: Vary; call
Extras: Beach, picnic area, barbecue, volleyball, bike rentals, television, VCR, camping

---

This hostel's a farm with a stellar view of the bay off Cook Inlet and some makeshift bunks for friendly travelers. Here's your chance to sleep on some straw in an actual barn. Better yet, the proprietor's name is "Mossy." Reason enough to stay. Always wanted to play a role on a working farm? Here's your chance: Get your hands dirty, put in your time, and the stay is free. Expect simple furnishings, don't be afraid to haul your own water or pick a few berries, and you'll be okay. (There are plenty of cabins at higher prices if you want more privacy and a little more comfort, though.)

The hostel suits the community well. Homer is one of those places where gruff,

Best bet for a bite:
Fish & chips on the boardwalk
What hostellers say:
"Lovely town."
Gestalt:
Home run
Hospitality: *A*
Cleanliness: *C*
Party index: 🎉

rugged fishing folk peacefully coexist with artists and writers. The television favorite *Northern Exposure* comes to mind. The hostel sits way toward the southern end on the Kenai Peninsula, offering 20 miles of scenic coastline for your recreational pleasure. Settle in, hang out, take your time; there's no rush here. Some folks drift in and wind up staying the season.

In addition to the barn bunks, you can secure a nifty cabin for a few more bucks or camp out on the seaside field.

How to Get There:
By car: From downtown Homer follow East End Road to the end (about 5 miles). Look for sign.

Juneau International Hostel
614 Harris Street, Juneau, AK 99801
(907) 586-9559

    E-mail: juneauhostel@gci.net
    Web site: www.juneauhostel.net
    Rates: $10 per person
    Credit cards: None
    Beds: 47
    Private rooms: 1
    Affiliation: None
    Office hours: 8:00 to 9:00 a.m.; 5:00 to midnight (5:00 to 10:30 p.m. winter)
    Extras: Storage, laundry, Internet access

*T*his hostel's housed inside a rambling, unremarkable-looking home in the Alaskan capital city. Actually, far away from the true downtown. But we digress. An efficient, tightly packed facility in the best Hostelling International tradition (though it's no longer a member), this place has all the essentials, plus decent management to keep you on your feet. The urban location tends to get rave reviews; just don't test the 11:00 p.m. curfew and don't think of dropping in during the daytime lockout. Showers will cost ya in the coin-op tradition. Put up with these strictures, and you'll enjoy the place, because it's quite clean and well-kept overall.

The hostel is a good base from which to explore the history and culture of Juneau, too. The city's waterfront is only a half-dozen blocks in one direction; downtown is a half-dozen blocks in the other. Popular spots include exhibits at the Alaska State Museum and the Perseverance Theatre. Renowned hiking is only 12 miles away at the Mendenhall Glacier. It's a popular hostel, so consider sending a deposit to snag a reservation ahead of time. And remember: They take credit cards to hold reservations, but *not* as payment at the door. Bring cash.

Best bet for a bite:
Alaskan & Proud supermarket
What hostellers say:
"Juneau what? It's not bad!"
Gestalt:
Capital appreciation
Hospitality: *B*
Cleanliness: *A*
Party index:

How to Get There:

By car: Hostel is 13 miles from the ferry wharf and 9 miles from the airport. Take Eagan Drive south into town and turn left on Main Street. Go up the hill to Sixth Street, turn right, and go 4 blocks to Harris Street intersection. Hostel is at the corner.

Eagle View Hostel ✺✺✺

2303 Fifth Avenue, Ketchikan, AK 99901
(907) 225-5461

   Web site: www.eagleviewhostel.com
   E-mail: info@eagleviewhostel.com
   Rates: $25 per person
   Season: April to October
   Beds: 10
   Private rooms: Sometimes
   Extras: Grill

---

*T*his wooden house with spectacular views of the Ketchikan area has potential, but it's also quite a small hostel—and, as a result, you're constantly crossing paths (and perhaps agendas) with the home's blunt owner, Dale Rogers, and the "house rules."

The hostel portion of the home consists of just three small bunkrooms, one of which is usually used for families or a couple. Rules are simple: Don't wear shoes. Make your bed. Pick up after yourself. Oh. And follow Dale's Way. No deviations. There's no breakfast here, but they do have a kitchen, and sheets and towels are included in the price. You also don't need to worry about a lockout or a curfew. If you can handle Dale's direct, tactless manner,

Best bet for a bite:
Alaska Brewing Co. brewpub (ask for directions)
What hostellers say:
"Hostel manager, ketch me if you can."
Gestalt:
Mr. Rogers's neighborhood
Hospitality: *D*
Cleanliness: *A*
Party index: 🎉

you might like it here. And Dale, a licensed boat captain, offers sightseeing, fishing, and remote-transportation boat charters, which can be a big plus. He'll hook you up with a kayak rental if you're interested (and qualified to paddle one).

Interestingly, this area was once an infamous hub of sin, offering up a defiant serving of alcohol and prostitution to visitors and residents alike. It has since transformed itself into a destination for folks interested in indigenous cultures: Totem poles are king around town, with the Totem Heritage Center being a designated National Historic Landmark. Check in with the Tongass Historical Museum, too, to learn about the intriguing history of this community. Can't get enough totemology? If you can catch a lift, head 10 miles north to Totem Bight State Historical Park to collect your thoughts in peaceful solitude among a collection of inspiringly crafted poles.

How to Get There:
By ferry: Hostel is ¾ mile from ferry terminal ($10 taxi ride). Contact hostel for transit details.

The Eagle Watch Hostel ✳✳✳
Mile 3 Oil Well Road (P.O. Box 39083), Ninilchik, AK 99639
(907) 567-3905
> **Web site:** http://home.gci.net/~theeaglewatch
> **Rates:** $13–$14 per person; $35 for private room

Credit cards: None
Season: May 15 to September 15
Beds: 31
Private rooms: 2
Affiliation: None
Office hours: 8:00 to 10:00 a.m.; 5:00 to 10:00 p.m.
Extras: Parking, storage, clam shovels, fishing rods, picnic area, barbecue

---

*F*ishing occupies this coastal community, and hostellers at Roswitha and Frank Miller's joint can pitch right in and test any of several waters for a potential catch. Two rivers, the inlet, and charter boats out in the ocean should keep you plenty busy. The hostel will also equip you with a shovel for your clam-digging pleasure during low tide.

Despite its local color, this hostel is a pretty bare-bones operation with about thirty beds and a view to kill for. The facility is set on a bank overlooking the Ninilchik River.

What else to do? Well, the local community has an interesting Russian background, which adds to the already rich Native American culture. You don't want to miss the Russian Orthodox Church that overlooks the old village and harbor.

> **Best bet for a bite:**
> *The general store*
> **What hostellers say:**
> *"Interesting stew of locals."*
> **Gestalt:**
> *Eagle eye*
> **Hospitality:** *B*
> **Cleanliness:** *A*
> **Party index:**

How to Get There:

By car: From Anchorage, take Alaska Highway 1 toward Homer to Ninilchik. Turn left onto Oil Well Road (paved road next to gas station), go 3 miles to the EAGLE WATCH SIGN. Hostel is on left.
By foot: Call for free pickup from "downtown" Ninilchik.

HAWAII

Backpackers Vacation Inn

59-788 Kam Highway, Haleiwa, HI 96712

(808) 638–7838

Fax: (808) 638–7515

E-mail: info@backpackers-hawaii.com

Web site: www.backpackers-hawaii.com

Rates: $27–$30 per person; $72–$290 for private room

Credit cards: None

Beds: 100

Private rooms: 15

Private bathrooms: 8

Affiliation: None

Office hours: Vary; call

Extras: Barbecues, snorkels, boogie boards, tennis, basketball, volleyball

*T*his hostel is located just minutes from the big waves of Oahu's north shore, a beautiful place if we've ever seen one. But beware. It's run-down, dirty, full of lizards and bugs, yet management still seems to feel they're doing us a favor with these "suites" and this "plantation village." Huh?? Friendliness is severely lacking, too. Inexplicably, it gets crowded both in summer (college vacation time) *and* winter (high-surf time), so it's best to book this place very early if you come. If.

The 'hood is certainly beautiful—you're so close to the beach, and the wonderful little town of Haleiwa (say hah-lay-ee-vah)—but this just isn't worth the trouble. We'll surf onward to a hostel back in Honolulu; it's only an hour (or less) to drive back to the city from here anyway.

Best bet for a bite:
Waialua Bakery

Insiders' tip:
Check out Waimea Falls too

What hostellers say:
"Spit. Welcome to Pipe."

Gestalt:
Haole haven

Hospitality: *D*

Cleanliness: *F*

Party index: 🎉🎉🎉

How to Get There:

By airplane: Free pickup at Honolulu airport.

By bus: Take #52 bus; get off one stop past Waimea Falls State Park. Call hostel for directions.

By car: Call hostel for directions.

Arnott's Lodge Hostel

98 Apapane Road (P.O. Box 4039), Hilo, HI 96720

(808) 969-7097

Fax: (808) 961-9638

E-mail: info@arnottslodge.com

Web site: www.arnottslodge.com

Rates: $25 per person; $60–$70 for private room

Credit cards: AMEX, DISC, MC, VISA

Beds: 50

Private rooms: Yes

Affiliation: None

Office hours: 8:00 a.m. to 8:00 p.m.

Extras: Tours, laundry, pickups, barbecue, television, DVD player, coffee, tea, camping, tours, kitchen, Internet access

This hostel, located in a seedy section of Hilo, has three twelve-bunk dorms and seven private rooms. Each bunkroom has its own bathroom and kitchen, and the private rooms have two bedrooms that share a kitchen, lounge, and bath. These are not particularly clean or private, and management's attitude ranges from rude to haughty to occasionally helpful. They also rank on their other competitors in town (see below) . . . even though it's much better, in our opinion.

Owner Doug Arnott has built a separate building as a television lounge/library area. That place provides a venue to meet other visitors and keeps the noise away from the sleeping quarters. And if you're looking for a quieter place for more intimate conversations, check out the house porch as well.

The hostel is located on the outskirts of rainy, voggy Hilo—not our ideal place to stay on the Big Island by a long shot. Yes, Arnott's is a short walk from a market and to the rocky coast that is typical on the Hilo side of the Big Island—but there are no swimming beaches nearby. The hostel's full-day tours are popular, and that makes sense: They show you Mauna Kea, the waterfalls and rain forests of the Hamakua coast, Hawaii Volcanoes National Park, and South Point/ Green Sand beach. All in all, this could be an awesome hostel but, sadly, it is not. The pushiness and disrepair are just not tolerable. We expect more.

Best bet for a bite:
Bears' Coffee
Gestalt:
Hawaiian punch
What hostellers say:
"This is the best island."
Safety: *B*
Hospitality: *D*
Cleanliness: *C*
Party index: 🎉🎉

How to Get There:
By airplane: Hilo airport is 3 miles away. Call hostel for directions.
By car: Call hostel for directions.

Hilo Bay Hostel ✴✴✴✴
101 Waianuenue Avenue, Hilo, HI 96720
(808) 933-2771

Fax: (808) 935-1183
E-mail: hawaiihostel@hawaiihostel.net
Web site: www.hawaiihostel.net
Rates: $25 per person; $65 for private room
Credit cards: JCB, MC, VISA
Private rooms: Yes
Affiliation: None
Office hours: 7:00 a.m. to 10:00 p.m.
Extras: Kitchen, television, patio, lockers, Internet access, free local calls, library

*I*n a restored 1913 hotel (and former speakeasy—cool), this newish Hilo hostel has Uncle Mo and Cousin Po . . . as in, momentum and potential. It's in an attractive historic building, extremely central in Hilo (if you really want to stay in Hilo), and features clean and airy dorms with views, surprisingly comfy beds, and walls painted in surf motifs.

Management has stocked the place with necessities like good-quality Internet stations, a really nice (and big) kitchen, and a patio for hanging out and meeting others. They even make their own T-shirts. This is near both the bus stop and a twice-weekly farmers' market—you can also read a book or use the Internet at the local library if it rains here, which it often does—and all in all, we can't think of anything bad to say about the place. Much better than the "other" choice in town. We'll repeat what we said last edition: So far, so good.

How to Get There:

By airplane or car: From airport, drive straight to Kilauea Avenue; turn right turn on Kilauea. Kilauea turns into Keawe Street. Hostel is located at corner of Keawe and Waianuenue Avenue. Park in city lot across street.

HONOLULU HOSTELS: A SUMMARY

	RATING	PROS	CONS	COST	PAGE
Honolulu University Hostel	★★★★	relaxed	distant	$18	339
Waikiki Hostel	★★★	central	attitudinal	$23	341
Polynesian Beach Club Hostel	★★	hoppin'	grimy	$25–$30	340

Honolulu University Hostel ✳✳✳✵

2323A Seaview Avenue, Honolulu, HI 96822

(808) 946-0591

Fax: (808) 946-5904

E-mail: hihostel@lava.net

Rates: $18 per Hostelling International member; $46 for private room

Credit cards: AMEX, MC, VISA

Beds: 43

Private rooms: 3

Affiliation: Hostelling International

Office hours: 8:00 a.m. to noon; 4:00 p.m. to midnight

Extras: Television, tours, laundry, patio, lockers, kitchen

*T*his good, environmentally conscious hostel—which is sort of a little-known adjunct to Hostelling International's beachside hostel in Waikiki—is located in a quiet, hilly residential area just a stone's throw from the nice University of Hawaii campus, a part of town known as Manoa. All the watering holes and eateries that cater to the college crowd are at your disposal, and hostel activities include such doings as hiking trips (good local waterfall) and weekend beach barbecues. There's a laundry and kitchen, too.

There's a three-day maximum stay limit here (too bad!), though they'll lock you out all day for cleaning purposes. Still, it's not bad. Think seriously about it when the other ones close to the water are booked solid; Manoa's really not all that far away by car or bus from the surf and nightlife action.

Best bet for a bite:
Local bento (Japanese) joints
What hostellers say:
"Off the beaten track but good."
Gestalt:
Oasis
Safety: *A*
Hospitality: *B*
Cleanliness: *A*
Party index:

How to Get There:

By airplane: Large airport outside Honolulu. From airport take bus #19 or #20, transfer to #6 or #18. Call hostel for directions; or call taxi.

By car: Drive Hawaii Highway east to exit 24B; then go north on University Avenue 3 blocks.

Polynesian Beach Club Hostel

2584 Lemon Road, Waikiki (Honolulu), HI 96815

(808) 922-1340

Fax: (808) 262-2817

E-mail: polynesianhostel@yahoo.com

Web site: www.hostelhawaii.com

Rates: $25–$30 per person; $54–$82 for private room

Credit cards: None

Beds: 74

Private rooms: 12

Affiliation: None

Office hours: Twenty-four hours

Extras: Pool, deck, boogie boards, barbecue, gift shop, television, laundry, tour discounts, bike/moped rentals, patio, lockers, snorkels, Internet access ($)

*S*ome love the Club, and some hate it. Depends on what you want: a clean bed, or a sociable time. In this case, you can't have your cake and eat it too.

The hostel features excellent proximity to Waikiki Beach and regular beach barbecues. It's a very hopping place, frequented by lots of young travelers drinking beers, exchanging surf and travel stories, and so on. If that's what you want, check it out. Also note the free snorkels and beach mats; you can rent bikes, mopeds, and other exploring gear or use Internet time for a fee as well.

Best bet for a bite:
Cha Cha Cha
What hostellers say:
"Da bes' kine, bra!"
Gestalt:
Poi dog pondering
Safety: *B*
Hospitality: *C*
Cleanliness: *D*
Party index:

Rooms come in configurations of dorms; a number of singles and doubles with shared bathrooms; and a private studio with its own bath, television, and kitchen. No dorm room has more than six beds, and each comes with a bathroom.

But on the cleanliness issue, we've got to draw the line. At times it's downright filthy, other times borderline okay. Staff didn't really seem to care either way. It basically depends on your own hygiene standards. But we give it the thumbs-down in this regard, and we'd stay elsewhere in town. Despite the happy-camper vibe, this is the most expensive hostel of the three in metro Honolulu—so it should act like it. But it's sadly underachieving.

How to Get There:

By airplane: Large airport outside Honolulu. From airport, take shuttle (#8) or #19 or #20 bus to Waikiki. Call hostel for directions.

By car: Call hostel for directions.

Waikiki Hostel ✹✹✹

2417 Prince Edward Street, Waikiki (Honolulu), HI 96815

(808) 926-8313

> **Fax:** (808) 922-3798
>
> **E-mail:** ayhaloha@lava.net
>
> **Rates:** $23 per Hostelling International member; $54 for single room
>
> **Credit cards:** AMEX, MC, VISA
>
> **Beds:** 63
>
> **Private rooms:** 5
>
> **Affiliation:** Hostelling International
>
> **Office hours:** 7:00 a.m. to 3:00 a.m.
>
> **Extras:** Laundry, television, tours, snorkel gear, Internet access

---

*T*his hostel couldn't be closer to fun Waikiki Beach: It's just 2 blocks away, and you can actually see the waves and surfers from the hostel's front door. Cool! But after that it's a mixed bag at best.

The good: covered parking (get there early). Video nights, island tours, nature walks. Decent facilities. A few private rooms that far undercut the price of hostels around here. The bad? Aging, beat-up bunks and private rooms. A bit of a seedy feeling in the neighborhood late at night, as hookers and cops cruise the Kuhio strip. And worst of all, some staff here continue to maintain a "take it, it's great" attitude of superiority (due to the location) when in fact we've stayed in *far* better places.

Why so smug, folks? You're okay, but this is hardly a palace and we wouldn't mind

Best bet for a bite:
Perry's (buffet-style)
What hostellers say:
"Shaka."
Gestalt:
Hawaii 5-0
Safety: *B*
Hospitality: *C*
Cleanliness: *B*
Party index:

dropping a few extra bucks for one of the zillions of condos (with private kitchens and pools!) that tower above and around you. We're on vacation, not at boot camp. Get real, kids.

But if it's hostelling you must do, this is the best close-to-the-beach pick on Oahu. (If you're bringing family, consider booking yourselves into Hostelling International's Honolulu University Hostel—see page 339—instead.) There's usually a three-night limit to your stay and no curfew—the latter is a nice bonus, and they do keep the office open really late—but you'd do best to reserve very early in advance, especially for a winter stay, since this hostel is super-popular during the colder months.

Plan, too, on hitting the scores of lovely beaches in the surrounding area (the hostel will lend you snorkeling gear), and don't forget to try your hand at something new. Take a surfing or boogie-board lesson, for starters. If you've got a car, hop in and cruise up to the North Shore, east over to the lovely windward (and windy) side of the island, and over the high Pali mountain pass with its gorgeous lookout. (Lock your car here and everywhere on Oahu, though; there have been lots of break-ins.)

How to Get There:
By airplane: Large airport outside Honolulu. From airport, take shuttle (#8) or #19 or #20 bus to Waikiki.
By car: Call hostel for directions.

 Key to Icons

Attractive natural setting	Comfortable beds	Visual arts at hostel or nearby
Ecologically aware hostel	A particularly good value	Music at hostel or nearby
Superior kitchen facilities or cafe	Wheelchair-accessible	Great hostel for skiers
Offbeat or eccentric place	Good for business travelers	Bar or pub at hostel or nearby
Superior bathroom facilities	Especially well-suited for families	Editors' choice: Among our very favorite hostels
Romantic private rooms	Good for active travelers	

Patey's Place Hostel ✳✳✳✳

75-184 Ala Ona Ona Street, Kailua-Kona, HI 96740

(808) 329-9663

Rates: $25 per person; $55–$130 for private room

Credit cards: MC, VISA

Beds: 35

Private rooms: 5

Affiliation: None

Office hours: 8:00 a.m. to noon; 4:00 to 10:00 p.m.

Extras: Pickups, television, table tennis, darts, free coffee, tours, kitchen, Internet access, Wi-Fi, laundry

"More marine life murals than any other hostel" is how Rob Patey (pronounced Pah-tay), owner and manager of Patey's Place, describes his hostel, and there isn't a wall in the place that is not covered. The murals are of a Wyland style and lend the place a trippy feel, especially at night when they are illuminated with black lights. This is the only low-cost lodging in the sunny, popular Kailua-Kona corridor of resorts, and we have to hand it to him—in the past few years, Patey has expanded his hostel, cleaned it up considerably, added a laundry, and hired better staff. There's even a vaguely New Agey feel to the place, which we don't have any use for but is surely better than the slightly strange/unclean vibe that pervaded before.

The hostel is located in quietish a residential neighborhood a ten- to fifteen-minute walk from the shops and restaurants of Kailua-Kona, the tourist center for the Big Island. The center offers a nighttime alternative to hanging around the hostel playing darts or watching television. The hostel has several kitchens, which makes cooking dinner simple; finding the necessary pots and pans can be a bit more difficult, though.

During the day snorkeling (you can rent equipment from the hostel, but for the same price you can do much better at one

> **Best bet for a bite:**
> *Kona Mix Plate*
> **What hostellers say:**
> *"Beautiful area, very good hostel."*
> **Gestalt:**
> *Boogie woogie*
> **Hospitality:** *A*
> **Cleanliness:** *B*
> **Party index:** 🎉🎉🎉🎉

of the shops in town), boogie boarding, or body surfing are the activities of choice at one of the many beaches in the area. The hostel also runs guided tours to more remote areas of the island if you can gather a group of four or more. Having seen the staff repairing the vans for the tours, though, we don't know if we can wholeheartedly recommend them.

Still, for this edition of the book, this is our Comeback Player of the Year. Good job, Rob!

How to Get There:

By airplane: Keahole-Kona airport is located 7 miles to the north. Call hostel for directions.

By car: Take Palani Road toward the water, turn left at second light onto Kuakini Highway, go left at first light onto Kalani Street, go 2 blocks to left on Alahou Street. Go 1 block, then take right onto Ala Ona Ona Street. The hostel is on the left.

The Kauai Beach House

4-1552 Kuhio Highway, Kapaa, HI 96746-1830
(808) 822-3424

> **Web site:** www.kauaibeachhouse.net
> **E-mail:** aloha@ www.kauaibeachhouse.net
> **Rates:** $30 per person; $65–$70 for private room
> **Credit cards:** None
> **Beds:** 9
> **Private/family rooms:** 3
> **Affiliation:** None
> **Office hours:** Vary; call
> **Extras:** Laundry, kitchen, hot tub, surfboard rentals, windsurf rentals, beach, pool, volleyball, basketball, bike rentals

A small operation set right on Kauai's Blue Lagoon, this two-and-a-half-story hostel has got position and a laid-back groove going for it. What it hasn't got—not yet, anyway—are many beds, but the owner says those will come when more guests do.

The owner, native San Franciscan chiropractor Jay Trennoche, came here more than thirty years ago, enthralled by the ocean, and never left. One look at his neighborhood and it's easy to see why: The building's surrounded by multiple decks and native palm and monkeypod shade trees, plus gorgeous views of blue, blue water. The dorm area contains bunks and one double bed closed off with curtains from the solo hostellers; there are also private and family rooms, many with little decks looking out onto either the water or the mountains. Unfortunately, cleanliness—as with so many Hawaii hostels—is an issue here, and so is staff attitude. We just don't get why they have attitude here.

Best bet for a bite:
Kojima's
What hostellers say:
"Aloha!"
Gestalt:
Blue Hawaii
Hospitality: C
Cleanliness: C
Party index: 🎉🎉

Sporting hostellers will like the availability of bikes, surfboards, and windsurfing equipment for rent, not to mention a swimming pool, sand beach, basketball net, and volleyball area. There's also a laundry, kitchens to cook in (one of which is open-air—or, as they like to say around here, "Hawaiian style"). You can walk to restaurants and bars, some with live Hawaiian music every night, but we'd probably hang out in a place like this instead; a grocery right across the road has food. To cap it all off, a carpeted hangout area on the hostel roof features amazing panoramic views of ocean and mountains—not to mention a hot tub.

During the day check out one of the many beaches on the island for good snorkeling, body surfing, or getting some tropical sun. Adventurous souls should try hiking along the Na Pali coast or in Waimea Canyon (it looks like a miniature Grand Canyon). Hey, they don't call this the Garden Island for nothing.

Too bad they're still getting the mix right at the hostel itself. It's got enormous potential, and it's way better than the other Kauai hotel, but still severely lacking for now.

How to Get There:
By airplane: Airport on Kauai; call hostel for transit route.
By bus: Island bus stops at hostel; call hostel for transit route.
By car: Call hostel for directions.

Kauai International Hostel

6532 Lehua Street, Kapaa, HI 96746

(808) 823-6142; (800) 858-2295 (in Hawaii)

Web site: www.vrbo.com/vrbo/861.htm

Rates: $20 for dorm room; $50 for private room

Credit cards: MC, VISA

Beds: 40

Private rooms: 5

Affiliation: None

Office hours: 8:00 a.m. to 10:00 p.m.

Extras: Pool table, laundry, television, VCR, airport pickup, tours, stereo, grill, kayak rentals, kitchen, Internet access

*K*auai is beautiful as a dream, but this hostel's management makes the place a nightmare. Avoid it; it's one of the worst in the islands, if not the worst, due to attitude problems.

The hostel promises a low-cost lodging alternative to the many resorts that are on the island. The hostel is in Kapaa, the major tourist town on the island. There are many shops and restaurants in the area, but they are spread out over a 3-mile strip, so this is not really a walking town; plan on supplying your own transportation.

Unfortunately, the owner walks around shirtless and lectures guests (or sidles up to them, if they're female). Then, if you call his bluff or get tough with him, he calls you a loser/tourist/ass. This is hospitality?

Oh, the hostel: It's separated into two buildings, one containing a nice kitchen and lounge area (the combination of people cooking, watching television, and just hanging out in this area can get a bit distracting) and a couple semiprivate rooms. The other building is divided into four dorm rooms, with eight to twelve beds in each. Each dorm has its own refrigerator, kitchen sink, and bathroom; the dorm buildings have private rooms. (In these private rooms,

Best bet for a bite:

Pono Market downtown

What hostellers say:

"Don't stay here."

Gestalt:

Kauai-bunga

Hospitality: F

Cleanliness: C

Party index:

you still share a bathroom with many more people.) One funny (well, not funny) thing: We noticed tons of local people living/staying here, and their friends visiting. Hey, isn't this supposed to be for travelers? This definitely detracted from the appeal of the place.

Kauai is the farthest west of the major Hawaiian islands, and for those willing to go a bit farther out of their way, it provides a wonderfully relaxing tropical paradise; those looking for action and nightlife should go somewhere else.

Those wanting to stay on Kauai and enjoy it should *also* stay somewhere else. Not here.

How to Get There:
By airplane: Lihue airport is 8 miles to the south. Call hostel for directions.
By car: Drive from airport through downtown Kapaa; at the far side of town make hard left turn onto Lehua Street; hostel is 100 yards on right.

Pahoa Hostel ✺✺✺

13-1132 Kumakahi Street (P.O. Box 2057), Pahoa, HI 96778
(808) 965-0317
   E-mail: edfunsurf@gmail.com
   Web site: www.pahoahostel.com
   Rates: $15 per person
   Credit cards: MC, VISA
   Beds: 10
   Private rooms: 2
   Affiliation: None
   Office hours: Vary; call
   Extras: Television, VCR, table tennis, boogie boards, grill, bikes, snorkel equipment, shuttle service, fresh fruit, free phone calls (sometimes), kitchen

---

*H*ostelling in the state of Hawaii has gotten more popular in recent years as the cost of hotels and resorts has skyrocketed. And the Pahoa Hostel, located on the Big Island of Hawaii—still relatively undiscovered by tourism entities, as Hawaii goes—is the latest to figure this out. This is a one-of-a-kind hostel, for sure.

Located beside owner Ed's home, the hostel offers a wide range of lodging options

Best bet for a bite:
Local fruit stands
Insiders' tip:
Hot ponds by the ocean
What hostellers say:
"Good beach for surf, yah."
Gestalt:
Organized chemistry
Hospitality: *A*
Cleanliness: *C*
Party index: 🎉🎉

including really cheap tent and car camping, bunkrooms carved out of two buses (!), private rooms featuring regular double beds or queen beds, and a well-equipped apartment. It's simple bunking, but there's a friendly groove.

There's lots to do for the intrepid traveler, and management has rentals of bikes and snorkel gear to help you discover the island more intimately. Kehena Beach is just 9 miles away. If you'd like, you can work on Ed's organic farm; some form of work exchange is almost always available. (That means lots of fruit for the picking, too.) And because the Big Island is less crowded than Oahu or Maui, you'll be free of the tour buses that plague those isles. Also nearby are beautiful waterfalls, black sand beaches, and hot ponds (which are sort of like hot springs) in which you can take a dip and rejuvenate yourself. Ed's also a huge surfer—big surprise there—so you can glean info on the most rippin' breaks from him, as well.

How to Get There:

By car: Take Highway 11 (left at airport) toward Keau Drive, continue 4 or 5 miles past Macadamia nut plant. Look for sign that says keau and make left; continue past stoplight to shopping center, then 3 more miles uphill toward Pahoa Town. After sign for Leilani Estates, take the third road on left to hostel.

Holo Holo In Hostel ✱✱✱✱✱
19-4036 Kalani Honua Road (P.O. Box 10) , Volcano, HI 96718
(808) 967-7950

Fax: (808) 967-8025
E-mail: holoholo@interpac.net
Web site: www.enable.org/holoholo
Rates: $17 per person
Credit cards: None
Beds: 14

Private/family rooms: 2
Single rooms: None
Affiliation: Hostelling International
Office hours: 7:00 to 9:00 a.m.; 4:30 to 9:30 p.m.
Extras: Television, deck, laundry, sauna, kitchen, Internet access

"*H*olo holo" means "leisurely journey," and this place on the Big Island provides that and much more: Basically, it's a big mountain house on the edge of the woods with a very homey kitchen and a nice sundeck set amidst lots of lush tropical foliage. Rooms here are small but clean, furnished with island-style chairs and dressers. All in all, it's among the very best hostels in all of Hawaii.

Best bet for a bite:
Fruit trees
What hostellers say:
"Howzit??"
Gestalt:
Lava camp
Hospitality: *A*
Cleanliness: *A*
Party index: 🎉🎉

Manager Satoshi Yabuki, a native of Japan and veteran round-the-world backpacker, runs the place with his friendly family; keeps it spic-'n'-span clean; and likes to tout the wide variety of natural splendors on the Big Island. And he's right. This town *is* very close to spectacular attractions such as Mauna Loa (the world's largest volcano, and still live), Mauna Kea (dormant, and often snow-capped), and other treats in the adjacent Hawaii Volcanoes National Park. No wonder this town is called Volcano; there's lava everywhere.

Go for a hike and check out the remarkable silversword plants that bloom on the volcanic slopes, or hit the black sand beach of a local county park. Afterward, for a fee, you can steam away—if Hawaii isn't warm enough for ya—in the hostel sauna.

How to Get There:

By car: From Hilo drive Highway 11 south toward Hawaii Volcanoes National Park. Turn right at Haunani Road in Volcano Village (between Mile markers 26 and 27), then turn left onto Kalani Honua Road. Holo Holo Hostel is next to the Old Japanese School House, second driveway on the right. Look for the yellow fire hydrant.

Pineapple Park Hostel ✱✱✱

3489 Pikake Street, Mountain View (Volcano), HI 96771

(877) 800-3800; (877) 865-2266; (808) 968-8170

Fax: (808) 323-2086

E-mail: park@aloha.net

Web site: www.pineapple-park.com

Rates: $25 per person; $85 for private room

Credit cards: None

Beds: 65

Private rooms: Yes

Affiliation: None

Office hours: Vary

Extras: Grill, television, VCR, videos ($), laundry, kitchen

*T*his rambling Hawaiian hostel strives to dispense some of the "aloha" spirit made famous by these friendly islands, and it partly succeeds at that thanks to its owners and a great location surrounded by rain forest close to one of Hawaii's best volcanoes. (In fact, the village the hostel is located in is *called* Volcano.)

It's run by the team of Annie Chong Park and Louis Doc Holliday; Annie speaks fluent Korean and Japanese and runs a fruit salad stand in Kona, at the Kona branch of this hostel (there's another in Hilo as well). So there's promise from the outset. There are simple bunk beds in airy, whitewashed six-bedded dorms; some quite good, little private rooms (all furnished in woody Hawaiian style); a TV room with VCR; a surprisingly nice kitchen; grills; and plenty of decks and patios—known locally as a *lanai*, of course. What to eat? Walk/drive around: There's literally fruit falling off the trees, and you can buy it at local markets or even by the side of the road.

Best bet for a bite:
Local produce stands and farmers' markets
What hostellers say:
"It's okay!"
Gestalt:
Fruity
Hospitality: *B*
Cleanliness: *B*
Party index: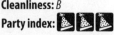

Only drawbacks? The management duo can sometimes be, let's say, a little idiosyncratic and autocratic: There are a lot of rules. But people seem to enjoy the place and its satellites in Kona and Hilo. Good enough for a look, and especially good if you're booking in a big group. Note that if you want to do some outdoor adventuring, stay at the Hilo branch (which is sorta so-so) or, better yet, the Kona branch: They rent kayaks and other outdoorsy stuff at those two hostels, but not here.

How to Get There:
By car: Contact hostel for directions.

Banana Bungalow Maui ✹✹✺
310 North Market Street, Wailuku, HI 96793
(808) 244-5090; (800) 846-7835
  E-mail: info@mauihostel.com
  Web site: www.mauihostel.com
  Rates: $25 per person; $71 for private room
  Credit cards: MC, VISA
  Beds: 73
  Private rooms: 32
  Affiliation: None
  Office hours: 7:00 a.m. to 11:00 p.m.
  Extras: Laundry, television, beach shuttle, tours, Jacuzzi, movies, table tennis, tropical fruit garden, hammocks, Internet access

---

NOTE: Free airport shuttle service has been discontinued.

Talking to the manager of the affordable Banana Bungalow hostel on Maui a couple years ago, you got the sense that this place was just about ready to spring big improvements on us. "I want to make this a little piece of paradise; clean and green with flowers and fruit trees surrounding the place," he said at that time, sincerely enough.

Well, we checked back, and it is improving . . . slightly. Fun? Oh yes. Pristine? Um, still no. Rooms have been redone and offer decent beds now. The bathrooms still tend to be overused and undercleaned. The real problem is a lack of lounge space to meet and mingle with other guests (other than a small indoor television lounge) and kitchen facilities (which consist of an outdoor propane stove, picnic tables, and a mold-culture refrigerator). Cleanliness continues to be an issue—with hostellers eating and drinking in a hot tub, crashing on the lounge couch, sometimes making a mess of things in the stuffy rooms and common areas. On the other hand, this is a place to meet fellow young people over a beer or in the tub, and almost everybody seems to walk away from this place with a smile in spite of the physical condition of the place.

What to do around here at night? Not much, other than watch television or hang with hostellers. Don't wander around at night: The town of Wailuku has almost zero to offer to the visitor (this is *not* the Maui you dream of, and in fact the hostel neighborhood is kind of seedy), even if the tiny downtown is a few blocks away. Just get a good night's sleep, if you can, then head out early to explore the island in the morning to get rid of your hangover. If you've got wheels, don't forget to drive up to Halehakala to see the sunrise. Or hook up with a tour outfit: They'll give you a lift by van to the *top* of the volcano, and then you coast back downhill. Unforgettable. Also don't miss the three-hour winding ride to Hana—again, unforgettable.

How to Get There:

By airplane: Kahului airport is 3 miles to east. Call hostel for directions.

By car: Take Hawaii Highway 32 to Wailuku from Kahului, turn right onto North Market Street; hostel is 3 blocks on right.

Paul's Picks

THE TOP U.S. HOSTELS

Albert B. Lester Memorial Hostel	Conway, New Hampshire	47
Buffalo Downtown Hostel	Buffalo, New York	65
Circle A Ranch Hostel	Cuba, New Mexico	205
Point Montara Lighthouse Hostel	Montara, California	252
Riverbend Hot Springs Hostel	Truth or Consequences, New Mexico	208
Sacramento International Hostel	Sacramento, California	260
Santa Monica Hostel	Santa Monica, California	243
Stanford House Hostel	Peninsula, Ohio	154
Tibbets Point Lighthouse Hostel	Cape Vincent, New York	67
Truro Hostel	Truro, Massachusetts	43

TOP RED-WHITE-'N'-BLUE AMERICANA HOSTELS

Eagle Home Hostel	Eagle, Wisconsin	156
Friendly Crossways Hostel	Littleton, Massachusetts	38
The Ranch Hostel	Vashon Island, Washington	315
Stanford House Hostel	Peninsula, Ohio	154
Weisel Hostel	Quakertown, Pennsylvania	94

THE BEST BEACH HOSTELS

Angie's Guest Cottage	Virginia Beach, Virginia	137
Clay Hotel International Hostel	Miami Beach, Florida	107
Robert B. Johnson Memorial Hostel	Nantucket, Massachusetts	40
Truro Hostel	Truro, Massachusetts	43

THE MOST OUTDOORSY HOSTELS

Bear's Den Trail Center and Hostel	Bluemont, Virginia	134
Blue Ridge Mountains Hostel	Galax, Virginia	136
Pitkin Hotel and Hostel	Pitkin, Colorado	178
Point Reyes Hostel	Point Reyes Station, California	259
Ranch House Inn Hostel	Tecopa, California	290
Redwood National Park Hostel	Klamath, California	223
The Yosemite Bug	Midpines, California	251

BEST URBAN HOSTELS

Buffalo Downtown Hostel	Buffalo, New York	65
Fisherman's Wharf Hostel	San Francisco, California	272
HI–Chicago Hostel	Chicago, Illinois	145
Northwest Portland International Hostel	Portland, Oregon	297
Sacramento International Hostel	Sacramento, California	260
Santa Monica Hostel	Santa Monica, California	243

THE MOST ROMANTIC HOSTELS

Hidden Villa Hostel	Los Altos Hills, California	224
Marin Headlands Hostel	Sausalito, California	286
Pigeon Point Lighthouse Hostel	Pescadero, California	257
Point Montara Lighthouse Hostel	Montara, California	252
Tibbets Point Lighthouse Hostel	Cape Vincent, New York	67

GREAT CYCLISTS' HOSTELS

Martha's Vineyard Hostel	West Tisbury, Massachusetts	45
Mid-Cape Hostel	Eastham, Massachusetts	36
Robert B. Johnson Memorial Hostel	Nantucket, Massachusetts	40
Seaside International Hostel	Seaside, Oregon	301

STRANGE-BUT-TRUE HOSTELS

THE BEST HOSTELS FOR SKIERS

THE BEST HOSTELS FOR BUSINESS TRAVELERS

THE BEST HOSTELS FOR FAMILIES

The Metropolitan Hostel	San Diego, California	264
Mid-Cape Hostel	Eastham, Massachusetts	36
Point Montara Lighthouse Hostel	Montara, California	252
Stanford House Hostel	Peninsula, Ohio	154
Truro Hostel	Truro, Massachusetts	43

THE MOST EARTH-FRIENDLY HOSTELS

Albert B. Lester Memorial Hostel	Conway, New Hampshire	47
Harpers Ferry Hostel	Knoxville, Maryland	63
Hidden Villa Hostel	Los Altos Hills, California	224
Hostel in the Forest	Brunswick, Georgia	120
Point Reyes Hostel	Point Reyes Station, California	259
Riverbend Hot Springs Hostel	Truth or Consequences, New Mexico	208
Seaside International Hostel	Seaside, Oregon	301
Stanford House Hostel	Peninsula, Ohio	154

EIGHT PLACES WE'D LIKE TO SEE A GOOD HOSTEL

Adirondack Mountains, New York

Berkeley, California

Dallas, Texas

Durham, North Carolina

Great Barrington, Massachusetts

Montauk, New York (Long Island)

Nashville, Tennessee

Portland, Maine

About the Author

Paul Karr is an award-winning editor and author/co-author of more than twenty-five travel guidebooks. He contributes regularly to magazines, owns his own media communications firm, and has twice been named a writer-in-residence by the National Park Service.

Travel Like a Pro

gpp
travel

To order call 800-243-0495 or visit thenewgpp.com

The Cheap Bastard's Guide to
NEW YORK CITY
MORE THAN 1,000 FREE LISTINGS

100 BEST
Resorts of the Caribbean

OFF THE BEATEN PA
VIRGINIA
A GUIDE TO UNIQUE PLACES

The Luxury Guide to
Walt Disney World Resort Second Edition
How to Get the Most Out of the
Best Disney Has to Offer

shifra stein's
day trips
from kansas city
fifteenth edition

NINTH EDITION
CHOOSE COSTA
FOR RETIREME

JOHN H

FUN WITH THE FAMILY
Connecticut
Hundreds of Ideas for Day Trips WITH THE Kids

INSIDERS' GUIDE
Florida Keys
and Key West

SCENIC DRIVING
COLORADO
STEWART M. GREEN